D. D. Guttenplan was born in Virginia and worked as an editor and writer in New York. He now lives in London. This is his first book.

The Holocaust on Trial

History, Justice and the
David Irving Libel Case

D.D. GUTTENPLAN

Granta Books
London

Granta Publications, 2/3 Hanover Yard, London N1 8BE

First published in Great Britain by Granta Books 2001
This edition published by Granta Books 2002

Copyright © 2001 by D.D. Guttenplan

A CIP catalogue record for this book is available
from the British Library.

1 3 5 7 9 10 8 6 4 2

Typeset in Caslon by M Rules

Printed and bound in Great Britain
by Mackays of Chatham plc

For Raul Hilberg

Contents

Acknowledgments

This book could not have been written without the cooperation, encouragement, and assistance of the following people:

Deborah Lipstadt and David Irving were both extremely generous in granting me extensive interviews before this case went to trial and in answering my often impertinent questions during the trial and after the judgment.

Anthony Julius and James Libson at Mishcon de Reya, Kevin Bays and Mark Bateman at Davenport Lyons and Helena Peacock at Penguin Books were all remarkably patient in helping a non-lawyer to understand both the libel process and the legal issues at stake. I am particularly grateful to Anthony Julius and Mark Bateman for their consistently generous and helpful responses to my questions.

Charles Gray, the trial judge, surprised me by granting a request for an interview before the trial began. We never spoke again, but his former clerk, Kim Janes, furnished me with a wealth of material relating to his career as a libel barrister, while his current clerk, John Lloyd, made sure I had access to the proceedings and then to the transcripts despite my being both a foreigner and a stranger to the courts.

Don Honeyman, Gitta Sereny's husband, allowed me access to material related to Irving's suit against Ms. Sereny and the

Observer; David Parsons of Lovell White Durrant, who represent Sereny and the *Observer*, helped me to understand how the two cases were related. Adam Bellow, who edited the American edition of *Denying the Holocaust*, helped me to make sense of the book's publishing history. Michael Rubinstein, who once represented Irving, helped me to make sense of Irving's legal history.

Christopher Browning, Richard Evans, Peter Longerich and Robert Jan van Pelt all answered my post trial questions with great candor and clarity. In the case of Evans and van Pelt this cooperation was all the more generous in that both men knew I was not unreservedly enthusiastic about their performance in the witness box; indeed Robert Jan van Pelt answered so many of my queries with such consistent kindness I felt constrained to remind him of my strictures. I am profoundly indebted to him and to his exemplary scholarship.

Writing for me is a way of thinking things through. My first attempt to understand what was at stake in this trial came in an article for the *New York Times*. I take great pleasure in acknowledging my debt to Patricia Cohen for commissioning that piece and for helping me to meet the *Times*'s standards of fairness and balance. She and I are both veterans of the late lamented *New York Newsday*, where such matters, though taken seriously, were perhaps less of a fetish. But my own roots are firmly in advocacy journalism, so it was with both amusement and amazement that I read an attempt in the *New Republic* to use what the magazine called my "fine relaxing balance" as a stick with which to beat both Ms. Cohen and the *Times*. Not every writer gets the satisfaction of such a speedy public response; for that, and for the incoherent ferocity of the attack, I am grateful to the editors of the *New Republic*.

My debt to the *Atlantic Monthly* is of a different order altogether. Jack Beatty commissioned 10,000 words to run on the eve of the trial, then accepted, edited, and printed over 15,000 words. Avril Cornel made contacting the magazine a pleasure rather than a burden. Amy Meeker and Yvonne Rolzhausen saved me from errors great and small, and particularly impressed my British sources with their tireless willingness to discuss nuances of meaning and their reverence for facts. None of this, however, would have been possible without the unwavering support of William Whitworth, a man I have still never met, and to whom I fear I never sufficiently acknowledged my gratitude for what was by any measure the most satisfying editorial experience of my journalistic career. For his initial queries, his consistently helpful advice, and most of all for his persistent questioning of whether what I wrote was what I really meant—his deep faith that it was in fact possible to get it right—I remain profoundly grateful.

It was my agent, Andrew Wylie, who first suggested writing a book about the Irving–Lipstadt libel trial. I thank him for that, for his serene confidence, and most of all for sticking with me through some long lean years. Thanks also to Zoe Pagnamenta, Helen Allen, Rose Billington, Georgia Garrett, Martha Lowe, and Emma Smart at the Wylie Agency.

Starling Lawrence at W.W. Norton and Neil Belton at Granta Books responded to my proposal to write about the trial with great enthusiasm and intelligence. I feel particularly fortunate to have editors on both sides of the Atlantic who understood immediately the importance of the trial, and who were both so willing and able to engage with the questions this book tries to answer. My thanks also to Sajidah Ahmad at Granta for guiding me through the production process, and to Drake Bennett at Norton for some crucial assists.

The United States National Archive cartographic division contains an extraordinary wealth of aerial photographs of Auschwitz and Birkenau, many of them digitized and available for viewing on-line at *www.nara.gov*. I thank Iris Cooper of the National Archive for helping me to reach the right person, and Sam Welch of the cartographic division for giving me permission to reproduce two aerial photographs.

I am a reporter, not a scholar. But in my various attempts to make sense of this trial I have benefited from the advice (which I have not always followed) and opinions (with which I have not always agreed) of the following scholars: Michael Berkowitz, Ruth Birn, Norman Finkelstein, Gerald Fleming, Michael Geyer, Eric Hobsbawm, and Jonathan Sarna. I am also indebted to Mark Mazower, both for his helpful comments and for the example of his own scrupulous, deeply engaged scholarship. Herr Dobblestein, of the legal section of the German Consulate in London, helped me to understand his country's laws against Holocaust denial. My cousin, the philosopher Samuel Guttenplan, helped to clarify my understanding of the epistemological questions. Sir Martin Gilbert, whom I met in the course of the trial, responded with characteristic generosity to my many requests for information. I should add that while I am indebted to all of them, none should be held responsible for the opinions expressed in this book or the mistakes that remain, which are entirely of my own making.

As an independent researcher I wish to thank the staff at the Wiener Library, who let me borrow one of the few copies of Peter Novick's book in Britain for months at a time; I am also grateful for the superb collection at University College London, where the American librarian, Ruth Dar, displayed similar indulgence. I also thank Dr. Eric Halpern, my supervisor at UCL, and Dr. Kathleen Burk, my director of studies, for allowing me to interrupt my studies in American History to write this book.

A trial is an enclosed universe, cut off from the rest of life by the protocols of court procedure and the fanatical attention paid by its inhabitants to meanings incomprehensible to the outside world. In the press section, Eva Menasse and James Buchan were singularly pleasant and stimulating companions whose understanding of the proceedings helped shape my own. Eva made it possible for a non-German speaker to follow the at times arcane arguments over the precise meanings of German words; Jamie first called my attention to the parallels between David Irving and Dio Chrysostom. Sam Tanenhaus, a visitor to the press section and newfound friend, proves you don't have to be a lefty to be a *mensch*. Dan Yurman's internet digest of trial coverage was a valuable resource, and Hilary Ostrov's e-mails kept me on my toes.

Outside the trial I have derived enormous sustenance from Peter Cariani and Becky Heaton, Duncan Bull, Edward Fox, Larry Friedman, Merle and Gene Mahon, Rosemary Moore and Josh Shneider, Andrew Patner, Joel Sanders, John Scagliotti, Gene Seymour and Marie Nahickian, Sheila Shulman, and Carl Strehlke. My old boss and friend Robert Friedman provided moral support at a crucial juncture, as did Victor Navasky. Karen Rothmyer and Katrina van den Heuvel, my editors at the *Nation*, have given me a congenial journalistic home. And though I take issue with him in these pages, I am grateful to my friend Christopher Hitchens for bringing David Irving to my notice, and for not taking our disagreement personally.

There are some debts that can never be repaid. My wife, Maria Margaronis, put her own work on hold to allow me to complete this book on time. This was a very difficult year and though I look forward to doing the same for her I doubt whether I, or anyone else, could have made the same sacrifice with equivalent grace. But I will try.

Our children, Alexander, Zoe, and Theo, all saw a great deal less of their father than they were used to. I thank them, too, for being so splendid throughout, and so nice to come home to. (Part of the credit here must go to Audrey Lematte and Martina Gjurekovic, "look-after-ladies" extraordinaire.)

My mother, Jacqueline Goldstein Guttenplan, was a great believer in asking questions. And if my father, Mitchell Guttenplan, didn't pass on his own piety he nonetheless continues to encourage his children and grandchildren in ways small and large to maintain their engagement with Judaism.

Long ago I realized that if I ever managed to write a book it would in large measure be due to the influence of Joseph Ormond, my teacher at Mayfair Elementary School in Philadelphia. As a parent I have seen yet again the importance of a teacher's influence, and as a writer I will always owe a great debt to Joe, and to Linda Jarrett of White Station High School in Memphis, and Sidney Morgenbessor, Michael Rosenthal, Edward Said and Catharine Stimpson at Columbia.

Finally I would like to thank Raul Hilberg. Anyone who writes about the Holocaust is in his debt. To me, Hilberg is heroic not just for his achievement as a historian, but as a moral figure, a man whose passionate commitment to the truth is undiminished despite bringing him—or the world—little comfort. To contemplate such darkness and remain unmoved would be inhuman. Hilberg struck me as profoundly aware of the dispiriting nature of his subject. Yet he persists, spurning rationalization or mysticism, seeking consolation only in his precious facts. The dedication of this book reflects only a portion of the enormous gratitude I feel for his work and for his assistance in clarifying my own thoughts about what will always remain his field.

January 1, 2001
Hampstead, London and Guilford, Vermont

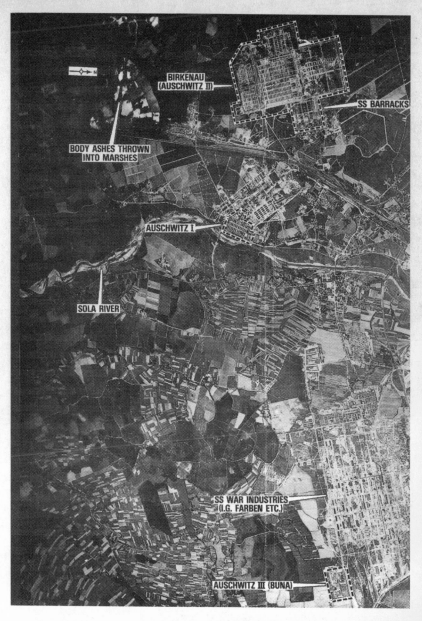

An aerial photograph of the Auschwitz–Birkenau complex taken on June 26, 1944 by the United States Air Force. The labels were supplied by the United States Central Intelligence Agency in 1978.

Four of the five triple muffle ovens from Crematorium 2, winter 1942.
Copyright © Auschwitz–Birkenau State Museum.

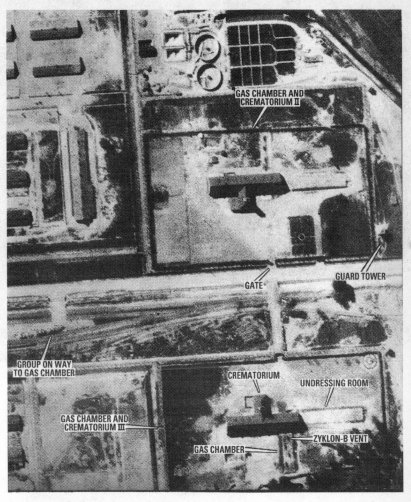

GAS CHAMBER AND CREMATORIUM II

GUARD TOWER

GATE

GROUP ON WAY TO GAS CHAMBER

CREMATORIUM

UNDRESSING ROOM

GAS CHAMBER AND CREMATORIUM III

ZYKLON-B VENT

GAS CHAMBER

Aerial photograph of Birkenau taken by the United States Air Force on August 25, 1944. Note the line of prisoners moving toward the gas chamber, and the four dark holes in the roof of Crematorium 3 (bottom right).

Crematorium 3, June 1943. Copyright © Auschwitz–Birkenau State Museum.

Introduction

This is the story of a trial. It is also a book about the Holocaust.

In July 1996 the British writer David Irving sued Deborah Lipstadt, an American academic, for libel. Irving is the author of *Hitler's War*, *The Destruction of Dresden*, and biographies of Erwin Rommel, Josef Goebbels, and Winston Churchill; his books telling the story of the Second World War from the German side have been praised by leading historians in Britain and the United States. In his massive study *The Second World War*, military historian Sir John Keegan calls *Hitler's War* "certainly among the half dozen most important books" on the period. But to Deborah Lipstadt, Irving's identification with his Nazi subjects went beyond scholarly empathy. In her book *Denying the Holocaust: The Growing Assault on Truth and Memory* Lipstadt portrayed Irving as a key figure in what she described as a movement to rehabilitate the Nazis by denying the historical reality of their crimes. In Lipstadt's account, Irving bends historical evidence "until it conforms with his ideological leanings and political agenda." Far from being a reputable historian, wrote Lipstadt, Irving is an extremist and a liar, "one of the most dangerous spokespersons for Holocaust denial."

The trial began on January 11, 2000 at the Royal Courts of Justice in London. By suing in London, Irving put Lipstadt at a multiple disadvantage. Not only did she have to travel thousands of miles from home, she also had to fight her case without the benefit of the First Amendment. In an American court Irving would have to prove that what Lipstadt wrote about him was false; he also would have to prove that she knew it was false. In Britain the libel laws favor the person suing. Here it would be up to Lipstadt to prove that what she wrote was true. And since Irving claimed that he couldn't be described as a "Holocaust denier" because the gas chambers themselves were a hoax, Lipstadt and her lawyers were, in effect, forced to prove the reality of the Holocaust.

This was a battle neither side could afford to lose. Irving, who represented himself, risked his reputation as well as his livelihood. Defeat would mean professional ruin, and probable bankruptcy. For Lipstadt and her British publisher (and co-defendant) Penguin Books, the stakes were even higher. Irving's strategy of putting the Holocaust itself on trial meant that Lipstadt and her lawyers had to defend not just her veracity, but the integrity of all of those caught up in the Nazi onslaught. If David Irving won, a British court would have lent its imprimatur to his version of events, in which the survivors of Auschwitz are branded as liars, and the suffering of the victims of the gas chambers is simply erased from the pages of history.

How serious was the danger of this happening? Serious enough for Penguin Books to spend over a million pounds on lawyers' fees, and hundreds of thousands more hiring expert witnesses. Serious enough for Steven Spielberg and a number of other American Jews to contribute to the cost of bringing Lipstadt to London for the three-month trial, and to the cost of hiring a prominent law firm to represent Lipstadt's personal interest. Serious enough that, for those of us who sat through the whole trial, the outcome remained in doubt until the last day.

Libel defense in Britain is always an uphill struggle, and part of Lipstadt's burden lay in having to prove things most of us take for granted: Adolf Hitler's murderous intentions, the horrifying efficiency of the death camps, the fatal consequences for the Jews. But the very act of taking so much for granted conceals precisely those questions which Irving's strategy was designed to provoke: How do we know these things really happened? What is the evidence? Who are the witnesses? How do we know they are telling the truth?

On January 27, 1945 the Red Army liberated Auschwitz. The camp itself was vast—a complex of barracks, factories, and satellite camps that covered roughly 15 square miles. At Auschwitz–Monowitz, a synthetic-rubber works, the Soviets found 600 slave laborers. (Among them was a young Italian Jew named Primo Levi, whose experiences would form the basis of *If This Is a Man*, one of the earliest, and most powerful, accounts of life in the camps.) At the main camp, there were 1,200 sick prisoners. At Auschwitz–Birkenau the Soviets found 32 enormous storage buildings burned to the ground. But in the four buildings that escaped the flames there were 348,820 men's suits, 836,255 women's garments, 13,964 carpets—and seven tonnes of human hair. Yet only some 5,800 sick prisoners remained. Whose clothing was this? Whose hair? Where did these mountains—of shoes, eyeglasses, false teeth, toothbrushes, children's toys—come from?

    The answer lay in ruins: four crematoria, dynamited by the retreating Germans, and within whose walls approximately one million people, most of them Jews, had been deliberately, methodically, gassed to death and then incinerated. What they found at Auschwitz stunned even the veteran troops of the First Ukrainian Front—but it did not come as a total surprise. The previous July the Soviet Eighth Guards Army captured Lublin, and in the suburb of Majdanek discovered a camp that the fleeing Nazis had been forced to abandon before it could be destroyed. In this much smaller compound the Red Army found furnaces and gas chambers still intact—and 820,000 shoes.

If experience had prepared the Soviets for what they would find at Auschwitz, ideology also played a part. In the German eagerness to extract everything possible from their prisoners, from the sweat of their labor down to the hair on their heads and the gold in their teeth, the Russians saw the logic of industrial capitalism reach its macabre denouement. These were not simple prison camps, or even concentration camps. These, proclaimed *Pravda*, were "factories of death."

The West was not prepared. The first British reporter to visit Majdanek had his story spiked as "a propaganda stunt." In the United States, the editors of *Christian Century* found the parallels between Majdanek "and the 'corpse factory' atrocity tale of the First World War . . . too striking to be overlooked." Lacking both the ideology and the first-hand experience, most Western commentators dismissed contemporary reports of the Nazi genocide as either Soviet propaganda or Jewish exaggeration. Deborah Lipstadt's first book, a scholarly study of this dismissal, is titled *Beyond Belief*.

It was as a corrective to such skepticism that General Dwight Eisenhower, deeply shocked by what he'd seen at Ohrdruf concentration camp, arranged tours of the camp for American Congressmen and newspaper editors. Eisenhower also sent photographs of the dead prisoners to Winston Churchill. As Belsen, Buchenwald, Dachau, and the other camps were liberated, a fuller picture began to emerge of the catastrophe which had struck European Jewry. Of the 8.5 million Jews living in Europe in 1939, fewer than three million were left alive. Thousands had died in uniform. A few hundred thousand managed to escape, mostly to the United States or Palestine or the Soviet Union. But the vast majority, between five and six million civilians—men, women, and children—had been murdered by the Nazis in their effort to eliminate European Jewry.

Most of those killed were not gassed. In the wake of Hitler's invasion of the Soviet Union some 1.3 million Jews, mostly

Russians and Poles, were murdered by shooting. Their killers were sometimes members of the *Einsatzgruppen*, mobile killing units sent in behind the attacking *Wehrmacht*. But regular army units, police battalions, and reserve police battalions all partici-pated in the slaughter. Other Jews were worked to death at Mauthausen, hauling boulders until they dropped. Still others were deliberately starved, or forced to live in typhus-infested ghettos and barracks until they succumbed. Toward the end of the war tens, perhaps hundreds, of thousands were sent on forced marches through the wintry Polish countryside without food or adequate clothing. For the victims, at least, the manner of killing was ultimately of little consequence.

History takes another view. With 40 million dead, the Second World War was the greatest conflagration in the history of the planet. Perhaps half of these deaths were civilians: the Soviet intelligentsia targeted by the *Einsatzgruppen* along with the Jews; the Polish intelligentsia decimated first by the Soviets and then by the Nazis; Russian civilians killed by artillery barrage and starvation at Stalingrad or Leningrad; Chinese killed by starvation in Manchuria; Greeks killed by starvation in Athens; English, German, Polish, Japanese, and Chinese victims of aerial bombardment. Even the dead of Hiroshima and Nagasaki, it could be argued, differed from the dead of London or Hamburg or Rotterdam only in their number.

To attempt to construct a hierarchy of such suffering is obscene. Yet there are still distinctions to be observed—dis-tinctions that shape both our view of the war and our response to its outcome. One such distinction is between the deaths of civilians, whether "inadvertent" or the result of a decision to terrorize the population, and the attempt to eliminate an entire population group. Not even those who see the bombing of Hiroshima (or Dresden or Coventry) as a war crime claim that they were intended to wipe out every Japanese (or German or

Briton). There is also a difference—a technological difference and a moral difference—between the direct, one-at-a-time action of shooting and the diffusion of responsibility introduced by the gas chamber. A man who kills with a machine gun still has to pull the trigger. The gas chamber introduces a chain of fatality from the bureaucrat in Berlin to the policeman who rounds up the deportees to the soldier who unloads the train to the prisoner who conducts the victims to the undressing room to the guard who locks the door to the doctor who pours in the gas pellets. Which one is the mass murderer?

Of all the nations engaged in the Second World War, only the Nazis tried to eliminate a whole people. And only the Nazis used gas chambers. These stubborn facts mark out the Nazi regime as something apart, a phenomenon that can't simply be weighed against the millions of Stalin's victims or the consequences of British or American imperialism. As the totem of this singularity, the gas chamber is both the emblem of Nazi inhumanity and the ultimate obstacle to any rehabilitation of the Nazi period.

Hitler's partisans have always known this. The Nazis themselves knew there was something different about the *Endlösung der Judenfrage*—the "Final Solution of the Jewish Question." Hence the strict secrecy: when Hans Frank, the Nazi Governor of Occupied Poland, tried to visit Auschwitz his car was stopped and he was turned back. Hence the deception: Auschwitz–Birkenau, the main killing center, was officially designated a camp for prisoners of war; Sobibór, a camp whose sole purpose was the killing of Jews, was officially labeled a transit camp. And hence the euphemism: in Auschwitz, the gas chambers and crematoria were known as *Spezialeinrichtungen* (special installations) or *Bade-anstalten* (bath houses); the killing itself was referred to as *Sonderbehandlung* (special treatment), the same term used for those shot by the *Einsatzgruppen*.

In the closing days of the war, and in the wake of the Soviet capture of Majdanek (which despite Western skepticism was still viewed as a propaganda disaster by Hitler), the Nazis raced to eliminate the evidence of what they had done. The camps at Belzec, Sobibór and Treblinka had already been reduced to rubble. Documents were burned. The *Sonderkommando*— prisoners who disposed of the corpses, tended the crematoria, emptied the gas chambers—were executed.

Like the secrecy itself, this effort was not entirely successful. In the millions of pages of captured documents the euphemisms sometimes slip. On a very few occasions the perpetrators spoke frankly of their deeds. And despite their best efforts, the Nazis were not able to eliminate all the evidence. Or the witnesses. A handful escaped during the war. Many more—a tiny remnant of the total, but too many to ignore— survived. Their testimony, and the testimony of those perpetrators who confessed their crimes either at Nuremberg or at subsequent war-crimes trials, forms the core of what we know about what came to be called the Holocaust.

Since the end of the war scholars have labored to construct a complete picture of the disaster and to provide explanations for what happened. In recent years, for example, Daniel Goldhagen's *Hitler's Willing Executioners* and Christopher Browning's *Ordinary Men* have offered opposing views on why the men who engaged in mass shootings of Jews—many of whom were given the chance to excuse themselves—chose to participate. There are no proofs in historical explanation, and such debates may never be resolved. Nor will we ever know the names of all the victims—or of all the perpetrators. Still, Raul Hilberg's magisterial *The Destruction of the European Jews*, first published in 1961 and subsequently expanded to three volumes as the passage of time has provided material for emendation, provides a remarkably comprehensive account. Hilberg, who fled Vienna with his parents in 1939, and served in the American infantry during the war, spent eight months at the War Documentation Project cataloguing captured Nazi archives. These, in conjunction with Nuremberg documents, were the basis of his research.

Hilberg lists the names of the men who designed Sobibór, the contractors who built Treblinka, and the chemist who supervised the killing at Belzec. He shows how the companies who manufactured poison gas divided the market, and explains how the two firms who collaborated on the building of the crematoria at Auschwitz parceled out the work. But in his description of the killing process, even Hilberg is forced to rely principally on eyewitness testimony.

"I'm not going to dispute most of what they say about the Holocaust," David Irving told me before the trial began. By concentrating his attack on the gas chambers at Auschwitz Irving hoped to present himself as a reasonable man with reasonable doubts. Irving knew that if he succeeded—if his doubts about the reality of the gas chambers were accepted as reasonable—the road would then be open not just to a normalization of our view of the Nazi regime, but to a broader revision of our understanding of what was at stake in the Second World War. He also knew that by focusing specifically on the gas chambers he was, in evidentiary terms, picking the opposition's weakest point.

A lot of what we know about Auschwitz comes from trials. The transcript of the Nuremberg Tribunal alone, for example, takes up 42 volumes, with additional volumes devoted to exhibits and evidence. Rudolf Höss, the camp commandant, was tried at Nuremberg. After his conviction he was extradited to Poland, where a separate trial devoted to Auschwitz was held. Dr. Jan Sehn, a judge of the Cracow court, led a year-long forensic investigation that brought together the confessions of Höss and other perpetrators with the testimony of numerous victims and those camp archives which had escaped destruction. Adolf Eichmann, described by Höss as "the only SS officer who was allowed to keep records" concerning liquidations, was captured in 1960. In 1972 the Austrians finally got around to trying Walther Dejaco, the man who designed the gas chambers. There was even an Auschwitz trial in England.

If you go into a bookstore today and pick up a copy of Leon Uris's novel *Exodus*, you will find the following description of life in Auschwitz: "Here in block X, Nazi doctors Wirths, Schumann, and Clauberg kept the human raw material for their pseudo-scientific experiments. Polish prisoner Dr. Wladislaw Dering performed castrations and ovariectomies ordered by his German masters as part of their insane program to find a way to sterilize the entire Jewish race."[1]

But if you go to a library, and look in the first edition, the wording is slightly different: "Here in block X, Dr. Wirte [sic] used women as guinea-pigs and Dr. Schumann sterilized by castration and X-ray and Caluberg [sic] removed ovaries and Dr. Dehring [sic] performed seventeen thousand 'experiments' in surgery without anaesthetic."[2] As Nazi war criminals, Wirths, Schumann, and Clauberg were in no position to object to Uris's description of their activities. In 1947 Wladislaw Dering had also been listed as a war criminal by the Polish authorities, but by the time *Exodus* was published he was practicing medicine in London after 10 years in the Colonial Medical Service, where his work had earned him an OBE.[3]

Dering sued Uris and his British publisher for libel, claiming that as a Polish prisoner he had no choice but to follow the Nazi doctors' orders. Dering, who'd been second-in-command of the camp's nationalist Polish underground, also maintained that the dossier which Uris had essentially transcribed into his novel was based on information from Polish Communists and vengeance-crazed Jews. He admitted performing forced sterilizations on Jews, but said these had only been a tiny fraction—about a hundred—of the 17,000 operations he'd performed at Auschwitz. He also claimed he'd used a proper anaesthetic.

The defense made extensive use of witnesses, including

several of Dering's victims. A prisoner–doctor who had refused to perform sterilizations—and who was not punished for her refusal—also testified. The witness accounts were sometimes contradictory, and in the end the jury found that Uris was unable to prove that what he'd written was true. The novel *QB VII* is Uris's own fictionalized account of the affair.

The judgment against Uris proved a pyrrhic victory since the same jury awarded Dering only a halfpenny's damages—at the time the smallest coin in circulation—and decreed he should pay his opponent's costs, which even in the 1960s ran to tens of thousands of pounds. But a pyrrhic victory for Irving would still be a disaster for his opponents—and a huge boost to those who, under the guise of historical revisionism, seek to rewrite the history of the Second World War, recasting Nazi genocide as a regrettably harsh response to Jewish oppression.

The gas chambers were not an issue in the *Exodus* trial. Nor was the existence of the gas chambers an issue at the trial of Walther Dejaco and Fritz Ertl, his collaborator in designing the crematoria at Auschwitz–Birkenau. Though their names are on the blueprints, and Ertl admitted he knew the designs were for "special actions"—a phrase whose real meaning he also admitted knowing—the Viennese court found neither man guilty.*

By suing Deborah Lipstadt for libel, David Irving hoped to make the existence of the gas chambers an issue, a controversy, an occasion for doubt. Of course everyone knows millions of Jews really did die in the gas chambers, not just at Auschwitz, but at Dachau and Belsen. The problem is, what everyone knows about the Holocaust isn't always true. There was a gas chamber at Dachau, but it was never used. There were no gas chambers at Belsen.

---

* The result, like the prosecutor's decision to charge Dejaco only with the murder of a single inmate on the building site, says more about Austria's difficult relationship with its own past than it does about the evidence for the Holocaust.

For a long time everyone knew the Nazis made soap from the fat of murdered Jews. In its first reports on the extermination camps in November 1942 the *New York Times* quoted Dr. Stephen Wise, head of the American Jewish Congress, who claimed that the bodies of the dead were being exploited for soap, fat, and lubricants.[4] In the Polish town of Piotrkow, as the transports of Jews passed through the town the locals would say "*Jada na midlo*." ("They travel on their way to soap.") After the war, the municipal museum in Prague displayed a bar of soap it said had been made from Jewish corpses.[5] It wasn't. The grisly tale of human beings rendered into soap, though it figured in some of the earliest accounts of events inside Nazi-occupied Europe, has long been rejected by historians as a recycled leftover from the First World War, when similar atrocity stories were staples of Allied propaganda.[6]

And we all know about the brave King of Denmark, who, after his country was occupied by the Germans, threatened to put on the yellow star himself if the Nazis insisted on imposing the badge on Danish Jews. As the historian Martin Gilbert writes in *Holocaust Journey*: "The King, and his people, courageously arranged for most Danish Jews to be smuggled across the water to Sweden on the eve of the planned deportation. But the episode with the yellow star never took place." The source for this inspiring but inaccurate episode: Uris's *Exodus*.[7]

The Danish King's gesture, though mythical, has become one of the "lessons" of the Holocaust, its parable of personal solidarity often serving as the uplifting counter to the German pastor Martin Niemöller's somber postwar confession: "First, they came for the Jews, but I was not a Jew. . . ." Niemöller's litany of indifference to the escalating brutality of life in Nazi Germany is one of the texts of our times, quoted by Republicans and Democrats, Jews and Christians, *Time* magazine and the *Encyclopedia of the Holocaust*. All of these versions agree: first, they came for the Jews. Only they didn't. And Niemöller never claimed they had.

When the Nazis came to power in Germany, "first, they came for the Communists"—a circumstance acknowledged by Niemöller, who actually went on to say:

> but I was not a Communist—so I did nothing. Then they came for the Social Democrats, but I was not a Social Democrat—so I did nothing. Then came the trade unionists, but I was not a trade unionist. And then they came for the Jews, but I was not a Jew—so I did little. Then when they came for me, there was no one left who could stand up for me.[8]

Why would so many sources mistakenly put the Jews first? Why would the version enshrined in the United States Holocaust Memorial Museum neglect to mention Nazism's first victims, the Communists? Perhaps because arguments about the Holocaust have always been about politics as well as history.

In *The Drowned and the Saved* Primo Levi recalls the taunts of a guard at Auschwitz:

> Even if someone were to survive, the world will not believe him. There will be perhaps suspicions, discussions, research by historians, but there will be no certainties, because we will destroy the evidence together with you. And even if some proof should remain and some of you survive, people will say the events you describe are too monstrous to be believed: they will say that they are exaggerations of Allied propaganda and will believe us, who will deny everything, and not you. We will be the ones to dictate the history of the Lagers [camps].[9]

In 1987 Levi fell to his death.

Who will write the history? Even while it was still going on, knowledge of the Holocaust was influenced—one is tempted to say fatally influenced—by the uses to which such knowledge might be put. It is now beyond doubt that both the British and the American governments knew at least the magnitude of the Jewish catastrophe, if not the precise means involved.[10] There were other, perhaps understandable reasons for keeping silent: the need to safeguard the fact that the Allies had broken Germany's codes, the probability that such "atrocity stories" wouldn't be believed, the fear that any move to rescue the victims would divert resources needed to defeat Germany on the battlefield. But there was also the fear that a campaign to persuade Germany to expel the Jews, rather than murder them, might succeed. In July 1944, when Jewish groups in Britain pleaded for the government to do something to stop the extermination of Hungarian Jewry, Home Secretary Herbert Morrison warned Foreign Secretary Anthony Eden it was "essential that we should do nothing at all which involves the risk that the further reception of refugees here might be the ultimate outcome."[11] Until the establishment of the War Refugee Board, very late in the war, American policy was little better.

Anti-Semitism was one factor that shaped how the facts of the Holocaust became known. Anti-Communism was another. During the war this meant refusing to acknowledge the reality of what the Red Army had discovered at Auschwitz and Majdanek. After the war, during the Cold War, it meant a resistance to Russian insistence on commemorating the "crimes of Fascism"—and suspicion toward anyone too eager to divert attention away from the more pressing struggle against Communism.

But if the fear of being considered insufficiently anti-Communist (or too zealously anti-German, at a time when Germany had been welcomed back in the Atlantic Pact) inhibited Jews from drawing attention to the Holocaust, Zionism gave many Jews a reason, and a license, to speak out. This was true both in Israel, where there was some effort to turn the disaster into political capital, and in the United States, particularly after the Six Day War, when support for Israel became a cornerstone of American strategic thinking in the Middle East, and when a mention of the Holocaust served both to ward off criticism of Israeli policy and to bolster claims that in the emerging "victimization Olympics," Jews had already been awarded the gold medal. Peter Novick's recent *The Holocaust in American Life* is a brilliant account of this transition from censorship to stridency.

Like all the Holocaust trials that came before it, *David Irving* versus *Penguin Books Ltd. and Deborah Lipstadt* is an argument about history, about what the Nazis did or did not do, and what did or did not happen in Auschwitz and elsewhere. Each side has its own reasons for pretending this is not so. Irving claims he is in court only to defend his reputation; the defense say the issue is Irving's veracity, not history. But Irving has used his reputation, his credibility as a historian, to advance the proposition that no Jews were killed in gas chambers at Auschwitz, which was merely a slave labor camp whose total of fatalities is dwarfed by the toll of Allied bombers over Dresden or Pforzheim. Anyone who claims differently, says Irving, is either a dupe or a liar. It is that thesis, and not any other errors or deceptions in his writing, that brought him to Lipstadt's notice in the first place. It is that thesis that brought the two of them to court. And it is that thesis that ensures that what happens in this London courtroom would be reported around the world.

The trial itself, however, poses other questions. Epistemological questions: Where does our knowledge of the past come from? How is it transmitted? Do documents deserve greater weight than the testimony of witnesses? If we use what we know about an event to interpret a document, yet we need the document to understand the event, what does this hermeneutic circle say about our ability to understand the past? If not all interpretations are equally valid, yet there is no

inherent standard of validity, on what grounds can any interpretation be ruled out?

It also raises political questions: Is the Holocaust the property of the Jews? Does a history of persecution create any
entitlement—for example, to legal protection from those who
would deny that history? What is the proper response to hate
speech? What is the connection between Fascism and anti-
Semitism? What is the connection between hate speech and
racial violence? Is the protection of free speech always a good
thing?

The trial raises questions for Jews: Is the Holocaust important for Jewish identity? How important? Why should we care
if Irving, or anyone else, wants to argue it didn't happen? Why
should anyone else care? How do Jews see themselves in relation to other groups in society?

And for non-Jews: How much does the Holocaust matter?
Why? How should we respond to Jews who feel threatened?
How should we respond to Jews who feel threatened by David
Irving? How do we see Jews in relation to other groups? How
did the Nazis see Jews? How do we feel about the implied
comparison?

And of course the trial poses—indeed, in some respects
hinges on—questions about historiography, about how history
is written. Many of these are technical, the historian's equivalent of malpractice: questions about footnotes, translations,
sources, statistics, the suppression of conflicting evidence.
There are questions about history as a discipline: What are
the standards of acceptable conduct? Who sets them? Who
enforces them? Are they the same for all kinds of history? Does
one position, however outrageous (for example the belief that
the Holocaust was a hoax), taint a historian's entire body of
work? Or can it be isolated, set to one side like a piece of
spoiled fruit?

Alongside all these questions, though, is the fundamental
challenge that haunted Primo Levi: Who will write the history?

History, the cliché tells us, is written by the winners. Yet the history of the Holocaust is a history without winners. The Allies may have defeated the Nazis, but they did not save the Jews.

Who will write the history? Every Holocaust trial offers a partial answer to that question, and the trial that is the subject of this book is only the most recent in a long series. There may well be others. But it is also something new: a Holocaust trial without victims and without perpetrators, a trial in which history is judged, as well as made.

1

Court Full

"Court rise!" With the clerk's shout we stop talking and struggle to our feet. *David Irving* versus *Penguin Books Ltd. and Deborah Lipstadt* opens on a gray morning at the height of London's flu season, and the packed courtroom is weighed down with soggy raincoats, mufflers, and sodden umbrellas. As the crowd quiets the clerk glances at an open doorway at the far end of the room and Mr. Justice Charles Gray enters, stage right, and walks briskly to the center of a raised dais with a long desk.

All trials are a kind of theater, but here the sense of costume drama is heightened by the judge's outfit. On top of his black silk robes Gray wears a scarlet sash, called a tippet. A white tie, of the kind favored by eighteenth-century New England divines, hangs from either side of his collar, and on his head is a pewter-colored horsehair wig. A patrician in fact as well as appearance (he was educated at Winchester and Trinity College, Oxford), Gray's handsome face, hound-dog eyes, and sash of office make him look like a leaner, more lugubrious version of Nigel Hawthorne, the actor who played the mad King George III.

The dramatic effect is also enhanced by the location. Court 37 is a crisp white modern chamber, with blond wood furniture and all the hi-tech paraphernalia of contemporary litigation: fluorescent lights and hanging microphones overhead, while a tangle of cables underfoot connect the laptops placed at regular intervals on the lawyers' tables with the stenographer's desk, allowing the transcript to be consulted instantaneously. As a set design Court 37 suggests a complex custody dispute or a protracted divorce (which is indeed what it is used for most of the time) rather than an argument about the writing of history or the fate of European Jewry. But the Royal Courts of Justice building—a Victorian Gothic pile with elaborate vaults, carved stonework, and towering spires—sits at the point where Fleet Street meets the Strand. We are, literally as well as figuratively, at the juncture of journalism and the theater district.

As if in recognition of this fact, most of the seats that are supposed to be available to members of the public have been taken by reporters, who overflow the press gallery on the left side of the room, filling up the back and right side as well, turning the normal proscenium arrangement into a thrust stage. The few spectators who do gain admission are crammed into the back rows, which in some cases results in elderly Holocaust survivors sitting cheek by jowl with skin-headed British neo-Nazis. Gray begins with an apology for the cramped conditions: "It is very desirable that everybody who wants to be here should be here and I am afraid they are not."[1]

One person who very much wants to be there is David Irving. Irving is the claimant in this case—in American usage, the plaintiff.

Suing somebody for libel in Britain is expensive. A Queen's Counsel (QC), the elite among barristers (trial lawyers), gets around £5,000 pounds a day. And just as most claimants consider it only prudent to hire a QC, most QCs require a junior barrister. Add in a complement of solicitors and the total once the trial gets underway can easily exceed £10,000 a day—a figure which makes libel the indoor equivalent of racing yachts or breeding thoroughbred horses as a rich man's sport. Though he comes to court in a £2,000 made-to-measure Gieves and Hawkes chalk-stripe suit David Irving is not a wealthy man, and it is an indication of just how much he wants to be there that he appears in court as a litigant-in-person, representing himself.

When wearing his lawyer's hat, Irving will sit alone at a long counsel's table, as he does now, peering over half-spectacles at some papers. Irving is an inventive and energetic self-publicist, and from time to time his glance lifts to the press seats, where he mouths greetings to some of the reporters. However, he never looks at the Second Defendant's table directly behind him, where Deborah Lipstadt sits glaring at the back of his neck. For her, this "day in court" has already meant a four-year interruption in her scholarly career. But if Lipstadt didn't seek this confrontation, neither did she shrink from it. Nor has she come alone to the arena.

Anthony Forbes-Watson, the owlish, sandy-haired managing director of Penguin Books (the First Defendant) is practically surrounded by lawyers. Most of them are solicitors, and wear ordinary business suits. But barrister Richard Rampton, who wears a short gray-blond wig and the silk robes of a QC, and his black-robed junior Heather Rogers, whose wig partially covers her own gray hair, add yet a further note of mummery to the proceedings.

The Second Defendant's bench is more modest, consisting of Lipstadt, a small, middle-aged woman in a sober, tan trouser suit set off by a colorful scarf knotted at the throat, seated between her two lawyers. James Libson, the younger of the two, also wears the solicitor's standard dark suit. Anthony Julius wears a plain black "stuff" robe, but no wig.

Directly behind them are a contingent of Lipstadt's supporters. There are friends from Atlanta, where she teaches at Emory University. There are also officials from the American Jewish Committee, the Board of Deputies of British Jews, the Anti-Defamation League of the B'nai Brith, and Steven

Spielberg's Shoah Foundation. Expert witnesses, reporters, interested parties, and one or two curious tourists fill the remaining seats, while several dozen disappointed spectators queue patiently in the hall outside.

All of these people—all of these interests—take up so much room that by the end of the week the trial, which has already been moved once to accommodate the anticipated crowds, will be transferred yet again to a still larger courtroom. Even so, on most mornings anyone turning up at the scheduled time of 10:30 will be greeted by a sign on the little vestibule leading into the court advising "Court Full." Just how full only becomes apparent when, in the course of some brief preliminary questions, the judge (and the spectators) learn that it has been agreed to divide the case into two parts: Auschwitz and "basically all the rest." There is some dispute about the ordering of this agenda, but when Irving remarks that "the most interesting part of the action in the light of history is, undoubtedly, the Holocaust and Auschwitz" the other side expresses no disagreement.

At that moment, history enters the courtroom. When it suits them, both sides will make energetic efforts to ignore it, to pretend that this trial is really about the interpretation of documents. Indeed the first of these attempts occurs just a few moments later, with Irving's contention that "we have to avoid the temptations of raking over the history of what happened in Poland or in Russia 50 years ago. What is moot here is not what happened in those sites of atrocities, but what happened over the last 32 years on my writing desk in my apartment off Grosvenor Square."

Irving's words are contradicted even before he speaks by a set of his own exhibits resting on an easel to his right. Roughly a metre square, and mounted on board, these blown-up black-and-white photographs do not show the interior of Irving's study or the papers on his desk. Nor do they show the books in Irving's library, or even his notorious Adolf Hitler self-portrait, or the swastika-topped swizzle sticks he likes to use to lend a politically incorrect *frisson* to his publication parties. What the pictures show, in the grainy, flattened way of aerial photographs, is one of those "sites of atrocities," in this case the camp known in Polish as Oswiecim, and whose German name, Auschwitz, has indeed come to serve as a synecdoche for the Nazis' deliberate, systematic destruction of European Jews.

In his bid to keep history out of the courtroom, Irving has the full support of both Mr. Justice Gray and the defense team. In an interview conducted in the judge's chambers before the trial Gray said he was determined to minimize that risk. "Judges," he said, "aren't historians." Defense counsel were as one in their declaration: "This trial isn't about the Holocaust." Why, then, did they commission a 700-page report from the author of *Auschwitz: 1270 to the Present*? Or another expert report on *Evidence for the Implementation of the Final Solution*, not to mention further separate reports on the systematic nature of the Nazi genocide and on Adolf Hitler's personal culpability?

Despite every determined attempt to usher it politely out the door of the courtroom, there will not be a single day in this trial when history is absent from the proceedings. And suddenly Court 37 is very crowded indeed. Here, in one of the dozens of boxes that line the room, are the records of the perpetrators: reports of the *Einsatzgruppen*, whose murderous record in Poland and behind the Russian front Irving does not deny. Here also are the documents recording a November 1941 shipment of a thousand Jews from Berlin to Riga, Latvia, where they were shot on arrival—men, women, and children. As it happens this particular transport and its fate are common ground to both sides—a small fraction of the hundreds of thousands of Jews whose deaths at the hands of the Nazis Irving also does not deny. Unable to speak for themselves, these silent witnesses will be invoked by both sides. Their presence fills the courtroom.

But they are the privileged minority, whose silence is not

taken for complicity in their non-existence. At least for the sake of argument, Court 37 must also find space to accommodate the more than two million Jews whose end—in the gas chambers of Belzec, Sobibór, Treblinka, Majdanek, Chelmno, and Auschwitz—Irving does deny. It is mostly the argument over their traces that, before the trial has even started, already fills the bookshelves and file boxes piled along every inch of free wall space in the courtroom. By splitting the trial in half, even if only procedurally, the two sides have made the status of these disputed Jews as much a matter of the court's concern as any of the questions of historiography which both sides would clearly prefer to debate. And as both sides know perfectly well, whatever Mr. Justice Gray decides about historiography, it is Auschwitz that will get the headlines in this case.

This poses a particular danger for the defense. Equivocation is a human impulse to which judges, notoriously, are not immune. If Irving loses on Auschwitz and wins on "everything else" that would still be a defeat for his opponents. In other words, if the judge finds that, though Irving was wrong about Auschwitz, his mistakes were honestly made, under the law he would be entitled to substantial damages. Lipstadt and Penguin would be forced pay Irving's costs; worse still, they might well be subject to an injunction not to repeat what they'd said about Irving's methods, on pain of imprisonment for contempt of court. But if a split decision goes the other way—if the judge finds that, despite Irving's flawed scholarship, the evidence regarding what happened at Auschwitz is simply too ambiguous to interpret with legal certainty—that would be a disaster. For the defense to win this case, they have to win it all.

The defense has other burdens as well. The English law of libel has its origins in the medieval crime of *scandalum magnatum*. A man convicted of speaking ill of his rulers—the crime later known as seditious libel—might forfeit his right hand, or his ears (the better to prevent him hearing any more slanderous gossip). In the seventeenth century the task of protecting the reputations of the powerful fell to the Court of Star Chamber, and it was partly that court's record of brutal repression—floggings and mutilation were common up to the eighteenth century—that sent American jurisprudence down a very different path. Under US law it is the plaintiff who must prove he or she has been falsely defamed.

This is not just a technical point. If Irving had sued Lipstadt in the United States (where her book was first published, and where he sells the bulk of his own books) the case would never have seen the inside of a courtroom. In an American court, Irving would either have to show that he'd never denied the Holocaust (a difficult task for a man who is on record claiming "more women died on the back seat of Edward Kennedy's car . . . than ever died in a gas chamber in Auschwitz"), or it would be Irving who had to prove that the events he denied had never happened. Besides, as a well-known author and commentator, Irving easily met the terms set by *New York Times* v. *Sullivan*, where the Supreme Court held that for a public figure to prove libel the allegations must be shown not merely to be false, but to have been made "in reckless disregard" of the truth.

An English libel claimant, on the other hand, must prove just three things: that the "words complained of" were actually published, that they could be taken as referring to the claimant, and that they were defamatory, i.e. that they tended to expose the claimant to hatred, contempt, or ridicule. Once those conditions have been satisfied—and in *Irving* v. *Lipstadt* no one disputes them—the burden of proof passes to the defendant.

The structure of the trial itself reflects this: a claimant in libel always has the last word, the last chance to persuade the judge and jury of his case. And because English law assumes that claimants are entitled to a good reputation unless and until proved otherwise, his lawyer has the first word as well. The aim is to introduce the judge and jury to the person free of any taint or shadow—to show, in Irving's case, an author of international reputation, the father of four daughters, a man whose books were prominently published and respectfully reviewed and whose company was eagerly sought by leading publishers in Britain and the United States.

Unusually for a libel trial, both sides have agreed to dispense with a jury. But as Irving opens his case it is obvious that, though the final decision will rest with Mr. Justice Gray, in Irving's mind the jury of public opinion is just as important. From his very first words Irving sets out an argument that runs on two tracks: to the judge, through the evidence he presents, and to the general public, by way of the media, who are interested less in the evidence than in Irving's manner. Though self-imposed, Irving's burden—and it is a real one—is to keep both his tracks running in parallel. He begins with a digression:

"My Lord, it is almost 30 years to the day since I last set foot in these Law Courts. . . . The occasion of that visit to this building was an action heard before Mr. Justice Lawton, which became well-known to law students as *Cassell* v. *Broome and Another*. It, too, was a libel action and I am ashamed to admit that I was the 'Another,' having written a book on a naval operation, *The Destruction of Convoy PQ17*. That was the only actively fought libel action in which I became engaged in 30 years of writing. There were two reasons for this abstinence, my Lord: first, I became more prudent about how I wrote and, second, I was taught to turn the other cheek.

"The man who taught me the latter lesson was my first publisher . . . Mr. William Kimber. Your Lordship may remember that Mr. Kimber and his author, Mr. Leon Uris, had become involved through a book which Mr. Uris had written, entitled *Exodus*, in a libel action brought by a London doctor who had been obliged to serve at Auschwitz. That case was also heard before Mr. Justice Lawton. There was one other similarity that closes this particular circle of coincidence: like me now, Mr.

Kimber was, in consequence, also obliged to spend two or three years of his life wading, as he put it, 'knee deep' through the most appalling stories of atrocities and human degradation.

"That day he advised me never, ever, to become involved in libel litigation. I might add that, with one exception that I shall later mention, I have heeded his advice."

Irving leaves the moral of this little tale unspoken. For the judge, it is that he has learned his lesson since *Cassell* v. *Broome*, when a jury found that not only had Irving libeled the commander of the ill-fated Convoy PQ17, which had been mauled by German U-boats in 1942, but that he had done so on the basis of a cold-blooded calculation that a libel suit might actually help the sales of his book. The result—an award of punitive damages on top of the libel damages—lives on in libel textbooks. Like a prosecutor whose star witness has a criminal record, Irving wants the judge to hear about this episode from him. He also wants to make the point that, despite press reports painting him as a litigious character, he is a reluctant claimant.

His mention of the *Exodus* trial is aimed at an altogether more complex set of targets. Wladislaw Dering's pursuit of Leon Uris ended up ruining Dering's reputation, his finances, and eventually his health. Irving's invocation of the most spectacular example of self-destruction through libel since Oscar Wilde sued the Marquis of Queensberry is a reminder that he, too, is running a considerable risk. But if his reference is partly a bid for sympathy—and partly, like his observation a few moments later that he and Uris had shared not only a publisher but also the lawyer Michael Rubinstein, a suggestion that he had once been on better terms with the Jews—it carries a harsher message as well. Uris's lawyers filled the courtroom with men and women who were able to describe what happened at Auschwitz from first-hand experience. And it still hadn't been enough to persuade the jury to find for their client.

This isn't turning the other cheek—Irving's unsubtle dig at his Jewish opponents—so much as throwing down the gauntlet.

"To justify her allegations of manipulation and distortion," Irving continues, "it will not suffice for Professor Lipstadt to show, if she can, that I misrepresented what happened, but that I knew what happened and that I perversely and deliberately, for whatever purpose, portrayed it differently from how I knew it to have happened.

"That is what manipulation and distortion mean, and the other, though fundamental, story of what actually happened is neither here nor there. In effect, this enquiry should not leave the four walls of my study."

Irving goes on to sketch a portrait of the artist as a wronged man. At times melodramatic: "My Lord, if we were to seek a title for this libel action, I would venture to suggest 'Pictures at an execution'—my execution!" At times grandiose: "My books have appeared between hard covers under the imprint of the finest publishing houses" (including Penguin Books, the First Defendant, which published Irving's *The War Between the Generals* in 1981).* But the overall effect is compelling. His income, once in excess of £100,000 a year, has fallen sharply: "By virtue of the activities of the Defendants, in particular of the Second Defendant, and of those who funded her and guided her hand, I have since 1996 seen one fearful publisher after another falling away from me, declining to reprint my works, refusing to accept new commissions and turning their backs on me when I approach.

"In private, the senior editors at those publishing houses still welcome me warmly as a friend and they invite me to lunch in expensive New York restaurants, and then lament that if they were to sign a contract with me on a new book, there would always be somebody in their publishing house who would object."

He has, in short, become a pariah, and though "I am not

* Penguin's corporate parent, Viking Books (at the time an independent company), published his book *Hitler's War* in 1977.

even denying that I may have been partly to blame for it myself" Irving hasn't come to the high court seeking absolution. Nor has he come solely to defend his reputation. David Irving has a "case" of his own.

"The Defendants did not act alone in their determination to destroy my career and to vandalize my legitimacy as a historian. That is a phrase that I would ask your Lordship to bear in mind. They were part of an organized international endeavor aimed at achieving precisely that. I have seen the papers. I have copies of the documents. I shall show them to this court. I know they did it and I now know why."

As he outlines it to the judge—and more importantly, to the press—Irving's "case" has two parts. The first part concerns the Holocaust, "an artificial label commonly attached to one of the greatest and still most unexplained tragedies of this century.

"I have never held myself out to be a Holocaust expert," he says. "If I am an expert in anything at all . . . it is in the role that Adolf Hitler played in the propagation of World War II, and in the decisions which he made and the knowledge on which he based those decisions." Nonetheless, "I intend to show that far from being a 'Holocaust denier'—the phrase in the title of the book—I have repeatedly drawn attention to major aspects of the Holocaust."

His voice rising in fury, Irving says that calling him a "Holocaust denier" was "particularly evil because no person in full command of his mental faculties, and with even the slightest understanding of what happened in World War II, can deny that the tragedy actually happened, however much we dissident historians may wish to quibble about the means, the scale, the dates and the other minutiae."

Baldly put, Irving's "case" on the Holocaust is that when he writes that Hitler had no knowledge of the Final Solution, or says that there were no gas chambers at Auschwitz, and that fewer people died there in four years than were killed in one night by the Allied bombing of Dresden, what he is doing is no different from a historian who argues that Lee was a better general than Grant, or an archaeologist who doubts whether the Greeks and Trojans really went to war over Helen of Troy. We may quibble about minutiae, says Irving, echoing Jean-Marie Le Pen, the French neo-Fascist, who called the gas chambers "un détail," but we are part of the conversation, and it is wrong to exclude us.

This is Irving at his most reasonable—quick to admit how much he doesn't know, ready to make concessions when confronted with evidence. But he is also very angry, and as the focus of that anger becomes clear, so does the second part of Irving's "case."

The label "Holocaust denier," he tells the court, "is a poison to which there is virtually no antidote, less lethal than a hypodermic with nerve gas jabbed in the neck, but deadly all the same. For the chosen victim, it is like being called a wife beater or a paedophile. It is enough for the label to be attached for the attachee to find himself designated as a pariah, an outcast from normal society. It is a verbal yellow star." At this there is an audible gasp from several spectators. But Irving isn't finished. "I shall invite the court to hear expert evidence on the relationship between the world's Jewish communities and the rest of us," he says. "The Jewish community, their fame and fortunes, play a central role in these proceedings."

Irving's "case" fits together to suggest that, in order to protect their fraudulent status as victims of genocide, which is threatened by "dissident historians" like himself, the Jews have fomented an international conspiracy aimed at silencing Irving and discrediting his views. Irving's problem is that his "case" deals with motives, but the trial—his "suit" as opposed to his "case"—deals with facts. If Irving wins, the judge will consider the Defendants' motives when awarding damages. Until then, Irving will have to argue his suit.

How he intends to do this—and vex his enemies at the same time—emerges in a neat little bit of misdirection about history.

"This trial is not really about what happened in the Holocaust or how many Jews and other persecuted minorities were tortured and put to death," says Irving. "It may be that I was totally ignorant on some aspects of World War II, and I hasten to say that I do not believe I was, but to be accused of deliberate manipulation, and distorting, and mistranslating, is perverse. The Defendants must show, in my humble submission, first that a particular thing happened or existed; second that I was aware of that particular thing as it happened or existed, at the time that I wrote about it from the records then before me; third, that I then wilfully manipulated the text or mistranslated or distorted it for the purposes that they imply.

"The Defendants must show . . . first that a particular thing happened." Using the British libel laws for leverage, Irving's legal jiu-jitsu means that, in effect, his opponents will indeed have to prove that the Holocaust happened.

With Irving still in full flow, the court breaks for lunch. When proceedings resume, he finishes reading out a document he calls the "Bruns report"—the transcript of an April 1945 conversation, secretly taped by British intelligence, between Major-General Walter Bruns and his fellow German prisoners of war. Bruns was in Riga on November 30, 1941 and witnessed the massacre of the thousand Berlin Jews: "When I arrived those pits were so full that the living had to lie down on top of the dead; then they were shot and, in order to save room, they had to lie down neatly in layers." The hellish scenes Bruns describes are full of convincing visual detail, and as Irving points out not only does he not deny them, he has quoted them extensively in three of his books.

He then turns to the question of anti-Semitism. Ironically, in her book Deborah Lipstadt never accuses Irving of anti-Semitism. But the rules of procedure call for both sides in a civil action to disclose in advance not only which documents they want to cite, and which witnesses they are going to call, but what those witnesses are likely to say. Irving knows he's going to be painted as a right-wing extremist, a bigot, and an anti-Semite, and he does his best to defuse such incendiary charges in advance. He cites his former lawyer, Rubinstein, "an enormously capable, energetic and likeable person," first introduced to him by William Kimber, who described him as "very Jewish, but a very Christian kind of a Jew, rather like Jesus Christ." He goes on to mention some Jewish friends, but stops short of claiming "some of my best friends are . . ." and lists instead the many Jews who have been happy to publish his books. Shifting to the attack, Irving describes various incidents of harassment over the years at the hands of Jewish groups.

Irving seems more comfortable on the attack, and after a lengthy recitation of how he came to acquire the original microfiche of Nazi propaganda minister Josef Goebbels's diaries from the Russian State Archives—a minor incident in Lipstadt's book, but one which evidently injured Irving's pride—he returns to the offensive. "I mention these facts, my Lord, to show that it was not just one single action that has destroyed my career, but a cumulative, self-perpetuating, rolling onslaught from every side engineered by the same people [i.e. the Jews] who have propagated the book which is at the center of the dispute, which is the subject of this action, my Lord." At 3:30 in the afternoon, David Irving sits down.

Before the defense can respond, Mr. Justice Gray has a question. Quoting with approval Irving's remark that "This trial is not really about what happened in the Holocaust," he adds: "Certainly as I see it, and I believe as the Defendants see it, that is right. This trial is not concerned with making findings of historical fact." Gray wants to know if Irving is arguing that the defense have to prove not just that an event happened, but that he had "actual knowledge" of the event. Can't they just show "you shut your eyes to it?"

Irving says no, and as he rises from his seat Richard Rampton agrees: "Your Lordship has it right. It is not that he is indolent. It is not that he falls into error. It is that he deliberately perverts the course of this particular episode in European history, including what happened at Auschwitz."

With his creased cheeks, thinning white hair and big round gold wire-rims, Richard Rampton could be mistaken for some-body's kindly uncle. Until he speaks. When he's "on his feet," as barristers say when they are addressing the court, Rampton's manner is the opposite of avuncular. He seems rather to com-mand a vast reservoir of irritability and disdain, which threaten at any moment to overflow the banks of tolerance, dissolving the object of his scorn in a flood of bile. As the trial progresses Rampton will wield his irritability like a weapon, snapping at his clerks and juniors, jumping impatiently from document to document. But as he opens his case, Rampton's tone is one of measured contempt.

"My Lord, Mr. Irving calls himself a historian. The truth is, however, that he is not a historian at all but a falsifier of history. To put it bluntly, he is a liar." Like the prosecutor in a murder case pointing to the accused, Rampton pauses and stares at Irving.

"Lies may take various forms," he continues, "and may as often consist of suppression or omission as of direct falsehood or invention, but in the end all forms of lying converge into a single definition: wilful, deliberate misstatement of the facts."

There are many ways to fight a libel trial. A defendant can claim that the words complained of have been misunderstood, in which case the trial becomes an argument about the meaning of words. Or a defendant can claim that the offending words were "fair comment"—not allegations of fact, but comments based on beliefs which are themselves substantially true, and which a fair-minded person might honestly believe. Deborah Lipstadt and Penguin, however, are pleading "justification"— that what she said about Irving in her book, though indeed defamatory, is also true.

As if to hammer home what this means, Rampton elaborates

his description of Irving's mendacity. "Mr. Irving has used many different means to falsify history: invention, misquotation, suppression, distortion, manipulation and not least mistranslation. But all these techniques have the same ultimate effect: falsification of the truth." While Rampton defames him, Irving huddles in his seat, arms wrapped around his chest.

Whatever Rampton says about Irving, one thing he won't do is underestimate him. As a litigant in person, Irving can appear outgunned, but any illusions Rampton might have had on that count were knocked out of him in the mid-1990s by a pair of penniless vegetarian anarchists who represented themselves in a libel suit brought by Rampton's client, the McDonald's burger chain. That trial began in April 1994 and lasted until June 1997, making it the longest trial in English history. When it finally ended the judge found that Dave Morris, an unemployed postman, and Helen Steel, a part-time gardener, failed to prove some of their allegations, and awarded McDonald's £60,000 in damages the company had no hope of ever collecting. But the judge also found that some of the allegations made against Rampton's clients had been proved, including the claim that McDonald's was cruel to animals and exploited children in its advertising campaigns. This public-relations disaster cost the fast-food Goliath £10 million in legal fees and expenses.

The centerpiece of Rampton's opening this afternoon deals with the same massacre in Riga mentioned by Irving a few minutes earlier. Slowly and methodically, Rampton takes the court through "one example of many to illustrate Mr. Irving's disreputable methods. In late November 1941 a train load of about a thousand Jews was deported from Berlin to Riga in Latvia, as part of a process which had been initiated earlier that year in accordance with Hitler's wishes to empty the *Reich* of its Jews."

Rampton quotes Irving's account of what happened next, from the 1977 edition of his book *Hitler's War*: "On November 30th 1941 he [Heinrich Himmler] was summoned to the Wolf's

Lair* for a secret conference with Hitler, at which the fate of Berlin's Jews was clearly raised. At 1.30 p.m. Himmler was obliged to telephone from Hitler's bunker to [Reinhard] Heydrich the explicit order that Jews were *not to be liquidated*; and the next day Himmler telephoned SS overall General Oswald Pohl, overall chief of the concentration camp system, with the order: 'Jews are to stay where they are.' That is what Mr. Irving wrote."

In the introduction to that volume, Rampton says, Irving claimed he had "incontrovertible evidence" from Himmler's private files that Hitler had issued an order protecting the Jews. "Mr. Irving had evidently read Himmler's notes, and Mr. Irving's German was then, as it is now, very good. So what did the notes actually say?

"The relevant part of the note for 30th November 1941 reads as follows: '*Judentransport aus Berlin. Keine Liquidierung.*' That is the German entry by Himmler. The unambiguous meaning of those words in English is: 'Jew transport'— the word is singular—'Jew transport from Berlin. No liquidation.'

"Thus so far from being a general prohibition against the liquidation of the Jews, it was merely an order from Himmler to Heydrich that the particular train load of Berlin Jews in question was not to be killed on arrival in Riga.

"The matter gets worse. What was the evidence that Himmler's order to Heydrich was derived from instructions given to him by Hitler at a secret conference at which the fate of Berlin's Jews was clearly raised? The answer is none. This was pure invention by Mr. Irving. Indeed, the fact is, as Mr. Irving later discovered, that Himmler did not meet Hitler until an hour after he telephoned this order to Heydrich.

"Thus the matter gets worse still. I repeat Mr. Irving's words: 'And the next day Himmler telephoned SS General Oswald

* Hitler's field headquarters at Rastenburg in what is now part of Poland.

Pohl, overall chief of the concentration camp system, with the order 'Jews are to stay where they are.'

"What does Himmler's note of his telephone call to General Pohl on 1st December 1941 actually say? It says this: '*Verwaltungsführer des SS haben zu bleiben.*'

"Does this mean, as Mr. Irving told his English readers, 'Jews are to stay where they are'? No, it does not. It means 'Administrative leaders of the SS are to stay where they are.' Nor is there in this day's entry in the Himmler log any reference to the Jews whatsoever.

"I repeat, Mr. Irving had, as he proudly announced, read the Himmler log and he has very good German."

From the charge of falsifying history Rampton moves on to Holocaust denial, and as he progresses through his account of Irving's 1988 "conversion" to the view that Auschwitz, described as "a monstrous killing machine" in the 1977 edition of *Hitler's War*, was, as Irving writes in the 1991 edition, merely "a slave labor camp," we begin to get some sense of what Rampton is up to. Though he represents the Defendants in this action, Rampton is not presenting a defense. In his entire opening, Rampton does not mention Deborah Lipstadt or Penguin Books once. He says not one word about his clients' character, their reputation, their methods, or their principles. Instead he continues his relentless attack on Irving, who sits and plays with a broken rubber band, like a naughty boy fidgeting in the principal's office, while Rampton demolishes the Leuchter report, the basis for Irving's conversion.

After a brief glance at some of Irving's more unsavory associates—"his audiences will often consist of radical right-wing neo-Fascist, neo-Nazi groups of people"—Rampton concludes his indictment: "My Lord, this is obviously an important case, but that is not however because it is primarily concerned with whether or not the Holocaust took place or the degree of Hitler's responsibility for it. On the contrary, the essence of the case is Mr. Irving's honesty and integrity as a chronicler—I shy away from the word 'historian'—of these matters, for if it be right that Mr. Irving, driven by his extremist views and sympathies, has devoted his energies to the deliberate falsification of this tragic episode in history, then by exposing that dangerous fraud in this court the Defendants may properly be applauded for having performed a significant public service not just in this country, but in all those places in the world where anti-Semitism is waiting to be fed."

When Rampton sits down, the judge makes one more valiant attempt to drag history out of the dock: "What is at the heart of the case is the manipulation allegation and that involves looking, to a degree anyway, at what the historical documents actually say and mean." In the coming days and weeks he will try again and again to shift the trial from the messy domain of history—in Leopold von Ranke's famous phrase, *"Wie es eigentlich gewesen ist,"* "how it really was"—to the tidier questions of historiography (how history is written) and interpretation (what the documents say and mean). But neither the judge, nor the defense, nor, perhaps surprisingly, Irving himself, make any serious effort to argue with the premise implicit in Rampton's manner: that whether he is there alone or in company, David Irving himself has also been put on trial.

The Claimant

There are not many comic moments in *Irving* v. *Lipstadt*, but one of them occurs at the point when, in an ordinary libel trial, the claimant's lawyer, having made his opening speech, would begin presenting his evidence. In an ordinary libel trial the theatrical aspects have a point, an audience: the jury. It is for their benefit that the show and tell of the trial take place. The rest of us are just bystanders.

But there is no jury in Court 37, only a judge. This means that what we do see and hear in court is but a fraction of the evidence, a situation hinted at by the judge when he observes that, "having now spent quite a lot of time with the papers, in a curious way [this] is a case that does not depend to a very great extent on the oral evidence." The heart of the case—the ground on which the trial will quite likely be won or lost—are the expert reports whose thousands of pages the judge has read before the first witness is sworn in. Since no representative of the daily press has the time to read these reports, media accounts of the trial have a certain air of unreality. Yet the script still has to be followed, the witnesses duly sworn. And what that gives rise to is the spectacle of David Irving standing at the counsel's table and calling his first witness, David Irving, who then strides to the witness box where the clerk asks him how he'd like to be sworn. He appears not to understand the question. "Which oath do you want to take?"

"C[hurch] of E[ngland]," Irving replies after a rather long pause. "I had to think for a moment," he explains.

The aim of Irving's testimony—his direct evidence—is the same as his opening statement: to present himself as a reasonable man who has been badly wronged. But the means are different. The opening was rhetoric, and although lawyers are supposed to be truthful, as counsel Irving wasn't yet under oath. What comes next is narrative, his story of how he ended up in this courtroom, and every detail has the added weight of being sworn to be the truth.

Irving is a talented storyteller, but after Rampton's opening he has some damage to repair. "The Defendants have chosen to refer to my politics and they wrongly categorize them. They say that I am extreme right-wing or something like that. I have never belonged to a political party, left or right, except I think I joined the Young Conservatives at University. My father stood as a Labour candidate in the 1945 General Election."

As for his own views, "I regard myself as a laissez-faire liberal. . . . I do not look down on any section of humanity, either coloured immigrants—I have regularly employed them—or females.

"I admit to having little patience with smokers and none at all with drug abusers," he adds. And then, lest he be accused of political correctness, he goes on: "This is not to say that I have applauded—I have to state this because I will probably be asked about it—I cannot say that I have applauded the uncontrolled tide of Commonwealth immigration into this country."

Irving's language might hint at the unacceptable—most Commonwealth immigrants are non-white—but his imagery is reminiscent of Enoch Powell, a former Conservative cabinet minister who prophesied "rivers foaming with blood" if immigration proceeded unchecked. The echo may well be deliberate since Powell, who died in 1998, though condemned as a racist during his lifetime, was eulogized by Prime Minister Tony Blair for his "brilliant mind" and "the strength of his convictions." Indeed, instead of the dangerous extremist described by the defense, in Irving's self-portrait the dominant note is nostalgia: "Like most fellow countrymen of my background and vintage, I regret the passing of the Old England. I sometimes think, my Lord, that if the soldiers and sailors who stormed the beaches of Normandy in 1944 could see what England would be like at the end of this century, they would not have got 50 yards up the beach. I think they would have given up in disgust."

Before the trial began, Mr. Justice Gray told me that part of his job will be "to ensure that [Irving] is not disadvantaged by not having the legal expertise available to the other side." As Irving begins giving his evidence, Gray suggests, "I think the best thing is if I give you a little bit of a steer, if I can put it that way."

"I'm not sure I need scaring," Irving replies warily.

"No," says the judge, "the word I used was 'steer' not 'scare', simply so that your evidence has a shape that might make it more comprehensible."

The judge's first "steer" comes after Irving complains that although he made his entire collection of reviews and press clippings available to the defense—"they were shown 16 ring binders full of chronologically organized, properly pasted-up reviews and press clippings in which, who knows, they might have found some goodies they could have used against me, I do not know—but they did not bother with them."

"Take your own course, Mr. Irving," says the judge, "but do you now want to deal with the publication of *Denying the Holocaust*?" His own course or not, Irving takes the hint. "The publication of the book. I paid no attention to that book, my Lord, until 1996. It did not come into my ken until 1996. I believe it was published in 1994, but in April 1996 we published in this country my Goebbels biography, *Goebbels: Mastermind of the Third Reich*. . . ."

In fact, Deborah Lipstadt's book was in Irving's "ken" long before 1996—and their encounter in the courtroom on the first day of the trial was not their first meeting. That took place in November 1994, in Atlanta, when Irving turned up at a talk Lipstadt was giving at DeKalb College. Lipstadt's text was the danger of legitimizing Holocaust deniers as "the other side" in historical debate—the theme of *Denying the Holocaust*, which had been published the previous year. Irving describes the encounter in his diary, which he later posted on his web site (and which in any case he had to disclose to the defense): *I then politely put up my hand. Invited to speak, I boomed in my very English, very loud voice to her: "Professor Lipstadt, I am right in believing you are not a historian, you are a professor of religion?" She answered that she was a professor of religion but (something special else) in history too. I then waded in with verbal fists flying: "I am the David Irving to whom you have made such disparaging reference in your speech."*

Brandishing a wad of $20 bills, Irving repeated his standard offer of $1,000 to anyone who could provide documentary evidence of Hitler's guilt in the extermination of the Jews. Lipstadt attempted to take other questions, but, again in Irving's account: *several times I wagged the bundle of $20 bills aloft, as she was speaking, and hissed: "One thousand dollars!"*

Irving goes on to savor his success in giving away 72 free copies of his Goering biography to the students, who duly lined up afterwards for his autograph: *Sweet victory. Then students came to me with copies of the printed invitation to autograph: I did so—they were blank, which meant that either they had not asked Lipstadt for her autograph, or she would have to sign after me. Total Victory! Revenge!*[1]

Why should Irving lie about such an easily checkable fact as his first encounter with Lipstadt? Perhaps because, as this account suggests, far from feeling aggrieved by his little skirmish with Lipstadt, Irving was enjoying himself. No matter how much Lipstadt "disparaged" him, as long as the question was "Why won't you debate me?" the advantage was with Irving—who saw no need to seek redress in a court of law. What changed his mind? Here his evidence came closer to the truth: "In April 1996 we published in this country my Goebbels biography. . . ."

David John Cawdell Irving was born on March 24, 1938, the youngest of four children. His father was a naval officer, and in some interviews Irving strives to give the impression of Country Life. "My mother," he told me, "was an artist." Then he caught himself. "A commercial artist. She did pen and ink drawings for *Nursery World*." For an Englishman with Irving's keen sense of social distinction, the difference is considerable. The Irvings lived in Essex—"Ongar, the end of the Central Line"—a dreary suburb made drearier by their lack of money.

Irving's family belonged to that nomadic horde of soldiers and bureaucrats who kept the Union Jack flying over what Britons of his generation still call "the pink bits" of the map. A maternal uncle was in the Bengal Lancers. A great-great-uncle on his father's side, Alfred Dolman, followed Livingstone to Africa where, on his second trip, somewhere in Bechuanaland, he was supposedly eaten by his bearer. Irving's father saw action in the First World War Battle of Jutland, and spent the 1920s helping to survey the Antarctic. "Two of the South Sandwich islands are named after my father and my uncle: Irving Point and Carey Point."

In the Second World War, when Irving was four years old, his father's ship, HMS *Edinburgh*, was torpedoed by the Germans. His father survived, but he never returned to his wife and family. "I saw my father about twice in my whole life. . . . During the war years we had a motorcar which was up on blocks, it was a Ford, and I remember as a child climbing through the door. Underneath the car I found a battered old board suitcase, which my mother had obviously thrown there, and it was full of a very musty naval uniform, which was beginning to rot, and ancient brown faded photographs of the Antarctic."

The war dominated Irving's childhood. "I remember standing on the beach at Southsea and watching the invasion fleet sail in June 1944. My mother said that most of them probably wouldn't be coming home." Recalling a time of rationing and genteel poverty, Irving said that by the end of the war he and his twin brother were so thin their mother told them "You look like Belsen children."

Sent as a day boy to "a minor public school," Irving was "beaten repeatedly. . . . The final beating came when I'd hung a 12-foot hammer and sickle flag over the main entrance to the school. They had to call the fire brigade to come and bring it down. . . . I was a scamp."

A year earlier, Irving had won the school prize for art appreciation. The award was a book of his choice—to be presented by the Deputy Prime Minister. "I filled in the form saying the prize I wanted to receive was *Mein Kampf*. I arranged for the local press to be there *en masse* to take a photograph of the deputy Prime Minister giving me a copy of *Mein Kampf*. I went up on stage and picked up this prize—and it was a German–Russian technical dictionary! I've never read *Mein Kampf* from that day to this."

Irving's desire to shock also got him into trouble at Imperial College, where he'd been given a one-year scholarship. The student magazine "ran a headline in 1956 that I'd said that 17 per cent of London university students were extreme left-wing or Communists. The figure of 17 per cent was straight off the top of my head. I just picked a prime number. I attained a certain degree of notoriety," he recalled. Irving lost his scholarship after failing his math examination—a failure he blames on his professor, "a known Communist."

To finance his second year of studies, Irving took a job on a concrete gang. He also joined "an organization called Common Cause. Rather like Aims of Industry or the

Economic League, bodies like that are funded by industry and given the task of keeping dossiers on troublemakers." In other words, he became a labor spy—a strange pastime for a "laissez-faire liberal." At a rally for Oswald Mosley, the former head of the British Union of Fascists, who was running for Parliament, Irving found himself entranced: "I was fascinated—fascinated by the techniques of it, fascinated by the mechanisms of street politics. Years later I'm working in Mussolini's archives and I found the evidence that he [Mosley] was being paid by Mussolini; then I was in Moscow and found he'd been paid by Hitler as well." An attempt to enlist in the Royal Air Force failed when Irving was turned down on medical grounds.

If Mosley was an odd inspiration for the son of a Second World War veteran, Irving's response to his rejection by the RAF was odder still. He wrote a letter to Krupp, the former Nazi armaments manufacturer, asking for a job in its steel mill.[2] Seized by the Allies after the war, the firm was unable to oblige. But Krupp's rival Thyssen, whose owners had fallen out with Hitler after helping him to power, offered Irving a year's work. His fellow steelworkers added a rough-hewn fluency to Irving's high-school German; one of them, a native of Dresden, gave Irving the subject of his first book.

This man had lived through the Allied fire-bombing of the city in February of 1945; his harrowing account of the raid came as a revelation to Irving, who set to work interviewing survivors and combing through German and Allied archival material. After a six-month stint in Spain as a clerk-typist for the Strategic Air Command, Irving returned to London, where he'd been given a place at University College to study political science and economics. To support himself he worked as a nightwatchman on the site of the Commonwealth Institute. "I slept in the pay hut—a little wooden hut with a cot and a table. During the day, I'd write letters [asking about Dresden] to the Air Ministry from 'The New Commonwealth Institute,

Kensington High Street'. They'd reply very deferentially; I got a lot of information out of them."

Published in 1963, *The Destruction of Dresden* was an immediate bestseller. The book's gruesome photographs of the Germans burning their dead, which Irving secured from one of his new contacts, ensured maximum press attention for Irving's claim that the Allied bombing raid of February 1945 had killed over 100,000 people—a figure that was more than twice official estimates.

"I imported Dresden into the vocabulary of horror," Irving says proudly. "So that people now say Dresden in the same breath as they say Auschwitz and Hiroshima. That's my small contribution to the vernacular."

In later years Irving's estimate of the Dresden death toll would fall as low as 35,000 and rise as high as 250,000, just as, in later years, he would sometimes make direct comparisons between Dresden and Auschwitz. "About 100,000 people died in Auschwitz," he told an interviewer in 1991. "So even if we're generous and say one quarter of them, 25,000, were killed by hanging or shooting. 25,000 is a crime, that's true. . . . But we killed that many people burning them alive in one night, not in three years, in a city like Pforzheim. We killed five times that number in Dresden in one night."[3]

At the time, however, *The Destruction of Dresden* was important to Irving for other reasons. The book's financial success prompted him to abandon efforts to complete his degree. Irving's publisher offered him a contract for two more books: a history of the German rocket program and a biography of Adolf Hitler.

Irving learned that Lord Cherwell, Churchill's scientific adviser, had kept tabs on the German V-weapons. Cherwell's papers were at Nuffield College, Oxford, and when Irving presented himself he was given the run of the archive. He soon realized he'd stumbled on the historian's equivalent of a treasure trove. He also discovered something else: "From the papers

it was obvious that we were reading all the German codes."
This was in the early 1960s, when the feats of Allied codebreakers were still top secret. Fearful that he would be found
out—or even worse, denied access to the archive—Irving "did
the unthinkable. I began borrowing documents, taking them
down to London to copy. But I always sedulously returned
them."

Since he had never been a government official, Irving was
not bound by the Official Secrets Act. The first draft of his
book *The Mare's Nest* contained an entire chapter about the
ENIGMA code, but "one night I was visited at my flat by men
in belted raincoats who came and physically seized the chapter.
I was summoned to the Cabinet Office, twelve men sitting
around a polished table, where it was explained to me why
[the information] was not being released and we appeal to you
as an English gentleman not to release [it]."

Irving withdrew his chapter. By then he had copied enough
material from the Cherwell archive "for my next three or four
books." Irving's willingness to co-operate paid a dividend. "Ten
years later I got a phone call from the Cabinet Office saying
'Irving, you're writing a book about Rommel, aren't you? If
you come around here we've got something for you.' I went to
the same room, and on the same polished table there was this
big, thick file. It was Rommel's personnel file—the original
file. The last entry on the file was Rommel's letter to Hitler
explaining why he was committing suicide."

During this period Irving learned his trade, applying what
are essentially the methods of a journalist—interviews, culti-
vation of sources, the ability to follow a paper trail—to the raw
materials of history. He also learned something else: for the
kind of books he was writing—popular history, military history,
books aimed at a mass readership rather than at the academic
market—there were essentially no rules. Despite the generosity of his cabinet sources, when Irving turned in his Rommel
biography, his American editor, Tom Congdon, felt the book

lacked immediacy. "He asked me to write a set-piece description of what it's like to be in a tank." Irving obliged, and as he'd never been in a tank, he simply made it up. "I'm the only one who knows it's completely phoney," he told me gleefully.

Throughout his long apprenticeship, Irving kept storing up contacts and material against the day when he finally felt ready to begin his Hitler biography. "I'd translated the memoirs of [Field Marshal] Wilhelm Keitel, who was hanged at Nuremberg. Keitel's son introduced me to Otto Günsche—the man who burned Hitler's body. He was Hitler's SS adjutant. And Günsche decided he would talk to me, because I was the Englishman who had written about Dresden. That gave me an edge."

Günsche became Irving's passport into "the inner circle—of all Hitler devotees—the servants and the adjutants and the colonels and the secondaries. Who would meet around the graveside when one of their number died. And the word was passed: 'He's okay.' And after a while they started producing their diaries and private papers." The result was *Hitler's War*, published in 1977.

Writing in *Time* magazine, Lance Morrow found Irving's portrait of "the Führer as a somewhat harried business executive, too preoccupied to know exactly what was happening in his branch offices at Auschwitz and Treblinka" diffficult to credit.[4] The historian Hugh Trevor-Roper's review in the London *Sunday Times* referred to Irving's "consistent bias" but went on to say, "No praise can be too high for Irving's indefatigable scholarly industry. . . . I have enjoyed reading his long work from beginning to end."[5] The military historian John Keegan called *Hitler's War* "Irving's greatest achievement . . . indispensable to anyone seeking to understand the war in the round."[6] The book reached number eight on British bestseller lists. Irving moved to Mayfair, and bought a Rolls-Royce.

There were dissenters. Martin Broszat, director of the Munich Institute for Contemporary History, thought Irving had misunderstood the nature of Hitler's authority.[7] But Broszat's lengthy article was never translated into English. Charles Sydnor's devastating critique of Irving's handling of documents appeared in 1979—in the journal *Central European History*.[8] The only noticeable dent in Irving's public credibility, however, came when writer Gitta Sereny and reporter Lewis Chester checked Irving's documents and re-interviewed his sources—including Otto Günsche—on assignment for the *Sunday Times*. Their article contains some damaging details— including Günsche's admission that "one must assume that he [Hitler] did know" about the extermination of the Jews—but ultimately posed little obstacle to Irving's continued prominence.[9]

One reason for this was the authors' focus on the narrow question of Hitler's personal culpability. Doubtless a response to Irving's much publicized $1,000 offer, the emphasis on Hitler diverted attention away from the issue of Irving's fidelity to his sources. And as a fellow writer on Nazi themes, Irving could—and does—simply dismiss Sereny as a jealous competitor. Finally—and perhaps most importantly—though his account of Hitler's role was hard to swallow (not even admirers like Keegan or Trevor-Roper took his behind-Hitler's-back thesis seriously), in 1977 David Irving's views on the Holocaust itself were fairly unexceptionable. Under "Jews: extermination of," the index to *Hitler's War* lists 17 separate entries. There are references to "the extermination camp at Chelmno" and "the extermination center at Treblinka." And Irving's argument that "the burden of guilt for the bloody and mindless massacre of the Jews rests on a large number of Germans, many of them alive today, and not just on one 'mad dictator,' whose order had to be obeyed without question,"[10] while debatable, is not very far from the thesis of Daniel Goldhagen's *Hitler's Willing Executioners*, another book whose dismissal by knowledgeable specialists has done little to hinder its success with the general public.[11]

But by 1981 it should have been obvious to anyone who looked that David Irving had a Jewish problem. In that year Irving published *Uprising!*, an hour-by-hour reconstruction of the 1956 Hungarian revolt. In the *Observer*, Neal Ascherson took issue with the book's "two insinuations: first, that Hungarian Communism up to 1956 was a Jewish dictatorship, and secondly that reforming Communists are more deadly enemies of liberty than the . . . Stalinists they try to overthrow."[12] Citing Irving's description of Hungarian dictator Matthias Rákosi as possessing "the tact of a kosher butcher," and noting his remark that before the war Jews "had overrun the more lucrative liberal professions," Ascherson concluded: "Irving is Jew-obsessed." Writing in the *New Statesman*, Kai Bird noted "Jews weigh heavily on Irving's mind."[13] Both reviewers also contrasted Irving's contemptuous treatment of the leader of the revolt, Imre Nagy—"a crop of hemorrhoids sprouting a Joseph Stalin moustache"—with his assertion that János Kádár, the Soviet puppet installed after the invasion, is "today one of Hungary's most genuinely popular citizens."

Bird, an American journalist who would go on to publish his own authoritative studies of John J. McCloy, the US High Commissioner for Germany, and cold warriors McGeorge Bundy and William Bundy, warned that, "if nothing else, *Uprising!* should lay to rest the charitable assumption made by gentlemen historians that men like Irving would never stoop to dressing up their evidence." Such strictures did little to dampen the enthusiasm of Peter Israel, who acquired the book for Putnams in the United States.

Besides, any damage to Irving's reputation was more than recouped by his involvement in the 1983 debacle over the "Hitler diaries," when *Newsweek*, the London *Sunday Times*, and the German magazine *Stern*, which had rushed to publish the diaries in a fanfare of publicity, were forced to admit they'd been conned—or in the case of *Newsweek*, which breezily declared "genuine or not, it almost doesn't matter," at least deeply embarrassed. Foremost among the victims was Hugh Trevor-Roper—by now ennobled as Lord Dacre—who'd authenticated the volumes for the *Sunday Times*. Irving crashed *Stern*'s Hamburg press conference in April 1983, and his comments casting doubt on the diaries' provenance were repeated on the "Today" show. It was his finest hour, recalled with glee by his defenders—most recently Christopher Hitchens in *Vanity Fair*, who cited the incident in support of his view that "David Irving is not just a Fascist historian. He is also a great historian of Fascism."[14]

A gratifying example of the amateur besting the specialist, this account, which turns up in most profiles of Irving, omits a few details. For one thing, it was Irving who first approached the *Sunday Times* in 1982 with an offer to go to Germany and inspect the diaries for the paper. And although he did denounce the diaries at *Stern*'s press conference, so had Lord Dacre. A week later Irving changed his mind yet again, and pronounced the diaries genuine—a dizzying sequence which shed little light on the fake diaries but generated a great deal of publicity for Irving's own *Adolf Hitler: The Medical Diaries*, an anodyne collection of notes by the Führer's physician, Theo Morrell, which just happened to be published that week.[15]

Whatever his merits as a historian, as a self-publicist Irving has few peers. Journalists across the political spectrum testify to his unfailing helpfulness, his willingness to make archives, clipping files, and documents available without any precondition.[16] On two occasions I was left alone in Irving's study for over an hour. If Irving has anything to hide, it is hidden in plain sight.

My first impression of Irving the man was unavoidably colored by sorrow. We had spoken on the phone several times, and had been exchanging e-mails for several months, before the gray autumn afternoon when I presented myself at his flat in a red-brick Victorian building off Grosvenor Square, just around the corner from the American Embassy. I'd read enough of his interviews to know that Irving could be provocative, truculent, or charming. But when I came to see him, he was none of those things. He seemed deeply tired (he was due to leave for a lecture tour of the United States the following day) and more than a little sad.

A few days earlier the oldest of his five daughters had committed suicide. Irving's first wife was a Spaniard; their daughter Josephine Victoria was born in 1963 on the anniversary of Franco's victory. She'd been schizophrenic, Irving said, for "half her life."[17] More recently she'd lost the use of both legs in a car accident. She'd seemed "level headed" lately, but there was, he said, no way to predict when "the meniscus of rationality" would break. "At the hospital they said to me, 'You know, she must have been very determined.' For someone who is legless to pull herself up and throw herself out of a fourth floor window. . . ." Irving stopped, then continued, responding to a question I hadn't asked: "Do you ever wonder whether you are mentally unsound or not? How do we know? There is no thermometer you can stick in your mouth that will say, oh, today I'm a bit unbalanced."

I'd been to his flat once in the summer to pick up some material, but Irving had been away. "Contact my staff (Bente) in London," I was instructed. Bente turned out to be the mother of Irving's youngest daughter, Jessica, who had to be collected from school, and so I was left there, seated in Irving's study leafing through his press clippings under the gaze of Franklin Delano Roosevelt, whose portrait on the wall above Irving's desk was flanked by a pair of framed front pages from the *Völkischer Beobachter*, the Nazi Party daily.

The lead story, Irving later told me with a certain amount of malicious pleasure, was headlined "Prophetic Warning To Jewry"—the paper's report of Hitler's famous January 1939 speech to the Reichstag:

Today I want to be a prophet once more: If international-finance Jewry inside and outside of Europe should succeed once more in plunging nations into another world war, the consequence will not be the Bolshevization of the earth and thereby the victory of Jewry, but the annihilation of the Jewish race in Europe.[18]

This time—perhaps in deference to his siblings, who, though embarrassed by Irving, had come to London for the funeral—the papers had been taken down. Nor was Irving's famous self-portrait of Hitler, given to him by the Führer's secretary, anywhere in evidence. Irving himself was a husky, square-jawed man with a weakness for martial metaphors. "It may be unfortunate for Professor Lipstadt," he'd remarked to me on the telephone, "that she is the one who finds herself dragged out of the line and shot." On the telephone, Irving had seemed both brusque and a bit wary. But when I arrived he was on his best behavior.

When he's among friends Irving's manners are less fastidious. At a meeting in Alsace a few years ago, he opened with a joke: *There's the one-man gas chamber, carried by two German soldiers looking for Jews alone in the Polish countryside. This one-man gas chamber must have looked like a sedan chair, but disguised as a telephone kiosk. How did they convince the victim to step, of his own free-will, into this one-man gas chamber? Apparently there was a phone in it which would ring, and the soldier would say, "It's for you!"*[19]

And there is his light verse, to be recited, according to Irving's diary—which he had to make available to Lipstadt's lawyers—when out with his daughter and "half-breed children" are wheeled past:

I am a Baby Aryan
Not Jewish or Sectarian
I have no plans to marry an
Ape or Rastafarian.

But since Jessica, now six, was barely a year old at the time, the intended audience was probably her mother, whose reaction, Irving noted with satisfaction, was "suitably shocked."[20] Irving later told me he knew I was a Jew "from the moment I saw you." So I was curious to observe how he would react when Jessica, who had been running in and out of his office, came and climbed into my lap. Irving barely noticed. In the American south, where I grew up, even "liberal" whites would get uncomfortable if their daughters got too close to a black man. Anti-Semitism is a different kind of racism, but there are certainly anti-Semites whose distaste for Jews is visceral. Irving, however, is not one of them.

Irving is a prodigious diarist, and though the entries I've seen read more like the first drafts of a press release than a record of his inner life, the need to fill up the pages does sometimes allow something personal to slip through. His love affairs, for example, are apparently recorded in a code based on the word "amiable" as in "Caroline came round and was amiable."[21] But even the sections cited by the defense in various expert reports hardly reveal a passionate Jew-hater. Irving believes in a worldwide Jewish conspiracy both to discredit him personally and to exploit the Holocaust for political and economic ends. He habitually refers to Jewish groups as "traditional enemies of the truth,"[22] and as far back as 1963, describing a speech by Oswald Mosley at Kensington Town Hall, noted: "Yellow Star did not make a showing."[23] But his recurring preoccupations are money and his career, not Jews.

Irving likes to point out that at one time both his lawyer and his publisher were Jews. The lawyer, Michael Rubinstein (who insists he is not Jewish), told me relations with Irving had been proper and professional. As for Lord Weidenfeld, the assumption of mutual utility can be gleaned from a letter he sent Irving after a newspaper article, obviously inspired by Irving, suggested that Weidenfeld had been pressured not to publish *Hitler's War*. "I have every reason to believe," Weidenfeld wrote, "that it was the reporter's tone and not your intention to disturb a businesslike and friendly climate of cooperation between us."[24] The firm of Weidenfeld and Nicolson went on to publish Irving's biographies of Field Marshals Erhard Milch and Erwin Rommel.

David Irving didn't sue Deborah Lipstadt because she is a Jew. On the same day in September 1996 that Irving issued his writ against Penguin and Lipstadt, he also sued Gitta Sereny and the *Observer*, which had published an article by Sereny accusing Irving of peddling "a clever mixture of truth and untruth" in his book on Goebbels. Sereny is not Jewish, and although the two complaints differ, Irving's reasons for suing both women are essentially the same, namely that, unlike his other critics, whose attacks merely raised his public profile, theirs had threatened his income. Because by 1996 David Irving had long since used up any credit he'd gained from the "Hitler diaries." Banned from Austria because of his views on the Holocaust, barred from archives in Germany for the same reason, his Rolls-Royce long gone and his Mayfair flat heavily mortgaged, Irving was, in every sense, seriously overdrawn.

The road that led David Irving to Court 37 began with a phone call from Toronto. The voice on the other end belonged to Ernst Zündel, a German immigrant to Canada who supplements his income as a commercial artist by distributing a selection of neo-Nazi and racist literature, including two works of his own: *UFOs: Nazi Secret Weapons* and *The Hitler We Loved and Why*.

In 1984 Zündel had been charged with contributing to anti-Semitism by knowingly spreading "false news" about the Holocaust—at the time a crime under Canadian law. Though Zündel's lawyer bullied and insulted the prosecution witnesses—calling Raul Hilberg "a historian of sorts" and hectoring one survivor to give him the full names of each of the 20 members of his family who had perished in the camps—

Zündel was duly convicted and sentenced to 15 months in jail. But the conviction was overturned on technical grounds, and for the 1988 retrial the defense team wanted reinforcements.

Would Irving be prepared to appear as an expert for the defense? A fan of *Hitler's War*, Zündel had been courting Irving for years. In 1986, when Irving visited Toronto on a lecture tour, Zündel picked him up at the airport. Irving, who knew Zündel only by reputation, was far from pleased. "He wanted nothing to do with me," Zündel wrote in a newsletter to his supporters. "He thought I was some 'Revisionist-Neo-Nazi-Rambo-Kook!'" Thirteen years later Irving saw no reason to revise his first impression. "Zündel is a Nazi," he told me. "There's no question about it. He's proud of it."

What prompted Irving to make common cause with a man he describes as "very far out on the branch which he's cut off"? Doubtless part of the impulse came from the same need to provoke that sent him up the ladder with that hammer and sickle as a schoolboy. Irving has a love/hate relationship with respectability. "You want to see egg on faces," he admitted.

Zündel also knew his customer. In 1986 he had kept his distance from Irving—and so had the press. In his letter commiserating over the meagre results from Irving's Canadian tour, Zündel sketched out a plan for Irving to turn his book audience—his "grassroots support"—into a distribution network "which you yourself would control and of course, make most of the editorial decisions and, in the end, retain most of the profit yourself."[25] The letter following up his request for Irving's assistance recommended he combine his testimony with a book tour "to take advantage of the publicity. . . . During the first trial, we received coast-to-coast coverage virtually every day."[26]

When Irving arrived in Toronto, he met Zündel's other new witness, an American named Fred Leuchter, billed as an engineer specializing in the design and operation of execution apparatus. Leuchter had flown to Poland with a cameraman, draftsman, and translator, and the group spent three days at Auschwitz–Birkenau and one at Majdanek chipping off bits of brick and concrete from a number of buildings. These "forensic samples," as Leuchter described them, were then taken to a lab in Boston, where the technician was told the material was from a workman's compensation case.[27]

Under questioning by the judge, it emerged that Leuchter's engineering training consisted of a few undergraduate science courses taken while completing his B.A.—in history—at Boston University.[28] His "report" purporting to demonstrate the non-existence of gas chambers—on which the defense had spent nearly $60,000—was ruled inadmissible. Leuchter was allowed to testify on the use of hydrogen cyanide (the gas which, under the tradename Zyklon-B, was used by the Germans) in American prison gas chambers, and to give his opinion that the structures he had seen in Poland "wouldn't have been efficient" if used as gas chambers, but the second jury was not convinced either, and Zündel was again found guilty.

Leuchter did acquire at least one convert. For David Irving, who followed him to the witness stand as an expert on German documents and the Second World War, Leuchter's account of his Polish field trip apparently struck with the force of a revelation. "My mind has now changed," he told the court, ". . . because I understand that the whole of the Holocaust mythology is, after all, open to doubt."[29] The Leuchter report, Irving declared, "is shattering in the significance of its discovery." Back in London Irving's new Focal Point press—the base of his "distribution network"—published the results of Leuchter's amateur chemistry experiment as a 66-page booklet with an introduction by David Irving. Irving also removed all mention of gas chambers from his revised edition of *Hitler's War*. "If something didn't happen," he said, "then you don't even dignify it with a footnote."[30]

Jewish groups were predictably outraged, but they hadn't liked Irving since *Hitler's War*. At the time, Irving dismissed the furor, which he said was only "because I have detracted from the romance of the notion of the Holocaust—that six million people were killed by one man."[31] He'd been through a few rough patches, but thanks to "Hitler's diaries" he'd bounced back triumphant. As publishers once again became hesitant, and newspaper editors once more stopped returning his calls, Irving plotted his comeback. His new book would do more than silence his critics—it would rewrite the history of the Second World War, not only proving that Hitler had indeed been led astray, but showing who was really behind the anti-Semitic outrages that still unfairly blackened the Führer's name.

Goebbels: Mastermind of the Third Reich was going to be the book that redeemed David Irving's career. Based on his usual prodigious mining of wartime archives, the book was nearly written when, in the spring of 1992, a German friend told Irving that the complete set of Goebbels's diaries, which had been microfilmed and stored on glass plates, had recently surfaced in the Russian State Archives. Armed with a commission from the *Sunday Times*, Irving raced to Moscow to secure his scoop. Though much of the diaries had already been published, there were substantial gaps, and Irving's "discovery" put him back on the front pages.

Not all publicity is good publicity. Irving's return to prominence courtesy of the *Sunday Times*, which agreed to pay him £75,000 to "edit" the Goebbels diaries, sparked a wave of protests from London to New York. The intensity of these protests lost Irving his fee from the *Sunday Times*, who cancelled their agreement; he also lost his American publisher, Scribners, and his British publisher, Macmillan, who not only rejected the Goebbels manuscript but also ordered the remaining stocks of two of his other books destroyed. All of this, it is worth noting, happened before Deborah Lipstadt published a word about David Irving.

Still, when St. Martin's Press in New York agreed to publish the Goebbels book in February 1995, Irving's rehabilitation appeared back on track. Tom Dunne, a senior editor, had read the book and was eager to go ahead. Even so it took until May to agree on the advance: $25,000, the first installment of which went directly to pay off the arrears on Irving's mortgage.* Dunne later claimed to be ignorant of Irving's history, but it's not as if he made a rushed decision. Besides, anyone with a library card or a modem could have predicted the ensuing controversy.

What perhaps couldn't have been predicted were the craven contortions and witless hypocrisy of St. Martin's as the book's publication date drew nearer. For months Irving heard nothing but praise from St. Martin's (who, having bought the rights to reprint the British edition, never planned to edit the book themselves anyway). When *Publisher's Weekly* pronounced Irving's book "repellent," and Jewish organizations expressed outrage, and the *Washington Post*, in a column attacking the book, quoted Deborah Lipstadt asking rhetorically if St. Martin's "would . . . publish a book by Jeffrey Dahmer on man–boy relationships?", the publishers stood firm. For about two weeks.

Sometime between the March 22 *Daily News* report, "Nazi Big's Bio Author Sparks Uproar," and Frank Rich's April 3 *New York Times* column calling Irving "Hitler's Spin Artist," Irving's publishers lost their nerve, announcing the next day that they were shocked—shocked!—to discover that the book they were on the very brink of shipping to stores was in fact not quite . . . kosher?

The principal effect of this decision, as Christopher Hitchens properly pointed out in a caustic résumé of the

---

* One of the most striking yet least remarked on aspects of the St. Martin's fiasco was the relatively small amount of money involved. That Irving, a supposedly bestselling author, would accept such a low advance is further evidence of his desperation.

scandal in the June 1996 *Vanity Fair*, was to transform a man with "depraved ideas" about the Holocaust into a poster-boy for free speech. One ancillary effect was to lend the Goebbels book the cachet of suppressed literature. Another was Gordon Craig's lofty declaration, in the course of a four-page review of the Goebbels biography in the *New York Review of Books*, that "silencing Mr. Irving would be a high price to pay for freedom from the annoyance that he causes us. The fact is that he knows more about National Socialism than most professional scholars in his field, and students of the years 1933–1945 owe more than they are always willing to admit" to his research. "Such people as David Irving . . . have an indispensable part in the historical enterprise, and we dare not disregard their views."[32]

Irving's defenders assumed that what he really wanted was a debate with his critics. If that were indeed his objective, all Irving had to do was bide his time. "Someone," Hitchens asserted confidently, "will no doubt pick up where St. Martin's left off."

What Irving did instead was sue Deborah Lipstadt and her publisher for libel in England (where even if she won Lipstadt's costs would amount to hundreds of thousands of pounds). At which point it became rather more difficult to defend the proposition that what was at stake was David Irving's freedom of speech.

The Defendants

On the second day of the trial two video clips are shown in court. The first is a black-and-white German newsreel from January 1948 reporting the judgment in the Auschwitz trial, held in Cracow after the war. The voiceover refers to "nearly 300,000 people from the most different nations [who] died in the Auschwitz concentration camp," and the point of the exercise is that number: 300,000.

The second clip is much more recent, a 1994 Australian current-affairs program, and shows a woman with reddish-brown hair and strong features. A man's off-screen voice asks if people who deny the Holocaust should be taken seriously. "What they're saying," the woman replies in an unmistakable New York accent, "is the equivalent of 'the Earth is flat' or 'Elvis Presley is alive and well' or 'there was no slavery.'" When the man asks "How overwhelming *is* the evidence for the Holocaust?" she answers, "The facts are beyond belief and beyond question." The voice belongs to Deborah Lipstadt, who sits silently in court watching herself on the video monitor. This is the only time her voice will be heard in the courtroom during the entire trial.

There is no obligation for a defendant in a libel action to testify. Leon Uris, for example, sat mute through the *Exodus* trial. Since there was no dispute about what the words he'd written might mean, or to whom they were intended to refer, there was nothing for him to add. *Exodus*, after all, was a work of fiction, and though that didn't protect its author from being sued for libel, Uris never claimed to be a historian.

But *Denying the Holocaust* is not a novel, and until the trial began Irving was under the impression he would have the chance to cross-examine Lipstadt. There were questions he wanted to ask her, and documents he desperately wanted to introduce in evidence, such as a 1992 letter from Yehuda Bauer, director of Hebrew University's Center for the Study of Anti-Semitism, which funded Lipstadt's research, complaining that in her first draft "Irving is mentioned, but not that he is the mainstay of Holocaust denial in Western Europe."

By not calling Lipstadt, the defense keeps the focus on Irving, his methods and his associates. They also spare their client what would doubtless have been an uncomfortable experience. In a jury trial, Lipstadt's silence might come at a price. At the very least, her lawyers would have to remind the jury not to hold it against her. With a judge sitting alone, the decision is much easier. Irving seems affronted; though Lipstadt's testimony would probably have made little difference to Irving's suit, it might well have helped his "case." But the judge's demeanor suggests he should have seen this coming:

MR. IRVING: Your Lordship will see that this interview provides the Second Defendant, Professor Lipstadt, with a chance to express her opinions unopposed.

MR. JUSTICE GRAY: Yes.

MR. IRVING: I feel it is appropriate to allow her some minutes of the court's time in this rather oblique manner to express her opinions.

MR. JUSTICE GRAY: Yes.

MR. IRVING: I understand that she will not be testifying in person in this case.

MR. JUSTICE GRAY: Yes.

An experienced barrister might still have made something of this, particularly in light of the defense claim that Irving is not a historian at all. In rough form the argument (which will be presented at great length and with considerable subtlety by Richard Evans, one of the defense experts, during his testimony) is that while credentials don't make a historian—Herodotus, after all, never got a Ph.D.—there are canons of conduct regarding the handling of documents, footnotes, and sources to which historians must adhere. All sorts of assumptions are folded up in this argument, such as how these rules get set and who enforces them, and though Evans will be fairly scrupulous in acknowledging this, Irving never presses the point.

A lawyer whose own ego wasn't at stake might have lifted his gaze—and the court's attention—to the shaky scaffolding surrounding this portrayal of history as a guild activity. After all, Irving's books sell in the history section of bookstores, and are shelved with history books in various university libraries. If, to take what might be called an operational approach, history is what historians do, then any definition which excludes Irving, who has spent years of his life in archives, is bound to seem arbitrary. Shifting the ground to whether or not he is a good historian might have helped Irving, if only by giving him an opening to examine Lipstadt's own handling of material.

But Irving is curiously unwilling to relinquish the spotlight even when it shows him to least advantage. So intent is he on proving that he is indeed a historian, with the kudos to prove it, that he never bothers to make the simple point that by some measures Deborah Lipstadt isn't a historian either.

On her father's side, Deborah Esther Lipstadt is descended from a prominent German rabbinical family. Erwin Lipstadt came to the United States from Germany in the 1920s "because of the economic situation. Nothing to do with anti-Semitism," she offers before being asked. Her mother Miriam was born in Canada. When Deborah was born in 1947 the family lived in Manhattan, but moved to Far Rockaway in Queens soon afterwards. "I went to Jewish day schools there, and got an intensive Jewish education, both at home and in school."

The Lipstadts considered themselves "modern Orthodox"—partly to distinguish themselves from the black-hatted, caftan-wearing Hasidim, and partly to signify that although they observed the Jewish dietary laws, and regulated their lives by the Hebrew rather than the secular calendar, they did not set their faces against modern life. "We were very much of this world," says Lipstadt. "Theater, opera, books, journals, museums."

Lipstadt grew up in a mixed neighborhood, but her interactions with non-Jews were limited. "When you're an observant family, you go to day schools, you keep kosher—just technically you march to the beat of a different drummer." Class may also have been a factor. The comfortable, parochial, culturally voracious, slightly smug yet socially conscious world of German Jews is difficult to convey to outsiders, though the fiction of Isaac Bashevis Singer provides a wry introduction. It would be unfair—and probably untrue—to say that German Jews look down on other Jews. Perhaps a better way to describe the self-consciousness of German Jews is as a kind of *mission civilatrice* —the Jewish version of *noblesse oblige*.

After her family moved back to Manhattan in the mid-1960s, Lipstadt says, I.B. Singer lived next door. But she is just as proud of the fact that civil-rights worker Andy Goodman's family also lived on her street. When Goodman's murdered body was finally found in Mississippi, along with those of his comrades James Chaney and Michael Schwerner, Lipstadt's father, who had a small headstone business, was commissioned to make his monument. "In the summer of the freedom rides," Lipstadt says, "I was too young to go down to the South, but I knew that if I had been older I would have. I remember going with my mother—this was . . . 1964 or 65—we drove up to Harlem on a Sunday to participate in a march. It was my mother's idea."

At City College, Lipstadt says ruefully, she was part of "the last generation where you could get a good education." She majored in political science and history, spending her junior year at Hebrew University in Jerusalem. "I took a couple of courses on the Holocaust, met more survivors than I'd met before—though I'd met survivors growing up, I didn't know they were survivors. . . . My parents had lots of German Jewish friends, but I didn't know them as survivors, I just knew them as the Peisers or the Ullmans."

According to Peter Novick, author of *The Holocaust in American Life*, such reticence was the norm until the late 1960s. As Art Spiegelman's father says in *Maus*, his "survivor's tale" in cartoon format, "no one wants anyway to hear such stories."[1] But Lipstadt's father had left five sisters behind in Germany, and tried desperately but vainly to get them admitted to the United States. Though all five survived the war, and though he, too, seldom mentioned the Holocaust, the emotional toll on him was evident every Passover.

"I remember as a teenager, at the Passover seder, my father would read a memorial prayer put out by the organization of the survivors of the Warsaw Ghetto, saying 'Tonight we remember the millions who died.' And he would cry as he recalled friends, relatives, and classmates with whom he had grown up in Hamburg who had perished. And I remember that as an adolescent this would be very unnerving to me. But I don't ever remember being sat down and told anything."

As Lipstadt's junior year in Israel was ending, the Six Day War broke out. "There was great fear. They dug 800 graves in Jerusalem," she recalls. The children's home where Lipstadt worked as a volunteer had a number of Holocaust survivors on staff, and suddenly, spurred by fear, they began to talk graphically about their experiences.

Lipstadt decided to remain in Jerusalem another year. "If I'd been there in June of '67, to go home in July '67 made no sense." After returning to City College to finish her B.A., Lipstadt enrolled in the graduate program in Jewish Studies at Brandeis. Her priorities were shifting, but the 1960s didn't pass her by.

"I lived in Cambridge! You had to be living under a rock not to have a Sixties. I even remember showing up at the synagogue my parents went to on the Upper West Side, wearing my SNCC [Student Non-Violent Coordinating Committee] button, and somebody yelling at me 'They're leftists, anti-Semites and terrible people!' I went berserk!"

Like many other Jews of her generation, Lipstadt's first steps on the path from civil rights to Jewish causes were prompted by the bitter 1968 struggle between the mostly black parents of Ocean Hill and Brownsville in Brooklyn and the largely Jewish teachers' union over community control of the schools. Neither side had a monopoly on racism—and there were Jews on both sides of the picket lines once the union went out on strike rather than cede power to the parents—but what Lipstadt saw was "overt anti-Semitism coming from people whose struggle you had always thought . . . cut to the core of America.

"Over the years finding myself more and more intellectually—and politically—first confused, and then to some degree angry and resentful, I became a sort of *New Republic* Democrat. I never went as far as *Commentary* and [Norman] Podhoretz—or saw it [black anti-Semitism] as a personal insight." And in the late 1960s, there were other reasons to take to the streets.

"Before I went to Israel and after I came back, I went on marches, I was at rallies [to protest America's involvement in Vietnam]. Was I a great activist? No. Was I at rallies? Sure. I remember coming home and my father was very excited. He'd gone out to walk the dog and there was a rally on the corner of 86th street and Broadway, an anti-war rally, and they were giving out candles and he stood with a candle, this very distinguished German-Jewish gentleman walking his cocker spaniel."

In 1972 Lipstadt visited the Soviet Union. On Yom Kippur, she found herself at the synagogue in Czernowitz, a city whose Jewish community had been decimated by the Holocaust. In her affidavit for the defense, she writes: "I lent my prayer book to an elderly woman. Shortly thereafter, an official of the synagogue who, I subsequently learned, worked for the government, accused me of being a provocateur . . . [and] of distributing religious ritual items, which was forbidden by Soviet law. . . . The next day . . . my traveling partner and I were taken from the hotel by the KGB police, brought to a remote train station outside of Czernowitz, held for an entire day, questioned separately, strip-searched, forced to sign statements about our contacts with Jews, and forbidden from contacting American authorities.*

"Though I was well aware that what I had seen could not be compared to the persecution Jews had suffered under the Nazis," she continues, "I became greatly interested in the invidious nature of anti-Semitism. I began to intensely study the history of the Holocaust."

Lipstadt's first book, *Beyond Belief: The American Press and the*

---

* Lipstadt, too, is an accomplished storyteller. So it is perhaps worth noting another version of this incident, from an article in the June/July 1993 issue of *Hadassah Magazine*. In this telling, Lipstadt is also at the synagogue on Yom Kippur 1972 and again she offers her prayer book: "One older woman indicated that the prayer book was useless since none of them could read Hebrew. I told her I would recite the prayer for her and when it came time to mention the name of the person in whose memory the prayer was being said I would pause so she could insert it. . . . For what seemed like an eternity Jews came forward so I could act as their mouthpiece. Emotionally drained at the end of the episode I realized that the small *siddur* [prayer book] had linked me with generations of Jews who had long been shut off from us." Titled "Benefits of Belonging," this uplifting account never mentions her subsequent detention and harassment.

Coming of the Holocaust 1933–1945, is a scathing indictment of American press coverage of the Holocaust. Even when confronted by the evidence, she argues, many correspondents were reluctant to admit "to themselves—and to their readers" the reality of genocide. Lipstadt attributes a least a portion of this reluctance to anti-Semitism.[2]

Like *Denying the Holocaust*, *Beyond Belief* can be found in both the history and Jewish studies sections of bookstores. Her first teaching job, at the University of Washington, was a joint appointment in history and comparative religion. But her next job, at the University of California at Los Angeles, was in Jewish studies. Denied tenure, she moved on briefly to Occidental College, a small liberal-arts college also in Los Angeles, where she taught courses on the Holocaust. At Emory, Lipstadt's chair is in the Department of Religion.

Unlike David Irving, Lipstadt is a bona fide academic, and her first degree, from City College, is in the related disciplines of political science and history. She long ago mastered the skills and methods necessary for admission to the guild of scholars. Her graduate degrees are in Jewish studies, a field which, like history, often concerns itself with the past, and with the interpretation of documents. But Jewish studies is not history; it isn't even—or always—Jewish history.

As an intellectual endeavor, Jewish studies is the confluence of two sometimes conflicting streams. One is wholly secular, and places Jewish studies among other minority and ethnic disciplines, such as gender studies, black or African-American studies, Asian studies, Hispanic studies, and women's studies. In the aftermath of the 1960s there was an explosion of such departments on campuses across the United States. Indeed in some famous cases the departments themselves were the results of campus revolts. Though there are no recorded instances of Jewish students rioting to demand the teaching of Jewish studies, once a university decided to fund

minority-studies programs Jewish studies was often among
the beneficiaries. To do otherwise would have meant discriminat-
ing among minorities—an unpromising route to a peaceful
campus.

Jewish studies was in a position to benefit from the turn
toward cultural studies because, unlike the more militant
disciplines, which in many cases were struggling for recognition
as well as funding, by the late 1960s Jewish studies already
had its own history. The field had its origin in the study of biblical texts that always formed part of the traditional rabbinic
training. By the twentieth century this training was already
moving out of the *yeshivot* and into the universities—especially
in Germany and the United States, where the non-Orthodox
branches of Judaism were growing in strength, and where it
was considered an advantage for a rabbi to have academic credentials.

The program at Brandeis straddles these two streams both
chronologically and temperamentally. At least in the early days
undergraduate majors generally went on to seminary training.*
But as the years passed students in the graduate department,
which awarded its first Ph.D. in 1958, came to have more in
common with their counterparts at Columbia, where Salo
Baron occupied a chair in Jewish history, or other purely secular institutions.

The inbuilt tension between the sacred and secular streams
is perhaps unique to Jewish studies, and distinguishes it from
similar programs in modern Greek studies or Italian studies or
Irish studies that in many cases also pre-dated and benefited
from the growing interest in ethnic studies. But what all these
programs, including Jewish studies, have in common, at least in
the United States, is their intellectual debt to nationalism, and
their more tangible debt to a politically conscious, financially

---

* My father, for example, who was in the first class to go all the way through
Brandeis, graduating in 1954, majored in what was then called Judaic studies
before entering Hebrew Union College, the Reform seminary.

assertive community of benefactors. During the 1930s, for example, Columbia University's Casa Italiana was a notorious center of pro-Fascist agitation.

Nowadays the pressures are likely to be more subtle. The Dorot Foundation, which funds Lipstadt's chair, "has a strong tradition of commitment to Israel [and] to the Jewish community in North America," according to its literature. And it is noticeable that when she comes to consider the actions—and inactions—of American Jewish leaders in *Beyond Belief*, Lipstadt's fury turns to sympathy and understanding.

Lipstadt herself views her close relationship with the Jewish community as essential to both her work and her personal identity. An observant Jew, Lipstadt describes herself as "not Orthodox." The exclusion of even the mention of women from so much of Orthodox ritual disturbs her. "I want them to at least acknowledge that you're only talking about the men. Because if the rabbi stands up and says, 'We need as many people as possible to come tomorrow morning,' I'll come." But her estrangement from organized religion—"I'm equally unhappy in any synagogue I go to," she jokes—does not extend to estrangement from organized Judaism. "My professional and personal lives are really integrated. Because so much of my personal life is tied up with being Jewish. Being a Jew and being Jewish. Culturally, religiously, intellectually—it's what I know best."

This coziness has prompted some academics to patronizingly dismiss Lipstadt's work as a "JCC [Jewish community Center] version of history." The implication is that while Lipstadt's books may make Jews feel better, or give them an opportunity to vent their anger, they have little to do with the hard work of presenting evidence, criticizing sources, and weighing interpretations that give history its analytical rigor and epistemological dignity. There is a measure of truth in such criticism, but there is a much greater measure of naïveté.

History, like war, is always a form of politics by other means, and it is perfectly proper, even prudent, to bear in mind a historian's known prejudices, political engagements, and sources of funding. But it is sheer intellectual laziness to suggest that such information obviates the need to come to grips with the work itself. Lipstadt's first book, *Beyond Belief*, though perhaps excessively kind to American Jewish and Zionist leaders, is nonetheless a pioneering work on how Americans came to learn the facts of the Holocaust. If her second book is more problematic, part of the reason may be that in *Denying the Holocaust* Lipstadt was following a fairly well-established route. Unfortunately for her, it was not always a clear path.

As Lipstadt herself documented, at the end of the Second World War the fact that there was something distinctive about the fate of Europe's Jews and their treatment by the Nazis was not widely acknowledged. In Edward R. Murrow's famous 1945 broadcast from Buchenwald, for example, the words "Jew" and "Jewish" are never spoken. Nor do they appear in the text that accompanied Margaret Bourke-White's photographs of the camp inmates. A reporter for *Life* described the prisoners liberated from Dachau as "the men of all Nations that Hitler's agents had picked out as prime opponents of Nazism."[3]

Lipstadt suggests this was willful blindness—a view whose partial truth is further diminished by Peter Novick's observation that, during the war, most Jewish organizations vigorously resisted attempts to describe Nazi persecution as specifically aimed at Jews. "It should always be pointed out," said a 1942 American Jewish Committee memorandum, "that Nazi tyranny does not discriminate between Jew and Pole." After Pearl Harbor, the director of the Anti-Defamation League of B'nai Brith worried about an increase in domestic anti-Semitism: "There will be hundreds of thousands of bereaved families, a substantial part of whom have been conditioned to the belief that this is a Jewish war."[4]

Besides, in the concentration camps liberated by American GIs or British Tommies—Dachau, Buchenwald, or Bergen-Belsen—Jews were a minority. In Buchenwald and Dachau only about a fifth of the prisoners were Jews. As the British historian Tony Kushner points out, the very term "concentration camp" lends itself to obfuscation: "In location, and sometimes even in name, those concentration camps could be seen as part of a continuum, however horrific they had become, with the Nazi atrocities of the 1930s" which had mostly been directed at Hitler's political opponents. When these camps were liberated, says Kushner, they confirmed a pattern which seemed to foreclose "the possibility of different camps in other localities—of death factories in Poland such as Treblinka."[5]

Though he speeds through the period covered by Lipstadt, Peter Novick's provocative survey of the Holocaust's post-war career offers a further reason for American reticence: with the realignment brought about by the Cold War, talk of the Holocaust was positively inimical to US interests. "In 1945," he writes, "Americans had cheered as Soviet forces pounded Berlin into rubble; in 1948, Americans organized the Airlift to defend 'gallant Berliners' from Soviet threat." The accompanying ideological retooling took place at breathtaking speed, but in 1950s America few besides Communists shouted "Remember the six million!" Mourners at the funeral of Julius and Ethel Rosenberg, executed as Soviet spies in 1953, sung the "Song of the Warsaw Ghetto." For most Americans, though, including American Jews, the Holocaust was, says Novick, "the wrong atrocity"—mention of it was at best an embarrassment, at worst a cause for suspicion.[6]

In Britain, where the wartime alliance with Stalin was even more of a shotgun marriage, suspicion of Soviet sources kept the Red Army's July 1944 liberation of Majdanek off the front pages. Majdanek was a death camp, a place where the Nazis had exterminated two hundred thousand people, yet even with the war still raging the BBC refused to broadcast a word about what the Soviets had found. Alexander Werth, the first British journalist to visit the camp, had his report spiked because "they thought it was a Russian propaganda stunt."[7] The liberation of Auschwitz by Soviet troops in January 1945 met with a similar reception in the West.

Location is as important in history as it is in real estate. At Sobibór, Treblinka, and Belzec the killers were efficient enough to leave only a handful of surviving victims: of the 600,000 men, women, and children deported to Belzec, there are precisely two known survivors. On Himmler's orders the camps themselves were razed to the ground before the Russian advance. But the fact that all the *Vernichtungslager*—the extermination camps—were behind what would become the Iron Curtain was at least as important a factor in obscuring the truth about what happened there as any cover-up by the retreating Nazis. Long after it had outlived its Cold War usefulness, skepticism about the evidence left behind at Majdanek, where the Red Army found the machinery of murder intact, or at Auschwitz, where efforts to efface what had happened were only partially successful, would resurface as one of the main strands of Holocaust denial.

Nowadays the Holocaust is ubiquitous. Films such as *Schindler's List* and *Sophie's Choice*, television programs, novels, memoirs, and works of history all add to the sum of what we know—or think we know. We need merely consider the reception of Binjamin Wilkomirski's *Fragments* to see how much has changed. Decorated with endorsements by famous academics, *Fragments* won the National Jewish Book Award for biography/memoir, beating out works by Elie Wiesel and Alfred Kazin. Even after evidence mounted that "Wilkomirski" was really Bruno Dössekker, a Swiss musician whose account of a childhood in the camps was completely fictional, *Fragments* continued to attract readers.[8] Such is the public appetite for Holocaust literature.

How did this change come about? Peter Novick mentions

various factors: a gradual easing of the Cold War, outbreaks of neo-Nazism in Germany, the 1952 publication of *Anne Frank: The Diary of a Young Girl*, later adapted to stage and screen. But the single greatest catalyst, he says, was the kidnapping and trial of the Nazi war criminal Adolf Eichmann. Here, too, initial response was negative: *The New Republic* said Israel should "confess error and hand Eichmann back" to Argentina. The *Wall Street Journal* worried that the proceedings would only benefit the Russians. But as the trial wore on, the sheer mass of detail evidently overcame such skepticism. The trial was televised, and for the first time the American public was confronted with the Holocaust as an event distinct from the general carnage of war.[9]

Much of what the Eichmann trial revealed was set out in even greater detail in Raul Hilberg's *The Destruction of the European Jews*. Hilberg's opus was first published in 1961 by Quadrangle Books, at the time a small independent publisher, but only after having been sat on by academic presses at Columbia and the University of Oklahoma, and rejected outright from Princeton, and only after a Czech refugee donated $15,000 toward the cost of publication. The book's early reviews were mostly hostile—with one notable exception.[10] Writing in *Commentary*, Hugh Trevor-Roper declared that Hilberg's analysis of the Nazi machinery of extermination carried "a profound social content." Trevor-Roper's review, which ran in the period between Eichmann's abduction and his trial, also contained a warning. The "most surprising revelation," he wrote, would also be "the least welcome"—namely Hilberg's depiction of the extent to which the Nazis relied on the Jews to assist in their own destruction.

The magazine, published then as now by the American Jewish Committee, hastened to counter Trevor-Roper's praise with an article by Harvard historian Oscar Handlin entitled "Jewish Resistance to the Nazis." Handlin accused Hilberg of "impiety" and "defaming the dead." This response became so widespread that in 1968, when Hilberg went to Israel on sabbatical, officials at Yad Vashem, the Israeli Holocaust memorial, refused to allow him into the archives (a situation anticipated by the way *Yad Vashem Studies* had treated his book. The review was titled "Historical Research or Slander?").[11]

Eichmann in Jerusalem, Hannah Arendt's report on the Eichmann trial, fared no better. Arendt's focus on Eichmann's ordinariness, on what she called "the banality of evil," struck some commentators as overly sympathetic. In the *New York Times Book Review*, Barbara Tuchman accused Arendt of "a conscious desire to support Eichmann's defense." The Anti-Defamation League of B'nai Brith condemned what it called an "evil book," reminding its members:

> It is common knowledge that Eichmann himself deliberately planned the cold-blooded senseless liquidation of an entire people. . . . Eichmann personally conceived the idea of liquidating Jews as a means of "solving" the Jewish problem. . . . He probably could have successfully proposed mass Jewish emigration to his superiors [but] instead he selected the gas chamber, the crematorium and the soap factory."[12]

These attacks, as Peter Novick points out, were "not just false but the reverse of the truth." Like Hilberg, Arendt was assailed for highlighting the role of the Jewish communal leadership in the tragedy—perhaps even more virulently than Hilberg, because in her view Jewish leaders had been particularly culpable. "Wherever Jews lived," she wrote,

> there were recognized Jewish leaders, and this leadership, almost without exception, cooperated in one way or another, for one reason or another, with the Nazis. The whole truth was that if the Jewish people had really been unorganized and leaderless, there would have been chaos and misery but

the total number of victims would hardly have been between four and a half and six million people.[13]

Once again *Commentary*, the voice of the American Jewish leadership, pronounced its anathema, with the editor, Norman Podhoretz, personally declaring Arendt's reports "complex, unsentimental, riddled with paradox and ambiguity"—all, in Podhoretz's mind, terms of abuse.[14]

In 1988 Arno Mayer, a professor of European history at Princeton, published *Why Did the Heavens Not Darken?* Subtitled "The Final Solution in History," Mayer's book intended to rescue the Holocaust from a "cult of remembrance" which in his view had "become overly sectarian" and thus impeded historical understanding. "Whereas the voice of memory is univocal and uncontested, that of history is polyphonic and open for debate," Mayer wrote. History "calls for revision."[15]

To the Anti-Defamation League, those were fighting words. Even worse, Mayer argued that the Nazis were motivated not by simple anti-Semitism, but by a hostility to "Judeo-Bolshevism"—the Nazi word for the belief that Jews controlled both Communism and capitalism. Mayer wrote that there was no evidence to suggest that when Adolf Hitler invaded Poland his objective was "to capture the maximum number of Jews for slaughter."[16] Indeed the Nazis went to great lengths to push Jews to emigrate. Contrary to Lucy Dawidowicz's *The War Against the Jews* (1975), which claimed that genocide was one of the Nazis' principal war aims, Mayer held that Hitler was far more concerned with his "crusade" against Communism, and that only after the failure of Operation Barbarossa, the invasion of the Soviet Union, did the Nazis vent their murderous frustration on the Jews of Eastern Europe.[17]

Mayer's thesis was sloppily presented. His book had no footnotes, and his contention that anti-Communism was more important in Nazi ideology than anti-Semitism was certainly open to argument, as was his account of events leading to the Final Solution. But argument was just what Mayer didn't get from his critics, who preferred insult and innuendo. "'A mockery of memory and history,' 'outrageous,' . . . 'bizarre,' and 'perverse'" were, said historian Richard Evans, reporting the controversy for a London newspaper, "just some of the more printable" responses. Leading the charge was *The New Republic*'s reviewer, a young Harvard graduate student named Daniel Goldhagen.

Goldhagen's rage seemed particularly aroused by what he called "Mayer's enormous intellectual error," namely his joint consideration of Nazi anti-Semitism and anti-Communism.[18] This is an old story, whose roots lie in the 1950s, when Lucy Dawidowicz was the American Jewish Committee's resident expert on Communism and the organized Jewish community resisted any suggestion of a shared fate.[19] Communist governments returned the favor, resisting efforts to even recognize Jews as a category among the victims, which is why the commemorative plaque at Auschwitz, like the many Soviet monuments to the Great Patriotic War, contained no mention of Jews. But the geography of the Final Solution wasn't just coincidence. On the eve of Operation Barbarossa Hitler issued the infamous "Commissar Order" authorizing the execution of Communist officials and "Jews in Party and State functions." This was followed by a directive enjoining "ruthless and energetic measures against Bolshevik agitators, guerrillas, saboteurs, Jews." The camp at Auschwitz–Birkenau housed Soviet prisoners of war before Jews were sent there; in the first mass gassings, in August and September 1941, the victims were Soviet POWs identified as political commissars.

The close association in Hitler's mind between Jews and Bolsheviks doesn't mean such a relationship existed in reality. But it doesn't mean there was no relationship, either. And since Hitler's views had fatal consequences, as when he told

Himmler in December 1941 that the Jews were to be
extirpated "as partisans," the tidy separation so dear to
Goldhagen, like the simplicity so cherished by Podhoretz, can
only be maintained at the cost of considerable distortion. Thus
Goldhagen writes that to the German soldiers at Auschwitz,
"the deaths of non-Jews were understood to have been incidental to the enterprise, mere tactical operations," yet even he
is later forced to acknowledge that at Auschwitz and elsewhere
such mere tactical operations "killed, mainly by starvation, 2.8
million young healthy Soviet POWs in less than eight
months."[20]

When aimed at their targets, this distortion is merely dis-
graceful. Hilberg, Arendt, and Mayer are all not just Jews but
refugees from the Nazis. There can be no doubting their obvious, sympathetic, personal identification with the victims of
the Holocaust. "By 1942, in her eighties and blind," Raul
Hilberg's grandmother "lay in bed most of the time," Hilberg
writes in *The Politics of Memory*. "Apparently that is where the
German raiders found her and where they shot her on the
spot."[21] Hannah Arendt had been arrested for illegal Zionist
activity, and interned by the Vichy French, before escaping to
the United States.[22] Arno Mayer's book opens with "A Personal
Preface" telling of his own hair-raising escape from
Luxembourg and occupied France, and of the fate of his grandfather, who refused to leave Luxembourg and died in
Theresienstadt.[23] Such personal bona fides didn't prevent the
Anti-Defamation League from including Mayer in its 1993
report "Hitler's Apologists: The Anti-Semitic Propaganda of
Holocaust Revisionism," where his work is cited as an example
of "legitimate historical scholarship which relativizes the genocide of the Jews." Mayer's crime is to "have argued, with no
apparent anti-Semitic motivation"—note how the absence of
evidence becomes itself incriminating—"that though millions
of Jews were killed during WWII, there was actually no pre-
meditated policy for this destruction."

Far more dangerous is the effect on what "enforcers" like Goldhagen or the Anti-Defamation League believe they are protecting. There is a kind of consolation in believing that the Second World War was really "a war against the Jews," just as there is a kind of comfort in the view that the whole German nation were uniquely and murderously anti-Semitic. But these are not the consolations of history. History is messy, complex, contingent. Emptied of its contingency, history becomes myth, which the French critic Roland Barthes defined as "depoliticized speech." In a myth, said Barthes, "history evaporates."[24] In other words, by describing a Holocaust outside politics, by reducing it to good Jews and bad Germans—or in Lucy Dawidowicz's formulation "the Devil and his hosts"—these writers have, however inadvertently, made the deniers' task easier.

"I'm always fighting. I'm a great dinner party guest if you want a lively dinner party; if you want peace and quiet, don't invite me." The voice of Deborah Lipstadt is a big instrument—big enough so that in the months between talking with her in the autumn and the opening of the trial I had in mind a much larger woman than the silent, actually rather petite person in a beige trouser-suit sitting between her lawyers.

In the preceding pages, as at the trial, Lipstadt's voice has been barely audible above the contentious chorus that surrounds any discussion of the Holocaust. Once the trial began, Lipstadt herself would become merely a figurehead—a hate figure for Irving's supporters, a heroine worthy of her biblical namesake to her admirers. Before that happened I wanted to get Lipstadt's sense of her own role. Did she see herself as a dragon-slayer? The victim of a legal mugging? A Jewish avenger?

What I found was a woman with a bad back and a New York manner—more Bette Midler than Bess Myerson—undiluted by her years in California and Georgia. A veteran of hundreds of interviews and dozens of television appearances, Lipstadt is perfectly at ease with the press, slipping on and off the record with the agility of a politician. She'd been forbidden to talk about the specifics of the case, but happily rehearsed the themes of her book: "Don't ask Stephen Jay Gould to get into a debate with people from Kansas who want to teach creationism. I'm not going to get into a debate with a denier."

But if Holocaust deniers are merely a nuisance, why bother to denounce them? "It's not that they are a clear and present danger," she replied. "I like to say they are clear and future danger." Pressed further, she responded with some heat: "Hello! I'm the defendant here. If I hadn't fought this he would have won by default. If he had won by default, he could have said—it would have been said—the High Court in London recognizes his definition of the Holocaust. Now some people would say, 'Oh that's ludicrous. Who would believe that anyway?' But it's naïve to think you can just say 'Oh, I'm going to ignore this.'"

Lipstadt did not seem naïve. However as we sat talking in the coffee shop attached to her London hotel she did give the impression of having been metaphysically wrenched out of her orbit. "I'd much rather be hanging out in the fall foliage in Georgia, hiking the Appalachian trail," she said. When we first spoke on the telephone she described her experience as "pretty chilling" and in free-speech terms that is hard to dispute. Though Irving tries repeatedly to make his right to speak an issue, it is Deborah Lipstadt who has had to put her own work aside, move to London, hire lawyers, do fundraising to pay them, and then sit and watch while men— all of the witnesses in this case are male—argue about words she wrote.

Before we met I thought perhaps it was conflict that made her uncomfortable. This illusion was swiftly dispelled. "My mother will tell you that she was called to the principal's office more times because of fights I'd gotten into, that had nothing to do with me," she said. This is very much her fight, "and if I'm going to fight it, you gotta fight it no holds barred." Remaining silent, letting others do the fighting for her—that will be the hard part.

Denying the Holocaust began life as a piece of commissioned research. In 1984 Yehuda Bauer, director of Hebrew University's Vidal Sassoon Center for the Study of Anti-Semitism, asked Lipstadt if she might be interested in undertaking a study of the historical development of "Holocaust revisionists, i.e. those who deny that the Holocaust happened." She replied with a three-page proposal on "the American school" of revisionists, focusing on "their historical and historiographic methodology." Among the questions Lipstadt proposed to answer in her monograph was how the writings of Harry Elmer Barnes, a once prominent historian and author of a revisionist account of the First World War, might have influenced "those such as David Irving who, though they do not deny the existence of the Holocaust, do shift the blame from Hitler."[25]

Completion was estimated for the fall of 1986, but in May of 1988 Lipstadt received an additional grant from the Center. By that time David Irving had testified in the Zündel trial, and Lipstadt had published her first book with the Free Press in New York. The editor-in-chief, Irwin Glickes, asked Lipstadt what else she was working on, and she mentioned her research project.

"I don't think she saw it as a book," says Adam Bellow, who became Lipstadt's editor. "We had a fascinating abstract collo-quy in Irwin's office" about whether publishing the study would do more harm than good. Lipstadt was worried that the ensuing "publicity would benefit the deniers." Bellow describes her as "reluctant to write it and reluctant to publish." Another complication was that, legally, the Sassoon Center owned the rights to Lipstadt's still-uncompleted research, and was already in negotiations with Pergamon Press, whose owner, financier Robert Maxwell, was a Center benefactor.*

By March 1991 terms had been agreed, and Lipstadt told Bellow she was "beginning to see the light at the end of the tunnel." Six months later she reported "the work is moving along nicely" but expressed concern about her January deadline. "I have also spoken to people in England who have a large cache of material on David Irving's 'conversion' to denial," she added, asking for extra time to "give a really contemporary slant to the story."[26] Bellow agreed.

"Deborah worked very hard for very little money," he says. In her affidavit Lipstadt says she received about $20,000 over the course of four years to cover travel, research assistance, and expenses. "According to my calculations I spent far more than that on my research," she adds, noting that despite an agreement calling for her to receive half of any royalties, "Hebrew University only sent me a small portion of the very first royalty payment they received (approximately 2,500 dollars). After that I received no royalties on this book. I received no other funds for the writing of this book. I received no funds when the rights to this book were sold to other countries, including the United Kingdom. I have earned nothing from this book since the first year in which it appeared, in 1994."

Lipstadt sent her finished manuscript to Yehuda Bauer in the fall of 1992. Bauer found it "well-written and fascinating," but complained that Lipstadt's perspective was too narrow, and asked her to include more material on Europe, especially relating to David Irving. "If you decide not to deal with it" Bauer suggested changing the book's title: "it is not about Holocaust

---

* Maxwell, a Czech Jew who began his career in Britain denying his Jewish origins, ended up buried on Israel's Mount of Olives. Maxwell's habitual use of the British libel laws to silence his critics—he once sued *The New Republic*, which at the time had a total UK circulation of 135—meant that the full details of his fraudulent dealings didn't emerge until after his death in November 1991.

denial, but about Holocaust denial in the U.S. and France."
Lipstadt dealt with it, writing in December 1992 to the head of
London's Institute of Jewish Affairs asking for additional material on Irving. When the book came out in 1993 Irving still
didn't get his own chapter (unlike American deniers Austin
App and Arthur Butz) but he was more than mentioned in
passing.

Though it may not have made much money, in every other
way the American edition of *Denying the Holocaust* was a publishing triumph. Hailing it on the front page of the July 11, 1993
New York Times Book Review as "important and impassioned"
reviewer Walter Reich wrote: "it illuminates, with skill and
clarity, not only the peculiarly disturbing world of the
Holocaust deniers, but also the methods they have used to distort history [and] the motives that have driven them to do so."
New York Newsday, the *Boston Globe*, and the *Atlanta Constitution*
agreed. The *Los Angeles Times* called the book "an antidote to
the moral and intellectual virus that has spread from the crack-
pot fringe to the very heart of public discourse." Lipstadt, who
arrived at Emory as an associate professor, was named to the
Dorot Chair in Modern Jewish and Holocaust Studies; she also
received a Presidential appointment to the United States
Holocaust Memorial Council.

Her British experience was rather different. In March 1995
Penguin issued a paperback edition, which sold 2,088 copies in
the United Kingdom in its first year. Outside the Jewish press,
reviewers ignored it. In 1996, the year Deborah Lipstadt was
served with David Irving's writ, net British sales for *Denying the
Holocaust* numbered exactly 21.

This put the First Defendants in an awkward position.
Penguin is owned by Pearson, a public company, and even if
they won, defending a libel action would cost Pearson's shareholders many thousands of times the book's minuscule earnings.
By the time lawyers' fees are figured in, the trial itself could
easily cost £10,000 a day—not to mention pre-trial expenses

like expert reports. The most cursory credit check would have made it clear how unlikely Penguin were to ever recover even a tiny fraction of this money from the much mortgaged David Irving.

As a purely business proposition a publisher involved in a libel action is nearly always advised to settle. Irving was well aware of this, having recently won a settlement from a London newspaper after a columnist attributed to Irving a phrase that had actually been a quote from Adolf Hitler. A settlement would be far cheaper than fighting the case even if Penguin won—and given the British libel laws, winning was far from certain.

Yet Penguin decided to defend the suit. Anthony Forbes-Watson, who became the company's CEO after a stint running its Ladybird Books, a juvenile division, cited a company tradition of "upholding the right to publish" running from the *Lady Chatterley* trial through Salman Rushdie's *Satanic Verses*. But Penguin's conduct regarding Rushdie, though perhaps understandable, was far from heroic. Subject to death threats themselves, Rushdie's publishers didn't disavow his book, or turn him over to the *fatwa*, but they declined to issue a paperback edition, or to reprint the book in hardcover.

Penguin may have stood by Lipstadt out of principle. Besides, controversial books often make money, and while *Denying the Holocaust* did not, a publisher known to cut and run at the first sign of a libel writ will have a hard time attracting certain authors—not to mention setting themselves up as easy pickings for would-be claimants. The unusual background of Pearson's CEO Marjorie Scardino, who published a crusading weekly newspaper in Savannah, Georgia that won a Pulitzer Prize before being forced out of business by the targets of its exposés, may also have helped to stiffen Penguin's resolve.

But there is one other factor worth mentioning. Lipstadt's American publishers had her manuscript read for libel—in other words they'd asked a specialist in defamation law to read it and flag potential trouble spots, suggesting changes if necessary. A routine precaution in the United States, libel readings are less common in Britain. Penguin hadn't bothered—a dereliction described as "unconscionable" by Adam Bellow, and which certainly would have increased Penguin's discomfort had they abandoned Lipstadt.

Discovery

Deborah Lipstadt isn't the only silent presence at the defense tables. While Irving gives his evidence, Richard Rampton can often be seen leaning to one side, his fingers massaging his wig back and forth over his scalp as he cocks his head toward a stocky, bespectacled man in a plain black robe and no wig. This is Deborah Lipstadt's lawyer, Anthony Julius.

In Britain, as in America, the law is a hierarchal profession. Trials in Britain are not televised, so there are fewer chances for lawyers to become household names in the way that Johnny Cochran or Barry Scheck or Alan Dershowitz have in the United States. But for the newspaper-reading public, at least, the most flamboyant courtroom advocates in Britain, like Michael Mansfield, QC, or Geoffrey Robertson, QC, have attained a measure of celebrity. These men are barristers; as a more formal society, Britain until recently maintained a strict division between barristers and solicitors, who were not allowed to appear in court. That was reserved for barristers, who got higher fees as well (with Queen's Counsels, the elite among barristers, at the top of the scale. A reasonably busy QC can depend on an income of hundreds of thousands of pounds.) What solicitors got was steady work. If you wanted to sell your house, or divorce your husband, or draw up a contract, then you needed a solicitor. Anthony Julius trained as a solicitor. When Princess Diana had to give up being Mrs. Charles Windsor she came to Anthony Julius to negotiate her settlement.

It is difficult for any foreigner to appreciate the armory of blandishments, threats, inducements, incentives, and wire-pulls available to the British royal family, even today. The Labour Party are pledged to reform the House of Lords, so faithful retainers can no longer expect that they—and their first-born sons, in perpetuity—will sit by right in the upper chamber. But no one has proposed taking away the Queen's power to create dukes, earls, viscounts, and all the lesser titles. Then there are the grace-and-favor residences. Not to mention the literally thousands of perks, patronage jobs, and gifts which will some day be Charles's to bestow—and which are already in the gift of his mother, whose disdain for her soon to be former daughter-in-law was notorious.

The Princess of Wales needed an outsider, someone who the British establishment would regard as "unclubbable," someone who couldn't be "gotten to." A Jewish partner in a Jewish firm, Anthony Julius got Diana a divorce settlement worth £17 million ($25 million). By way of a thank you, Diana sent him a silver blotter from Asprey's. Her patronage made him the most famous lawyer in Britain. She also made him executor of her will.

It was Alan Dershowitz who told Deborah Lipstadt she needed her own lawyer. When a newspaper or a magazine is sued for libel, the writer and the publication are often represented by the same person. The economics of book publishing, however, mean that the interests of writers and their publishers do not always coincide. A publisher may be tempted to cut its losses at the writer's expense—not necessarily in terms of money, since as Michael Rubinstein has written, "publishers . . . normally bear the brunt of the claims," but in terms of credibility or reputation.[1] Though he later acted for David

Irving, in the *Exodus* case Rubinstein was the publisher's lawyer; Leon Uris used somebody else.

Penguin has a team of in-house lawyers, headed by Cecily Engle, a former libel lawyer, and Helena Peacock. They also had outside counsel: Kevin Bays, a litigation partner at Davenport Lyons, a big London media and entertainment firm, and Mark Bateman, an associate at the firm. Bays and Bateman were in court every day; Engle and Peacock were there most days. Penguin told Lipstadt they would be happy to represent her; she was also welcome to retain her own counsel, but in that case she would have to pay for it herself. Lipstadt approached the Board of Deputies of British Jews for advice. Lord Mishcon, the name partner of Julius's firm, Mishcon de Reya, had represented the board for many years. Julius was asked if, at least initally, he'd be willing to represent Lipstadt on a *pro bono* basis and he said he would.

"I betrayed my vocation," Anthony Julius says self-mockingly one morning a few weeks before the trial, "so I might as well be a lawyer." Though the desk in his Bloomsbury office is a lawyerly clutter of files and documents, some belonging to his client Deborah Lipstadt, every other surface is covered by a blizzard of art books that fall from tables and chairs onto the carpet forming drifts around our feet. Julius is writing two books on modern art, but art was not his vocation. "English was my vocation; I thought I would like to teach. The only reason I ended up doing law is because I didn't think I could get a good enough degree to stay on and do research."

The oldest of four sons, Julius eventually graduated from Cambridge with first-class honors and could easily have done a Ph.D. But he'd already been accepted at law school. Then his father, a menswear retailer, suddenly died of a brain tumor, so after taking six months off to help in the family business, Julius says, "I stuck with law." Though his rise in his unwanted profession has been meteoric, he remained wistful, and returned to literary studies on a part-time basis, completing his doctorate a few years ago.

His thesis on *T.S. Eliot, Anti-Semitism, and Literary Form* was published by Cambridge University Press. It begins:

> Anti-Semites are not all the same. Some break Jewish bones, others wound Jewish sensibilities. Eliot falls into the second category. He was civil to Jews he knew, offensive to those who merely knew him through his work. He wounded his Jewish readers, if not the Jews of his acquaintance, to whom, apparently, he was "not disagreeable." Though worth noting, this is not a distinction that yields a defence to the charge of anti-Semitism. If the work, or some notable part of it, is anti-Semitic, it is the work of an anti-Semite.[2]

Every culture has its own stereotypes. In America, Jews are variously supposed to be clever, grasping, clannish, or pushy, with sexual and political associations ringing the changes from Bolshevik bohemians to reactionary patriarchs. In Britain, Jews are supposed to be touchy. Touchy about having to sing hymns at school, touchy about innocent remarks—like when Harold Macmillan described Margaret Thatcher's cabinet as containing "more old Estonians than old Etonians"—and touchy about little things like quotas or the assumption that to be English you have to be a white, Christian Anglo-Saxon. By taking on T.S. Eliot, an icon not only of English literature but (though he was actually a native of St. Louis) of the very idea of Englishness, it is as if Julius is saying, "You want touchy? I'll give you touchy!"

To his detractors, Julius's patient separation of the several strands of anti-Semitism found in poems such as "Gerontion" and "Sweeney Among the Nightingales" is just "oversensitivity."[3] But the touchiness, or, to put it more neutrally, the extraordinary attentiveness, of his reading is precisely the great strength of Julius's approach. The history of anti-Semitism has been rehearsed many times; so has August Bebel's dictum that, politically, anti-Semitism is the socialism of fools. What Julius does is attend to anti-Semitism as a language, a medium for communicating certain ideas, a discourse. This is important because, in a tolerant society like Britain (where, for example, mixed-race couples are far more common than in the United States), prejudice mainly shows itself at the level of speech rather than violence. It is also important because, particularly in Britain, literature has always played a significant role in repeating and elaborating on Jewish stereotypes.

From Christopher Marlowe's *Jew of Malta* and Shakespeare's *Merchant of Venice* to Hilaire Belloc, who wrote a whole book attacking Jews, and Rudyard Kipling, who wrote poems on a similar theme, to the novelist John Buchan (whose hero, Richard Hannay, learns in *The Thirty-Nine Steps* that "the man who is ruling the world just now" is "a little white-faced Jew in a bathchair with an eye like a rattlesnake") there is what might be called a tradition of literary anti-Semitism. Most of the more recent practitioners have been Tories,* but then the party of Disraeli (and Thatcher) has long given its anti-Semites cause for complaint. Indeed it is this culture of complaint, whose most prominent representative in recent years was the late Alan Clark, Tory MP and latter-day advocate of a negotiated peace with Hitler, that constitutes David Irving's intellectual hinterland.

In his scrupulous dissection of the way in which anti-

---

* But not all. The visibility of the Rothschilds made attacks on Jewish capital irresistible for some on the left, even as the prominence of socialists like writer Harold Laski and publisher Victor Gollancz drew attacks from the right. George Orwell, who wrote that "neo-tories and political Catholics are always liable to succumb to anti-Semitism" was baffled by the persistence of prejudice on the left. Orwell himself was far from immune, writing in the Labour newspaper *Tribune* in 1940 that "for the time being we have heard enough about the concentration camps and the persecution of the Jews."

Semitism not only influenced Eliot, but actually inspired some of his most powerful verse, Julius's manner is critical, not prosecutorial. But in his mapping of the mechanisms behind other scholars' blindness to Eliot's offensiveness, as in his approach to Irving's anti-Semitism, the professionalism of Julius's approach masks a cold fury that is entirely personal.

There was a "Jewish quota" at City of London, the private secondary school that enabled Julius to become the first member of his family to go to university. "I know there was a quota," he told me, "because the school wrote to my father and said: Your son passed the [entrance] exam. We've given him a reserve place, and we'll see if any other Jewish boys drop out."

With his large, close-cropped head, ambling gait, and slightly stooped posture, Julius looks a bit like a bear in a pinstripe suit—that is if you can imagine a bear who, though capable of tearing you apart, would much rather simply persuade you of the error of your views. When I ask him, with my tape recorder running, why this case matters, his response is guarded, deliberately offhand: "Does this case matter? To who? It matters to Deborah Lipstadt because she's being sued." When I turn the tape recorder off his words are equally careful, but there is a flash of anger in his manner that is actually frightening in a man otherwise so perfectly contained.

Something of a polymath, Julius recently stepped down after nearly a decade as his firm's managing partner in order to pursue his interests in writing and art. He has written a study of poet Philip Larkin, and recently gave the Neurath Lecture at the National Gallery. An essay responding to critics of his book on Eliot is dedicated to the painter R.B. Kitaj. But his fame has come at a price: though Julius donated his own time spent administering the Diana memorial fund, that didn't stop the tabloids from attacking Mishcon de Reya's fees for the firm's work on the fund. More unwelcome attention came when Julius left his wife after he fell in love with a woman whose father Julius represented in a libel action. She and Julius later married.

When Deborah Lipstadt came to see him, Julius's life was still in turmoil. Irving had filed libel claims against the *Observer* and writer Gitta Sereny at the same time as suing Lipstadt and Penguin. Ironically, Sereny's article, "Spin Time for Hitler," spent nearly as much space attacking Daniel Goldhagen's "hymn of hate to the Germans" as it did warning readers away from Irving, "a man of talent, both as a researcher and a writer," but a master of "deliberate falsehood."[4] Since the cases seemed to overlap, Penguin's outside counsel had begun meeting with lawyers from Lovell White Durrant, another firm with a big media practice who represented Sereny and the *Observer*. When Julius and James Libson, a Mishcon partner, joined them, they might have noticed three things: None of the other participants were Jewish. None of them seemed in a hurry to go to trial. And none of them had any experience with David Irving.

The first reply to Irving's claim had been drafted before Mishcon came on board, and was essentially identical to the reply in the *Observer* case. It quoted from Irving's books and published interviews, and gave the Goebbels diaries episode considerable attention. Though hardly a surrender document, it seemed drafted in the hope that Irving, once he realized the other side was willing to go to trial, would simply give up. It was defensive, in every sense of the word.

Anthony Julius knew that David Irving wouldn't go away. In 1992 Irving was expelled from Canada, and one of the documents he later obtained under Canada's Access to Information Law was a dossier on his activities compiled, Irving claimed, by the Board of Deputies of British Jews and sent to the Canadian authorities. Irving wanted to sue for libel, but Julius, who acted for the Board, says that Irving was "sadly too late" in filing the proper papers. Julius doesn't look too broken up by this. Indeed when Irving went to court to seek permission to file "out of time," Julius not only opposed him, he convinced the judge that Irving should pay the Board's £10,000 costs, and then, when Irving failed to pay, moved to have him declared bankrupt. Irving came up with the money.

Deborah Lipstadt will not be saved by the bell. Her case would have to be fought, and fought hard. Julius immediately took steps to prepare for litigation, applying to become one of the first solicitor-advocates under new rules that allow properly qualified solicitors to argue cases before the courts. There was no guarantee that Penguin's lawyers would support the more aggressive—and more expensive—strategy he and Libson had in mind. As a solicitor-advocate, Julius could, if he had to, argue the case himself. He also took over "Discovery," the pre-trial stage where, under the rules of procedure, both sides are obliged to make available any relevant evidence or documents to the other side's lawyers. The burden of proof was against him, and if Julius had to go to court on the basis of the documents he had so far—Irving's books and the other material cited in the first reply to Irving's claim—he'd probably lose.

> Discovery is the nastiest stage you get into in a High Court action because it's when you are required by law to open your innermost secrets, your innermost files and documents: I had to provide copies of all my telephone logs and private letters and diaries, and nobody can—I don't mind, because I've got an open conscience.
>
> David Irving, speech to the Clarendon Club,
> September 19, 1992

As he'd reminded the judge in his opening speech, David Irving was an experienced litigant. In 1992 he'd sued the *Sunday Times* after the paper refused to pay him the balance of his fee in the Goebbels diaries episode. Though that case never went to trial, Irving, as he told his supporters at the Clarendon

Club, knew all about discovery. Or so he thought. To Irving, discovery was about documents, and as one of the world's great document hounds, he had nothing to fear. "As a researcher," wrote Gitta Sereny, "he is good enough to make it difficult for anyone to fault him who doesn't know the material he uses as well as he does—and let us face it, few do."

Lipstadt's lawyers wanted—needed—access to Irving's material. "We decided that in order to win this case we needed to see what Irving had in his study," said James Libson. But they also needed to get inside Irving's head, and documents alone wouldn't get them there. To Mishcon de Reya, discovery wasn't just—or even primarily—about documents. Discovery was about control.

"We wanted to control the course the proceedings took," said Julius. "First of all because when you are defending it's very easy to be reactive." Reactive was the strategy he'd discarded. Irving's complaint made it clear he intended to put the Holocaust on trial. Instead, Julius would use discovery to put Irving on trial, to "take the initiative. Run it as if it was a history seminar and Irving was a rather unintelligent student." The aim throughout was to make the trial about David Irving's methods, rather than Deborah Lipstadt's book.

To lead his seminar Julius needed a QC who could master the material as well as the part. In the summer of 1997 he and Libson went to see Richard Rampton. They took with them a single sheet of paper on which they'd outlined their new strategy: to use academic experts to investigate Irving's historiography and the evidence upon which it purported to rest, and to use Irving's own words—in speeches, interviews, and diary entries—to show he was an extremist.

Barristers operate under the cab-rank principle, meaning they are supposed to take whatever comes up. But they have ways of making themselves unavailable. Rampton had written a textbook on libel. Known for his ability to master detailed briefs, he had an unfulfilled ambition to write a biography of

Mozart, but no pretense to being an intellectual, and, for a barrister, a notable lack of flamboyance. In his seminar, the attention would be on Lipstadt's experts. Might he be available? Rampton, intrigued, told them to come back if the case went to trial.

Now they needed an expert. Sereny's lawyers had recommended Eberhard Jaeckel. A leading authority on Hitler, Jaeckel was Professor of Modern History at the University of Stuttgart, and the author of *Hitler's Weltanschauung*. But in 1981 he'd been duped by Konrad Kujau, who forged the "Hitler diaries," into putting bogus poems into a collection of Hitler's early writings.[5] Though Jaeckel had publicly admitted his error, Irving could have used the incident in cross-examination. Besides, Jaeckel had already written an attack on Irving.[6] The proposal that Jaeckel serve as pointman for the defense case was one reason Julius decided to run the discovery.

"I had the sense," said Julius, "that we had to engage with Irving three ways: historical, historiographical, and the political. So I had already separated out those categories. I also had the sense that they represented a hierarchy, and that the historical and the political were the bases of a pyramid, and that the apex was the historiographical. So it was important to get a historian who was at home in the historiographical, but who was also a Germanist."

Since the trial would take place in London, they wanted someone reasonably local. And they needed someone who could start work as soon as possible. "We needed experts before discovery, to advise on discovery," said Libson, who studied English and Arabic at Leeds University. "We didn't want generalists," Libson added. He and Julius needed someone who not only knew how to interpret wartime German documents, but also knew where to look for them. Ian Kershaw, author of a monumental biography of Hitler, was too busy; he was also rumored to be advising Sereny.

Similar considerations ruled out Jeremy Noakes, editor of a massive edition of source documents on Nazism.

Ideally they also wanted someone who couldn't be seen as Irving's rival. As Julius quickly realized, they wanted Richard Evans. "I'd read his book *In Defence of History* which I very much liked. And I'd also read bits of *Rituals of Retribution* (a study of capital punishment in Germany)." Professor of Modern History at Cambridge, Evans is a Fellow of the British Academy and of the Royal Historical Society. He is, as they say, familiar with the literature—hardly surprising considering he wrote much of it, including standard works on German feminism and the German underworld and two books on German historiography: *Rereading German History: From Unification to Reunification, 1800–1996* and *In Hitler's Shadow: West German Historians and the Attempt to Escape from the Nazi Past*.

In the fall of 1997 Julius and Libson met with Evans, whom they found to be "a person of intellectual confidence and composure." Better still, though he'd worked on the Nazi period in several of his books, Evans had never come across David Irving personally and had no prior opinion of his work. On the stand, Evans's intellectual confidence would get him into trouble, but as a guide to the deeps and shallows of Irving's documents he was invaluable. Evans brought in two of his graduate students, Nicholas Wachsmann and Thomas Skelton-Robinson, to help with the task of reading through all of Irving's books—in English and German—in order to draw up a "wish list" of documents to look for in discovery. Evans also recommended Hajo Funke, Professor at the Free University of Berlin and an expert on the contemporary German right.

"We mounted a gigantic disclosure* operation," said Libson.

---

* The Woolf Report on Access to Justice (1996) recommended a number of changes in the discovery process, including its name, which became "Disclosure." But since Parliament did not act on these changes immediately, *Irving* v. *Lipstadt* took place under the old regime, properly called "Discovery," and I will generally follow that usage here.

Under the rules, both sides were required to make available to the opposing side any material either party had in its "possession, custody or power related to any matter in issue."[7] Discovery itself is automatic. But if either side feels the other is holding back, they can apply for a court order to enforce "fuller and better" discovery; penalties for failure to comply can include dismissal of the entire case, striking off one of the parties (at one point Irving applied to have Lipstadt excluded, leaving Penguin to defend the case on its own), even imprisonment for contempt.

The first stage, the exchange of lists, took place in the late winter and early spring of 1998. "Irving's first discovery was just a list of his books, plus commendations of his work by other historians and some historical documents," said Libson. "There was no record of his contacts with right-wing extremists, and there were no diaries." Julius made an application for a court order to force Irving to produce more material. He would have to persuade a special judge, called a Master, that Irving had held back documents, and that these were relevant to the case.

"I wanted to make the applications myself," said Julius. "But I also wanted to make them conservatively because it was very important we should win every application. We didn't want to give him [Irving] any morale victories. That's . . . the psychological battle." Mishcon's strategy of going on the attack depended on ammunition they could only get through discovery. Without it, what they had was the legal equivalent of sticks and stones. Lipstadt's case now hinged on whether Julius could get the right order on discovery. Irving's first list had given them little more than a tiny lever, but Julius would use it to pry open Irving's citadel.

Before they faced the Master, there was one other question that Libson and Julius had to decide.

Like the *Exodus* trial, *Irving* v. *Lipstadt* was in part an argument about what had or had not happened at Auschwitz. In order for the jury to have vividly before them the horrors committed by Dr. Dering, the *Exodus* lawyers called a succession of his victims to testify. These men and women told of the terror of having testicles or ovaries removed, often without adequate anesthesia, amid the generally unsanitary and chaotic conditions of the camp. The women spoke of the pain of childlessness. That many of them were unable to say with certainty it had been Dering behind the surgeon's mask was unfortunate for the defense, but the witnesses were credible and their stories were generally believed by the jury. How better to underline the absurdity of Holocaust denial than by calling survivors, eyewitnesses who could say: "I am the man. I saw! I suffered!" Hadn't Elie Wiesel said that "any survivor has more to say than all the historians combined about what happened"?[8]

Though fewer in number, and nearly half a century older, there were still Auschwitz survivors who would have been willing and able to testify if asked. Julius decided not to ask. One reason was forensic: "We're not out to prove the parameters of the Holocaust. To an extent we had to do some of that—particularly with Auschwitz," said Libson. "Survivor testimony would have pulled the case further in that direction." Excluding survivors helped keep the focus on Irving, and on his evidence.

Then there was what Julius described as a "moral reason: Why should we expose survivors to cross-examination by a belligerent anti-Semite?" In the event, Irving conducted cross-examination with relative decorum (aside from asking Lipstadt's experts if they were "in the pay of the Israeli government," a gauche but not terribly incendiary way of referring to Yad Vashem or the Sassoon Center). But at the Zündel trial, attorney Doug Christie had subjected survivors to a sustained verbal assault, and Libson and Julius felt it would be "obscene" to risk that happening again.

There was an additional reason, though both Libson and Julius are too tactful to mention it. As every police reporter knows, just because a witness isn't lying doesn't mean they are telling the truth. Deborah Lipstadt told me: "Lots of survivors who arrived at Auschwitz will tell you they were examined by [the infamous Dr. Josef] Mengele. Then you ask them the date of their arrival, and you say, 'Well, Mengele wasn't in Auschwitz yet at that point.' There were lots of doctors . . . [somehow] they all become Mengele." One shaky witness, one survivor who, over half a century after Auschwitz, became confused about whether the crematoria at Birkenau had four ovens or five, whether the door to the gas chambers opened in or out, probably wouldn't lose Lipstadt her case. But it wouldn't help.

Besides, unlike Penguin, who simply wanted the case to go away, or their lawyers, who simply wanted to win, Julius, like his client, knew the case had to be won the right way. Convincingly. On the evidence. And in a way that would make the next person who wanted to rehabilitate the legacy of the Nazis have to work that much harder to get a hearing. In a few years—maybe 10, almost certainly 20—there won't be any survivors left. Nor any perpetrators either. No witnesses. Perpetrator trials are probably already finished. Survivor testimony would have made *Irving* v. *Lipstadt* the last trial of its kind. Instead it is the first of a new generation: a trial about the Holocaust in history instead of a trial about the Holocaust.

The discovery hearings were scheduled to begin on September 10, 1998 before Master John Trench, in the judge's chambers. Over the preceding spring and summer Libson and the two graduate students made regular visits to Irving's flat to inspect the material that was in his first list.

"I went to Irving's flat every day to look at documents," said Libson. "Nick and Thomas came too. I looked for obvious stuff; they did the more difficult job. We spent a total of two months going through the list."

Some of what they wanted was in plain sight. The existence of Irving's diaries, for instance, was hardly a secret. Over the years he'd shown extracts to favored journalists, and would even publish portions on his website. Irving's position on the diaries—like his position on many other items—was minimalist. If the lawyers let him know which dates they wanted, Irving promised to take a look and see if there was any relevant material. If he found any, he'd be happy to disclose it. Anything broader, he argued, would open his diaries to a fishing expedition by the defense.

In his affidavit before the hearing, Julius didn't exactly deny this. Rather he argued that since Irving brought this case, and the law said his client had a right to defend herself, that gave him a fishing license. It would be up to Master Trench to decide who was right.

But most of what the defense needed was, if not concealed, far from obvious. Irving's first list made reference to his "Action Reports"—an irregular publication circulated among his supporters. He hadn't actually listed the whole set, but some of them were on his website, and it would have been foolish to ignore them. Among the "Action Reports" he did mention were scattered references to the Institute for Historical Review (IHR), a pseudo-academic think-tank in California that, along with the Committee for Open Debate on the Holocaust, was one of the main channels for the distribution of literature contending that the Holocaust was a hoax. Libson knew that Irving had spoken at IHR conferences, and been an invited guest at IHR events, but there was no correspondence to or from IHR officials on Irving's list.

Irving denied having any correspondence with Robert Faurisson, the French author of articles on "The Problem of the Gas Chambers" and "The Rumor of Auschwitz" and Irving's fellow witness at the Zündel trial. Though he kept detailed phone logs, Irving's list made no mention of telephone conversations with Zündel. In court papers Irving denied having extremist views; he implied his relations with Faurisson and Zündel were distant and claimed he had "taken issue" with their views.[9]

Evidence of Irving's unsavory associations was only part of what Libson was looking for. The task of figuring out what source materials to ask for was much more complicated, involving a kind of documentary dead reckoning from the sources Irving had listed to those that were missing. Several of Irving's books contained accounts of *Kristallnacht*—November 9–10, 1938, the "night of broken glass," when Germany's synagogues were set alight, Jewish homes and businesses vandalized, and Jews arrested, beaten, and killed. In part these accounts were based on interviews Irving had conducted with a number of Hitler's adjutants. "He'd cited these in his books," said Libson, "and since he'd interviewed them himself, there was no question about that, and he gave us transcripts or interview notes. But he'd also used other sources, and those he didn't disclose."

What Irving did instead was to produce a mass of documents having little or nothing to do with the suit, but which Libson and his assistants were forced to read in order to rule them out. Irving's first discovery produced nothing, for example, regarding his relations with the National Alliance, an American white-supremacist organization under whose aegis he'd given a number of lectures. But there was a whole sheaf of material detailing his invitations from various school and university groups, including a letter to the secretary of the Durham Union Society, a university debating club, listing "female candidates with the necessary attributes to attract the male vote, if not intellect," to speak in opposition to Irving on the motion "A woman's place is in the home." He also volunteered a video-tape recording the birth of his daughter, and audiotapes relating to the Kennedy assassination.

By the time Irving found himself in front of Master Trench he'd been playing cat and mouse with Mishcon for months. Indeed the weekly, sometimes daily serve and volley of motions, summonses, and documents might well have come to seem like a game. When Irving told me the story of his brush with the Official Secrets Act, he described his interrogators as "Officers and gentlemen, the whole bunch. They play cricket with a straight bat." Discovery, he was about to learn, was a whole different ball game.

The hearings before Master Trench take two days. Julius opens with a sketch of the issues in the case, quoting from the pre-trial pleadings and from Lipstadt's book calling Irving "a dangerous spokesperson for Holocaust denial . . . a historian who . . . distorts historical evidence . . . an Adolf Hitler partisan." This, Julius points out, "is happily one of those trials where there is no essential dispute between the parties on the meanings. And that allows everyone to be sensible and just concentrate on the issue of justification."

There is no reason for Irving to disagree. Everything Julius has said so far is true. And as he continues to summarize his own affidavit, once again Irving has no reason to speak. But as Julius continues talking, outlining the six different classes of defect in Irving's discovery, and Irving remains silent, control over the course of the hearing comes to rest firmly in Julius's grasp. When Irving does finally speak up, on page 11 of the transcript, it is merely to confirm that he is indeed still looking for some photographs not yet produced. The next time Irving addresses the Master it is on a convivial note:

MASTER TRENCH: I see one of the letters was a letter to Leo Gradwell, the magistrate.

MR. IRVING: A charming man.

MASTER TRENCH: Yes, I have appeared in front of him previously. Have you had to?

MR. JULIUS: No, I have not, Master. (Laughter)

MASTER TRENCH: He has a V[ictoria] C[ross] I think, does he not?

MR. IRVING: Yes, sir, he is a real hero.

Irving's affable manner may be intended to sustain the illusion that he and the Master are social equals, fellow Englishmen, and military history buffs. Irving's diary for the day, posted on his website, describes Julius as having "the manners and delivery of a hod-carrier." In any event, his pose of superiority has cost Irving his only chance to derail Julius's game plan.

"When we got into court we were so well prepared," said Julius. "We broke down the kinds of documents into categories, and we gave the Master a draft order we wanted him to make at the very beginning of the case." In a way, from that point Irving lost it. With the Master already in "I'm making an order" mode, the rest of the hearing just became an argument about terms.

The argument about terms takes two days. On most items, the logic of Julius and Libson's drafting is so compelling Irving offers only token resistance, asking that any order to disclose correspondence be limited to a fixed period of time (Julius proposes "his entire career") and complaining that his diaries "occupy very many feet of shelf space, individual diaries, eight or nine hundred pages per year of single space typescript. If you look through twenty years of diaries for the name Zündel or something like that, it would be a major task."

Julius is having none of this: "Professor Lipstadt is entitled to read all diary entries relating to the issues. It is not for her to have to request specific passages. There is no question of such an entitlement being oppressive. If Mr. Irving was not prepared to give discovery of those parts of his diaries that relate to the pleaded issues, he should not have brought the case. Oppression arises, in this instance, not in the obligation to disclose, but in *not* disclosing the entries." Subject to suitable language restricting the order to relevant material—"We do not seek the irrelevant," says Julius, volunteering to draft the required clause—the Master agrees.

On the question of his contacts with various figures on the far right, Irving puts up stiffer resistance. "You must be aware," he tells the Master, "that if you make such an order this imposes on me an immensely onerous task, which will last many months." He proposes instead limiting the order to a specific list of names, and objects specifically to Ewald Althans, a German skinhead activist, and Arthur Butz, author of *The Hoax of the Twentieth Century*, on the grounds that Lipstadt's book does not connect him with Butz. Julius points out that Butz, like Althans, is mentioned in Lipstadt's pleadings. "That seems sufficient to bring him in, does it not?" asks Trench. "If they are named people, I do not think you can possibly object.

They have barely returned from lunch on the first day when Julius begins a line-by-line presentation of the order he and Libson have prepared. Owing to the evident personal hostility between Irving and Julius, there are still some tense moments. Julius cites a "plan of Colditz Castle" as an example of the kind of irrelevant document Irving has produced. Irving says the plan isn't irrelevant; it "has a gas chamber on it." Julius asks him where this is. "In the caption at the bottom," Irving replies, "it says: 'Delousing shed.' . . . Every prison camp had a delousing shed in it in which the clothing was treated with cyanide gas." Trench asks: "Auschwitz was not a prison camp, was it?" Irving turns to Julius: "Mr. Julius? Auschwitz prison camp?" This is too much for Julius. "Look, I think your views are completely absurd," he replies. When Irving attempts to continue, he interrupts: "You see, Master, this is where we penetrate beyond the fringes of madness."

On the second day, Irving, perhaps seeking revenge, implies that Lipstadt's lawyers can't be trusted. They are discussing the Goebbels diaries, which Irving describes as his "stock in trade." He tells Trench he is "reluctant to part with the content of these diaries . . . with valuable trade secrets which the opponents are now asking under legal pretext to have a look at." It is, he says, as "if somebody wants to know the secret formula to Coca-Cola on some pretext."

Generally, however, both sides manage to maintain civility, Julius keeping his contempt in check and Irving acting as if haggling over the precise terms of discovery really is somewhat beneath him. As it becomes more and more obvious that the hearing is going against him, Irving becomes more and more detached. Julius, drafting on his feet, proposes various forms of wording in response to Trench's questions; Irving makes a few half-hearted sallies, then contents himself with either pedantic observations or the odd attempt at self-mocking humor. Asked the whereabouts of some wartime interrogation transcripts, he replies: "I had them at one time and. . . ."

"And sent them to the *Bundesarchiv*?" offers Master Trench.

"In my kind-hearted neo-Nazi way," says Irving, "I gave all my records to the German government and that is where they are now."

On the afternoon of the first day, when Julius complains about how much irrelevant material they have been saddled with—"Master, I think a jury will begin to tear its hair out if it has to look at this"—the judge asks: "Is there going to be a jury in this action?" Irving says he hasn't decided yet. Later, outside the session, Julius approaches Irving. "Obviously it's got to be a judge only because of the complexity of the case," says Julius. To his amazement, Irving agrees. "Of course. Of course," says Irving.

Julius had always wanted to dispense with a jury. Partly for financial reasons: "The trial would have been three times as long," he said, which would place an even greater financial burden on his client. But the issue of control was never far from Julius's mind. With a jury as his audience, Irving might be tempted to grandstanding, which would also have drawn out the trial. Finally, a judge has to spell out the reasons for his verdict. A "reasoned judgment" that went against him would be much harder for Irving to brush off. "The closest you get to a judgment in a jury trial is the judge's summing up," said Julius, "but that's immediately lost in the jury verdict."

Why did Irving agree so quickly? Given the class background of most high-court judges, perhaps he felt he had a better chance of getting a sympathetic hearing. As Irving frequently remarked, Mr. Justice Lawton, the judge in both *Cassell* v. *Broome* and the *Exodus* trial, had once been a follower of Oswald Mosley. Perhaps he felt that the average Briton—the proverbial man on the Clapham omnibus—was more likely to be anti-German (German domination of Europe being a popular theme on tabloid front pages) than an anti-Semite.

Gratified at having achieved another of his principal strategic objectives—without an argument—Julius was sufficiently surprised by Irving's agreement to write asking him to confirm his position. "It is my belief," Irving replied, "that the issues before the court, particularly in matters of semantics and the German language, are sufficiently complex to require the attention of a learned judge, and too complex to confront a jury with. I further believe that any attempt to prejudice a fair trial of this case by the introduction of emotional or colourful evidence about the Holocaust and other horrors of World War II would be better withstood by a judge than by a jury."

His considerable capacity for self-delusion notwithstanding, David Irving is an intelligent man. He'd now gone two rounds with Anthony Julius, who bloodied his nose in the Board of Deputies suit and outboxed him in discovery. Time for a change in tactics. During the lunch break on the second day of discovery, Irving approached Penguin's lawyers. He would be willing, he told them, to settle the case for £500. Were they interested? Later that evening, Irving sent his terms in writing to Mark Bateman, the young lawyer from Davenport Lyons, Penguin's outside counsel: If Penguin would write him "an open letter withdrawing the allegations made" in *Denying the*

Holocaust, would promise not to republish the book, and would "as a token of apology . . . pay the sum of £500 to the British Limbless ex-Servicemen's Association in the name of my daughter (who lost her legs)," Irving would drop Penguin from his action.

"It is quite apparent to me," he wrote, "that your client does not share the bitter hostility of Ms. Lipstadt and Mr. Julius." Irving proposed keeping the terms of any settlement confidential, adding "I do not intend to settle with Ms. Lipstadt."

Whatever his personal feelings about Irving, Kevin Bays, head of litigation at Davenport Lyons, and Bateman's boss, had to take Irving's offer seriously. The enormous expense of going to trial means that most libel actions settle out of court. The satirical magazine *Private Eye*, a Bays client, often runs tiny boxes apologizing to one or another of its many targets, frequently with the stipulation that "a substantial sum" has been paid to the offended party. Robert Maxwell threatened *Private Eye* many times, usually over stories that were true, but couldn't be proved. Maxwell generally settled, and the one time he insisted on going to trial nearly bankrupted the magazine. For Bays, who had recently concluded a settlement between his client the *Daily Mirror* and singer Michael Jackson concerning articles about Jackson's alleged plastic surgery, settlement was all in a day's work.

Penguin, too, had to take the offer seriously. In May Penguin's lawyers and Mishcon de Reya had concluded a formal agreement about how the case would be paid for. Penguin was already responsible for the cost of their solicitors at Davenport Lyons as well as a junior barrister, Heather Rogers, who would work with Rampton at the trial. Though Rampton would be representing both defendants, the publishers had agreed to cover all of his fees too. Penguin also agreed to pay all fees and expenses associated with the experts, who had grown in number over the past few months as discovery documents began to trickle in. That left only Mishcon de Reya's fees to be paid by Lipstadt.

Letting the book go out of print was not a problem.* And at the rate of £150 an hour that Penguin was paying its many experts, the settlement would improve the company's balance sheet within an hour of acceptance. The problem was the apology. If Penguin did walk away from the suit—and there were sound business reasons to at least consider doing so—that would be a serious blow to Lipstadt's credibility. Which is what Irving hoped for. What he didn't know (since he assumed "international Jewry" bankrolled his opponents) is that it would have also cut off the defense's funding.

Irving's offer came on a Friday. On Monday afternoon, Penguin turned him down. Three weeks later he made a formal "Part 36" offer to settle the case on the same terms, though this time, interestingly, the offer was addressed to both defendants. Once again the offer was refused.

How seriously had Penguin considered settlement? Helena Peacock, the company's legal director, says Penguin never wavered in its resolve. This now seems clear. But at the time Anthony Julius wasn't taking any chances. He and Libson only found out about Irving's offer via Irving's website, and when they phoned Bateman for an explanation he confirmed that Irving had approached him but said he was still awaiting instructions from Penguin. At a meeting after the initial offer had been turned down, Julius told Davenport Lyons that if Penguin had settled on Irving's terms, he would have moved to bind them back into the case—on Irving's side. If St. Martin's had made fools of themselves by first embracing Irving, then disavowing him, the consequences of reversing the process would have been a public relations nightmare for Penguin. Cricket or not, this was hardball.

* When I called Penguin publicity in London in June 1999 and asked for a copy, the woman I spoke with said, "I very much doubt it's still in print." This was not, strictly speaking, true, but there were very few copies left.

A paper Eichmann?

When David Irving looks down from the witness box he does not see a friendly audience. There are a handful of his supporters scattered through the courtroom: a pair of tall, balding men in shapeless sweaters, one of them wearing a swastika ring; the pock-marked, scholarly-looking man in perpetual need of a shave who runs Irving's website; a bullet-headed man in a leather jacket. After the first few days an elegant older blonde woman, whose presence at Irving's table prompts several reporters to mistake her for his wife, can usually be found seated incongruously beside a couple of students in cheap suits and a short, plump man who keeps wiping his forehead with a large silk handkerchief.

But there are also a number of men with *yarmulkes*—the skullcap worn by observant Jews—and some young Asian men, one wearing a turban. There is a stylish young Israeli woman, dressed entirely in black, from the Shoah Foundation, and a very tall, white-haired American who is married to Gitta Sereny. Several elderly men and women have numbers tattooed on their forearms. They are survivors of the concentration camps: Dachau, Buchenwald, Belsen, or Plaszow, where Oskar Schindler's workers lived. One or two may even have been through Auschwitz—a vast complex that included mines and slave-labor factories as well as the extermination camp at Birkenau.

Irving ignores both of these groups. His testimony is directed at the judge, and the tourists in the public gallery, and most of all at the reporters in the press seats. He tells of his struggle to learn who was behind the campaign against him. "It was," he said, "like trying to put a hook in a custard pie." And he refers, yet again, to his expectation that he would "be able to cross-examine Professor Lipstadt when the time comes . . . and, of course, now we will not." But mostly what he does is tell stories.

Irving's stories have several aims. Some are war stories, meant to illustrate links in what Irving calls his "chain of documents, of varying magnitudes of integrity and weight, which indicate that Hitler"—far from being the instigator of the Jews' destruction—"was a negative force in this matter."

Some are designed to portray Irving the intrepid researcher: "I visited the widow of Ernst von Weiszäcker, Ribbentrop's private secretary. . . . She had all her husband's diaries and letters, which she made available to me. I was rather puzzled that she had not made them available to the German historians, and her reply was, 'Mr. Irving, they never asked.'"

Some are designed to distance him from his associates. The problem with Ernst Zündel, Irving tells the judge, is that "you had to realize that he was a man with a certain intellect, a certain sense of humour and execrable private opinions. That is the only way that I can characterize him." To Irving, Zündel's lapses in taste, however regrettable, don't make him an extremist. "In my book," he explains, "an extremist is somebody who plants bombs under motor cars, somebody who plots the overthrow of governments, somebody who goes around with a gun in his pocket. Somebody who holds views which are extreme—this is a very subjective concept. It depends on which viewpoint you view those views from."

Irving tells the judge that in his view the whole fuss over

numbers—whether of the dead at Dresden or the victims of the Nazis—is meaningless. "My Lord, 35,000, 135,000—you may disagree with me, but I see no difference between these figures. Any more than somebody who says it was not six million who died in the Holocaust, it was only one million. Which is the kind of sentence I would never utter because each one of those people being killed is a crime."

This may be special pleading. It was after all Irving who not only drew attention to Dresden but, according to the defense, hyped the figures to do so. Just as it is Irving who makes speeches and publishes literature taking issue with the numbers killed at Auschwitz. But it is special pleading of a very high order. How high becomes clear when Irving turns his attention to the question of what it means to deny the Holocaust.

"The Holocaust," he says "was the tragedy that befell the Jewish people during World War II. I would set it as broadly as that. One could even set it more broadly and say the Holocaust was the whole of World War II and that the people who died and suffered in that Holocaust were not necessarily confined to the Jewish religion, but any number of innocents, whether Gypsies, homosexuals, the people in Coventry, the people in Hiroshima. I think it is otiose to try and define the Holocaust just the way you wish to define it in order to snare somebody, which appears to be what happens in a case like this."

The judge tries, in a non-adversarial way, to get Irving to be more precise. "I understand what you are saying about the Holocaust being a term you could apply to World War II generally," he says, "but if you take it as meaning, for the purposes of this question anyway, a systematic program of exterminating Jews . . . can I just ask you this, do you accept that there was any such program first?"

"No, I do not, " Irving replies.

"The systematic program to exterminate the Jews," he explains, "is the cause, whereas the Holocaust, the word

'Holocaust' as I would see it is the effect, the result, the tragedy that results. When we are looking at the Holocaust we are looking at the victims. We are looking at the mass graves. We are looking at the people being machine gunned into pits. The Holocaust in my submission is not the machinery which produced the result, it is the suffering and not the murderer, shall we say."

Mr. Justice Gray tries again, inviting Irving at least to agree that there was a systematic character to this slaughter. Irving demurs. "I am not caviling, but these are important definitions, my Lord. If the definition—if by using the word 'systematic' you are implying that the system, the Third Reich as such originated these massacres, then I would have to quibble with that."

The judge's questions are designed to identify common ground on the Holocaust, thereby keeping history in its place. But even when they do elicit, for example, Irving's acknowledgment that killing by poison gas was also one of the "effects," this apparent concession soon evaporates.

MR. JUSTICE GRAY: Can I ask a similar question? Do you accept or deny totally that there was any systematic gassing of Jews in gas chambers, whether at Auschwitz or elsewhere? I know we are not dealing with Auschwitz but I think that that ought to be part of—

MR. IRVING: Yes, I think if we can leave out the word "systematic" which is contentious, I do not deny that there was some kind of gassing at gas chambers in Birkenau, it is highly likely that there was.

MR. JUSTICE GRAY: —on a solely experimental basis or—

MR. IRVING: That is the word I have used to give an indication of scale and to give an indication of the authority on which it was conducted, and, well, I leave it at that.

In a sense, Irving's argument—his "suit"—is that he has

every right to "leave it at that." Tall and stocky, Irving squares
his bulk against the wooden witness enclosure like a sailor
heading into the wind, presenting himself as a reasonable man
who has made his fair share of mistakes. "I admit I made a
mistake in the transcription," he says of the Himmler phone
call concerning the Jews from Berlin. The Holocaust, he told
me before the trial, is "not my patch." Why then should he be
expected to adhere to some orthodoxy about an event whose
causes are still the subject of intense historical controversy, and
whose deplorable effects he neither condones nor disputes?
On its face this is a fair question, and if Irving can keep the trial
on this ground he will prevail.

Irving ends his testimony with one last story. "My Lord, I
had the great misfortune in September to lose my eldest
daughter. After we buried her, I received a phone call from the
undertakers that another wreath had come. When the wreath
was delivered late that afternoon, it was a very expensive and
elaborate wreath of white roses and lilies . . . with a card
attached to it saying, 'This was truly a merciful death,' signed
'Philipp Bouhler and friends'." Philipp Bouhler, Irving
explains, was the name of the head of the "Nazi extermination
program for the mentally and physically disabled—the
Euthanasia Program."

If the whole of Irving's evidence can be seen as an attempt to
take and hold the high ground, Rampton's cross-examination is
an attempt to push him off. He rises irritably to his feet. "This
is the most ghastly inconvenient and uncomfortable court I
have ever been in," he complains. The witness is too far away
from his documents, there is a column blocking his view, and
the steamy, overheated courtroom gives Rampton "the feeling
I'm being boiled alive.

"I am sorry to be a little facetious," Rampton says, smiling
and turning toward Irving. "Mr. Irving, that is an elegiac story
that you told us just now. I do not mean that sarcastically at all;

it is perfectly true. It is." Rampton pauses. "You blame that appalling note on the wreath on Deborah Lipstadt's book, is that right?"

Irving counters with a reference to a "climate of hatred." Rampton, undeterred, and with the same wan smile, asks, "If what the book said about you is true, then it would not—perhaps you would agree—be the book's fault but yours, would it not?

"In 1977, when *Hitler's War* was published," asks Rampton, shifting gears, "you accepted the Holocaust in all its essential details in its ordinary sense . . . its generally understood sense?"

Irving asks what he means.

"The systematic mass murder of millions of Jews by the Nazi regime during the Second World War," Rampton replies.

"I do not accept the word 'systematic,' but for the rest of it, then that is an accurate précis," Irving says.

Rampton tries again: "Until 1988 you accepted the Holocaust, however it be precisely defined (and I am not quibbling about minutiae) in its generally understood sense, that is to say, a mass killing of Jews by the Nazis during World War II, did you not?"

"I did not use the word 'Holocaust,'" says Irving, "but I did quite definitely accept that the Nazis engaged in mass killing of Jews during World War II."

Rampton then asks Irving about a speech he made in connection with the 1991 publication of a revised edition of *Hitler's War*: "And did you regard that proposition, that the Germans had factories of death with gas chambers, plural, in which they liquidated millions, plural, of their opponents, at this date in November 1991 as a lie?"

"A big lie, yes."

"A big lie?"

"Yes."

Rampton quotes from Irving's speech: "If you look at my great Adolf Hitler biography here, this bumper Adolf Hitler biography that we have only just published, in fact, it literally arrived off the printing presses today, you will not find the Holocaust mentioned in one line, not even a footnote. Why should we? If something didn't happen, then you don't even dignify it with a footnote."

"Do you accept," Rampton asks, "that the Nazis killed, by one means or another—and I am not talking about hard labor or exposing people to typhus—shot, murdered, gassed, kicked to death millions of Jews during World War II? Or not?"

"Yes," says Irving

Rampton, confused: "You do?"

"Yes, whether it was of the order of millions or not, I would hesitate to specify, but I would say it was certainly more than one million, certainly less than four million. But that is not a very useful answer to you, the limitation I put on that. I do not want you to say, 'You said *millions*, therefore, it is more than two million,' for example."

"Would you accept," Rampton resumes wearily, "that one version of the Holocaust which is generally understood, accepted and perceived—"

Irving interrupts: "Will you avoid using the passive voice so we know precisely who is generally accepting, understanding and perceiving?"

"Call it the public at large," says Rampton, "the audiences to whom you speak."

"Have you stood in Oxford Street with a clip board asking them, the public at large?" Irving asks.

"You will not commit yourself to a generally understood sense of the Holocaust then?" says Rampton.

"I do not know what the generally understood sense of the Holocaust is," Irving replies. "I have given my version of it. You are giving the court your version of it."

Rampton keeps coming. "You deny that the Nazis—do not let us talk about Germans, let us talk about Nazis—that the

Nazis killed millions of Jews in gas chambers in purpose-built establishments?"

"Yes." Rampton finally gets the answer he wants, but his satisfaction is short-lived. "Is the reason really why you deny that," asks Mr. Justice Gray, "because you do not accept there were any such purpose-built factories?"

"Well," says Irving, smiling, "the word 'purpose-built' made my answer much easier, my Lord. You will understand why I say that when we turn to the architectural drawings and we bring in the evidence that I have."

"And Leuchter?" asks the judge.

"Leuchter I think is something that I am not going to rely on at all," Irving replies. At this Rampton begins tugging on his ear and shifting his wig forwards and backwards with his hands. "As I said in my introduction to the Leuchter report," Irving continues, "the Leuchter report is flawed. We now have very much better expertise."

Rampton erupts. "Mr. Irving, you do tempt me very sorely. When Leuchter first swam into your view, you had no expertise about Auschwitz or about gassing or extermination or anything like that, did you?" Rampton reads from Irving's remarks at the conference to launch his publication of the Leuchter report: "After Fred Leuchter did his truly epoch making investigation of the gas chambers at Auschwitz, the forensic laboratory tests . . . yielded the extraordinary result which converted me, made me into a hardcore disbeliever."

Rampton looks at Irving. "It was Mr. Leuchter's report and the bit about the laboratory tests which converted you into disbelief that there were gas chambers at Auschwitz, is that right?"

"That is correct."

"As a consequence of that," Rampton continues, "you have come to believe, perhaps it was a matter of protest, perhaps not, I do not know, that the Nazis did not use gas chambers for the extermination of Jews—let alone millions of Jews?"

"Yes, I have become very skeptical of that element of the story."

"And you have publicly expressed your disbelief?"

"Skepticism, yes."

"So if and in so far as that forms a part of people's belief about the Holocaust, you are a Holocaust denier?"

"No."

"Are you not?"

"No," Irving repeats. "You do not have to believe in the whole to be a believer. How many of us are Christians who do not believe in every aspect of the Christian ethos?"

For the moment, Rampton is beaten. "All right. I do not think we ought to argue metaphysics, Mr. Irving."

In *The Technique of Advocacy*, a handbook for lawyers, the barrister John Munkman sets out four possible aims of cross-examination: (1) to destroy the evidence-in-chief; (2) to weaken the evidence; (3) to elicit new evidence; (4) to undermine the witness. In the movies, aggressive cross-examination can break down witnesses, force confessions, win cases. But in real life, says Munkman, "even the most devastating cross-examination" seldom succeeds on its own.[1] Irving's obduracy made the first three objectives impossible; even undermining his credibility would take time.

Rampton needed help—which, eventually, he would get, thanks to the documents thrown up by discovery. When it was the defense's turn to call witnesses, there would be no shortage of new evidence with which to challenge Irving's version or to demonstrate the selectivity of his vision. Until then, Rampton was reduced to trying to refute Irving using internal evidence—the inconsistencies in Irving's own account of events—and appealing to the court's common sense, to what "everyone knows" about the Holocaust, to counter Irving's claims.

Irving's stubbornness, the complexity of the case, the efforts of the Nazi perpetrators to cover up their crimes, their frequent resort to what Eichmann called *Amtssprache* (bureaucrat-ese) and euphemism—Rampton's "seminar" faced many obstacles to understanding. But none, perhaps, so persistent as the belief that we already know all about it.

In a way, a little metaphysics in the courtroom might have helped. Because despite Irving's claims, the fundamental difficulty in "proving" the Holocaust isn't an absence of evidence. The destruction of European Jewry was, in Raul Hilberg's central insight, essentially a bureaucratic process, the result of "a series of administrative measures." In their pursuit of the *Endlösung*—the Final Solution—the Nazis left all the detritus of any large organization: memoranda, requisition forms, purchase orders, files, and blueprints.

Approximately one million Jews were murdered at Auschwitz, for example, and all of them had to be taken there by train from somewhere else, in the middle of a war in which the railways were the lifelines of the German army. The gas to kill them—Zyklon-B—had to be paid for. The trucks that delivered it had to get travel permits. And the ovens that disposed of the bodies had to be specially built—by Topf and Sons, a German firm that patented the design. Finally, for each *Stück*—"piece," as the Nazis referred to a Jew—processed, certain items had to be accounted for: money, jewelry, personal effects, dental gold, hair.

Hilberg's mapping of this bureaucracy fills three volumes, but the essential facts of the Holocaust are contained in a series of tables at the end. "Deaths by Cause," for example, shows that more than 800,000 Jews died as a result of "ghettoization and general privation," more than 1.3 million were killed by "open-air shootings," and up to 3 million were murdered in camps—as many as 2.7 million of these in specialized extermination camps. By comparison Hilberg says that 150,000 died in other camps, including concentration camps such as Dachau and Buchenwald. In "Deaths by Country," Hilberg's list ranges from the up to three million Jews of Poland to the fewer than

1,000 from Luxembourg, and in "Deaths by Year" he charts the genocide's rise and fall. But in all three tables the total is the same: 5.1 million Jews.

Other historians dispute Hilberg's arithmetic, arguing for a figure closer to six million. Scholars also remain divided on exactly when and why the Nazis shifted from a policy of encouraging Jewish emigration (which saved half of Germany's Jews) to a policy of extermination (which murdered perhaps 90 percent of Greece's Jews). And they argue about the role of the camps in the German economy. They even disagree about Hitler's role in the decision-making process.[2] Irving makes use of these divisions—just as he makes use of ambiguities in the Auschwitz complex, where factories run by Krupp and IG Farben all co-existed with Birkenau, a highly specialized killing center in which nearly a million people were gassed to death. But his argument is something different.

The first glimpse of a chink in Irving's armor comes on the third day. Rampton opens his cross-examination by returning to Himmler's November 1941 telephone log, with its order that a trainload of Jews were "not to be liquidated." The previous day, Irving had admitted he'd made a mistake, transcribing *Judentransport*, a German singular noun meaning "Jew transport," as the plural *Judentransporte*, which he'd translated as "transportation of Jews" in *Hitler's War* (turning an order against killing one trainload of Jews into general prohibition). It was, Irving said, "a silly misreading"; he'd brought in a letter from 1974 to demonstrate how long ago in the past the mistake had occurred. After noting that his previous testimony had been "sworn evidence on oath," Rampton asks Irving to turn to that 1974 letter, where, it turns out, "you have transcribed it correctly."

"Yes."

"The answer you gave yesterday was wrong, was it not?"

"That is correct."

Rampton presses hard on the implication that Irving deliberately mistranslated the phrase to falsely suggest that Hitler opposed the killings, but at this early stage the judge has no reason to deny Irving the benefit of the doubt. Later that morning Rampton takes up another document from Irving's opening statement, the remarks of Major-General Walter Bruns, secretly taped when he was in British captivity. Rampton reads from a transcript of the conversation filed in the Public Record Office in London: "I told that fellow Altemeyer—in fact, Altemeyer, whose name I shall always remember and who will be added to the list of war criminals—'Listen to me! They (that is Jews*) represent valuable manpower.' Altemeyer: 'Do you call Jews valuable human beings, sir?' I (that is Bruns*) said, 'Listen to me properly. I said valuable manpower, I did not mention their value as human beings.' He said (Altemeyer said*), 'Well, they are to be shot in accordance with the Führer's orders!' I said: 'Führer's orders?' He said, 'Yes!' whereupon he showed me his orders.

"Now that"—the mention of "Führer's orders"—"has never appeared in any of your books, has it?" asks Rampton.

"Too true, yes, absolutely right," Irving replies.

"Why not?"

"I discounted it."

"Why do you discount it?"

"Ah, at last," Irving says. "Because other evidence shows that Hitler had not issued the order. Firstly I said that nowhere in all the documentation of all the world's archives has any such order turned up."

"That's not evidence," says Rampton, "that is an absence of evidence."

"It is evidence in a very powerful sense," says Irving.

"It is a negative piece of evidence."

"I hate to remind you of the basic principle of English law that a man is innocent until proven guilty. Am I right?"

"Hitler is not on trial, alas," observes Rampton.

* Rampton's interpolation.

Which prompts Irving to ask: "Is Hitler somehow excluded from this general rule of fair play?"

The question of fair play recurs repeatedly when the trial resumes on the Monday. Gray has managed to get the proceedings moved to Court 73 in the newly refurbished East Block, a more spacious courtroom specially reserved for cases involving a large number of documents. Before resuming cross-examination, Rampton mentions he has not yet received Irving's "bundles"—the selection of documents upon which he and his experts will rely. "We will do so with the utmost reluctance," says Irving, "but if it is the law, then we will do so. But it is rather like playing poker with the other person having a mirror over your head."

"Mr. Irving," says Rampton, "may be under a misapprehension about the way litigation is conducted nowadays in these courts. . . . Of course, litigation is not poker any more. All the cards have to be on the table anyway. It is like playing—what is the other game?—patience."*

The morning's topic is Hitler's responsibility for the massacres of Jews in Poland and the Soviet Union. In his previous day's testimony, Irving had claimed the shootings "appeared to be chaotic, disorganized and arbitrary." Rampton shows Irving another Himmler note, this time from his desk diary, recording a meeting with Hitler on December 18, 1941.

MR. RAMPTON: Himmler has written "*Judenfrage*"?
MR. IRVING: The Jewish question.
MR. RAMPTON: And under "*Führer*" in the right-hand column he has written "*Als Partisanen auszurotten*," has he not?
MR. IRVING: "To be wiped out as partisans."
MR. RAMPTON: . . .This is evidence that Hitler gave authority for the massacre at least—

---

* In America the game is known as solitaire.

MR. IRVING: Of Jews.

MR. RAMPTON:—of Jews in the East?

MR. IRVING: Yes. . . . I do not think there is any dispute between the parties on this.

This clearly comes as a surprise to Rampton, as does Irving's readiness to agree that "at least half a million, and probably as many as one and a half million" Jews were killed by shooting.

At this point the judge intervenes. "Berlin must have known that the shootings were continuing on, as you would accept, a massive scale?" he asks.

"I accept this, my Lord, yes," says Irving.

"To that extent, would you accept it is systematic," asks Gray, "or would you say not?"

"I think to the extent that My Lai was systematic," says Irving, "the Vietnamese war was systematic, and these things happen. They are subsequently covered up by the people in charge."

Rampton, understandably, finds this unsatisfactory. He shows Irving an order from Heinrich Müller, chief of the Gestapo, to the *Einsatzgruppen*—the mobile killing squads—stating that Hitler would be kept constantly informed of their activities. Dated August 1, 1941, the order advises *Einsatzgruppen* commanders to be on the lookout for "visual materials" to supplement these reports. Irving says the document is interesting but that he'd never seen it before.

Rampton next asks Irving about one of these reports, which has survived the war. *Meldung* 51, sent from Himmler on December 29, 1942, lists 16,553 "partisan accomplices and suspects" taken prisoner, of whom 14,257 were executed. Under the category "Jews executed," the report gives the total as 363,211. The document, retyped on the special large-type "Führer typewriter," bears a handwritten notation attesting it has been *vorgelegt* ("laid before") Hitler.

This, too, Irving accepts—perhaps less surprisingly since he quotes these figures himself in *Hitler's War*, though in the 1977 edition he never identifies his source. In his own book, Irving referred to Himmler's "report to Hitler"; here in the courtroom Irving argues Hitler may never have seen it. Or if he saw it, he was too busy to notice it. Besides, says Irving, the document is "an orphan, because it is so totally impossible to fit it into the general framework of all the other documentation which is of equal evidentiary weight."

Again Mr. Justice Gray breaks in: "I must say, that I hesitate to accept. For this reason: it is quite a simple document, and it is referring to the killing by shooting of 300,000 Jews. Well, you have to be quite a man to just pass over that, do you not?"

"My Lord," Irving replies, "as is quite evident from a study of the history of that period, at this moment in time . . . Hitler's primary concern was focused on saving the Sixth Army in Stalingrad.

"Mr. Rampton," Irving continues, "this [Meldung 51] is not a hanging document. I think if this document were to be shown to an English jury in a murder case they would say, well, it is interesting and probably the guy did it, but I will not send him to the gallows just on the basis of this one document." Rampton in turn reminds Irving that "Hitler, as we observed before, is not on trial here," before resuming his enumeration of the evidence for Hitler's responsibility.

Finally Rampton reads out an excerpt from a lecture Irving gave to the Institute for Historical Review in 1992, where he'd said that the gas chambers were "Hollywood legends" but that "there were certain My Lai-type atrocities by troops in Russia." He asks: "The words 'My Lai-type massacres' mean this, do they not, to any educated or half-educated audience? These massacres were done by criminal gangsters . . . in the East without the approval, consent or knowledge of the people in Berlin?"

"That is correct," says Irving.

"That is correct, and it was wrong, was it not?"

"That was wrong, yes."

"And you knew that it was wrong?"

"No, I did not, not at this time."

"Not in 1992?"

"No."

"When did you learn that it was wrong, Mr. Irving?"

"I suppose once I began studying the documents for this case in detail."

On the fifth day of the trial Rampton begins his cross-examination by reading Irving's account, in *Hitler's War*, of a document known as the Korherr Report on the Final Solution to the Jewish Problem in Europe. Richard Korherr was Himmler's statistician, and in March 1943 he informed his boss that "of the 1,449,692 Jews deported from the Eastern provinces, 1,274,166 had been subjected to *Sonderbehandlung* (special treatment) at camps in the General Government."*

Rampton then points out that, when the report was retyped on the "Führer typewriter," Himmler ordered the words "subject to special treatment" changed to "channeled through the camps" to Russia. Why?

Irving suggests Himmler "does not want Hitler being told, he does not want his nose being rubbed in it." Rampton disagrees; he argues Hitler knew perfectly well what was happening. But Irving has already conceded Rampton's main point, namely that while to our ears "special treatment" is a euphemism, to Himmler or Hitler its meaning was obvious to the point of crudity.

Rampton then takes Irving through all the places Jews were sent for "special treatment," quoting again from a passage in *Hitler's War*: "Hitler might still be dreaming of Madagascar, but the head office of the Eastern Railroad at Krakow reported since July 22nd one train load of 5,000 Jews has been running

* The General Government was the name given to those portions of Poland not destined for incorporation into the German Reich.

from Warsaw . . . to Treblinka every day and in addition a train load of 5,000 Jews leaves Przemysl twice a week for Belsec [Belzec]." There is a brief exchange about whether, when Hitler proposed sending Europe's Jews to Madagascar, he meant it seriously, and then Rampton asks what Irving thinks happened to the Jews on those trains.

"The documents do not tell us," Irving replies, "but perhaps it might be useful if we had a look at a map which will show us exactly."

Rampton hands up a German army railway map. He then calls out a series of routes: from Warsaw via Malkinia to Treblinka; from Lublin via Chelm to Sobibór; or Lublin via Zamosc to Belzec. "Those, Mr. Irving, were little villages in the middle of nowhere, and from the 22nd July 1942, if these fig-ures you have given in your book are right . . . hundreds of thousands of Jews were transported from Lublin and Warsaw. . . . What were those Jews going to do in these three villages on the Russian border?"

"The documents before me did not tell me," says Irving.

Rampton invites Irving to "construct in your own mind, as a historian, a convincing explanation." When he declines, Rampton says his next exercise will be to show the scale of the operation, and to demonstrate that "anybody who supposes that those hundreds of thousands of Jews were sent to these tiny little villages, what shall we say, in order to restore their health, is either mad or a liar."

"Mr. Rampton," Irving responds, "can I just draw one paral-lel and say during World War II large numbers of people were sent to Aldershot, which is also a tiny village, but I do not think anybody is alleging there were gas chambers at Aldershot."

"I suggest, Mr. Irving," Rampton responds, "that anybody— any sane, sensible person would deduce from all the evidence—all the available evidence, including, if you like, the shootings in the East which you have accepted—would conclude that these hundreds of thousands of Jews were not being shipped to these tiny little places on the Russian border in Eastern Poland for a benign purpose?"

"Mr. Rampton, what possible other conclusion could somebody have drawn from reading that page in my book? You are implying that the reader is being invited to draw a different conclusion."

"No, I am wondering what your position is, you see, Mr. Irving, because if it is simply this: 'I accept that the Germans systematically murdered Jews in vast numbers throughout 1941, accelerating through 1942, 1943 and reaching a crescendo in 1944, but I simply do not accept there were any gas chambers,' then I am not bothered because it does not matter how it is done, the fact is it is a systematic genocide. I want to know whether you accept that; if you do accept it, then we can forget Professor van Pelt and all his works and everything else beside in relation to Holocaust denial." (Robert Jan van Pelt is an expert witness for the defense, and the author of a 700-page report to the court on Auschwitz.)

Earlier, Rampton chided Irving for comparing the trial to poker. But this offer is surely a bluff. A position that affirmed the systematic murder of millions of Jews but denied that any of them had been killed in gas chambers might make sense rhetorically. Indeed, Irving's fluctuating numbers—"certainly more than one million, certainly less than four million"—at times seemed to flirt with such a position. But as a symbol and a historical fact, Auschwitz is far too important to both sides.

Irving doesn't accept. "It is my belief," he says, "that Professor van Pelt's purpose in coming here is prove to us that the gas chambers at Auschwitz existed."

Irving sends a note to the judge. A magistrate's court in Weinheim, Germany, has issued a request for his extradition based on a 1996 indictment for racial incitement. It seems that in 1990 Irving made a speech in Weinheim arguing that Hitler had not been to blame for the war and that the gas chambers were a hoax. Günter Deckert, a right-wing politician who shared the platform with Irving, has already been imprisoned under Section 130 of the German Criminal Code, which says that "any person who publicly denies the historicity, expresses approval or plays down the importance of the racial murder committed under the National Socialist regime in a manner calculated to disturb the public peace is liable to a prison sentence of up to five years or a fine."

Irving suspects that the warrant's timing is designed to discredit him. He worries that, as the British government has apparently given permission for the request to go forward, he might actually be extradited in the middle of the trial. Mr. Justice Gray assures him this won't happen. But the incident is also a reminder that Irving's "case"—and the whole controversy over the gas chambers—has a history outside Britain and the United States.

In France, like Germany a country with a guilty conscience about the fate of its Jews during the Second World War, those who seek to deny or denigrate their suffering are also subject to criminal penalties. In the late 1970s French intellectuals were convulsed over *l'affaire* Faurisson, which began when Robert Faurisson, a professor of literature at the University of Lyons, published an article in *Le Monde* proclaiming the "good news" that the gas chambers did not exist. "The alleged Hitlerian gas chambers," said Faurisson, "and the so-called genocide of the Jews form a single historical lie whose principal beneficiaries are the State of Israel and international Zionism and whose principal victims are the German people, but not its leaders, and the Palestinian people in its entirety."[3]

Faurisson's only previous claim to fame was as a literary critic, the author of "A-t-on lu Rimbaud?" (Have You Read Rimbaud?), an essay maintaining that the poet's celebrated "Voyelles" was really the disguised erotic reverie of a young schoolboy, and that Rimbaud's play with vowel sounds—the *voyelles* of the title—was actually a coded reference to female anatomy, with "A" standing for the genitalia and "E" signifying a woman's breasts. Published under a pseudonym—at the time Faurisson was teaching at a girls' high school in Vichy—the essay achieved a kind of *succès de scandale*, and was followed by a book, *A-t-on lu Lautréamont?* (Have You Read Lautréamont?) performing a similar operation on the author of *Les Chants de Maldoror*.[4]

As an interpreter of history, Faurisson was far less original, deriving some of his arguments from the English neo-Fascist Richard Verrall's booklet *Did Six Million Really Die?* and the writings of Arthur Butz, and the rest from Paul Rassinier, a French socialist who spent the war as a political prisoner in Buchenwald and Dora and emerged with admiration for his jailers. Faurisson was physically attacked, and his classes at Lyons were suspended after the university authorities pronounced themselves unable to guarantee his safety. He was also prosecuted, once by a private citizen, who accused Faurisson of defaming the dead (an offense under French law), and once under a new law making it a crime to teach a false history of the Second World War.[5]

Though his aims were the rehabilitation of Nazism and its collaborators, Faurisson's public supporters were found mostly on the far left of French politics—which is what gave the affair its *frisson*. When the linguist and political activist Noam Chomsky lent his name to campaigners defending Faurisson's freedom of expression, the controversy became a trans-Atlantic one.

At the time Chomsky was under constant fire for his early and outspoken criticism of America's policy in Vietnam, and for his early and lonely advocacy of the Palestinian cause. So when Chomsky went further, and allowed a statement he'd written defending Faurisson's rights to be used as a preface to Faurisson's pre-trial *Mémoire en défense*, the thunder of hoof-beats from his critics on their high horses was positively deafening. While Chomsky could dismiss most of these attacks as just further evidence of the kind of intellectual bad faith he'd been writing about for years, one of his critics was far more formidable.[6]

Pierre Vidal-Naquet is a classicist, France's greatest living authority on the history and culture of ancient Greece. He is also the author of a number of books denouncing the French government's use of torture during the Algerian war. His credentials as an *engagé* and as a man of the left, in other words, were fully the equal of Chomsky's. He, too, is a long-standing supporter of Palestinian rights. However, perhaps because both his parents had died at Auschwitz, Vidal-Naquet felt it was just as important to expose Faurisson's lies as it was to support his right to lie.[7]

To Vidal-Naquet, Chomsky's actions were "scandalous" because they furthered the charade that Faurisson's claims were "findings"—the "result of a historical investigation, one, that is, in quest of the truth." Chomsky's remark that, "as far as I could judge, Faurisson is a sort of relatively apolitical liberal" sent Vidal-Naquet into a fury.* Yet note his conclusions: "To live with Faurisson? Any other attitude would imply that we were imposing historical truth as legal truth, which is a dangerous attitude available to other fields of application.[8]

"Confronting an actual Eichmann," Vidal-Naquet continues, "one had to resort to armed struggle and, if need be, to ruse. Confronting a paper Eichmann, one should respond with paper. . . . In doing so, we are not placing ourselves in the same ground as our enemy. We do not 'debate' him; we demonstrate the mechanisms of his lies and falsifications, which may be methodologically useful for the younger generations."

The parallels are imperfect. Lipstadt's immense debt to Vidal-Naquet is clear the moment we set the above passage from *Assassins of Memory*, his elegant, restrained, yet devastating

---

* The inspiration, perhaps, for David Irving's incredible description of himself as "a laissez-faire liberal"?

response to Faurisson, beside a similar passage from *Denying the Holocaust*:

> Not ignoring the deniers does not mean engaging them in discussion or debate. In fact, it means *not* doing that. We cannot debate them for two reasons, one strategic and the other tactical. As we have repeatedly seen, the deniers long to be considered the "other" side. Engaging them in discussion makes them exactly that. Second, they are contemptuous of the very tools that shape any honest debate: truth and reason. Debating them would be like trying to nail a glob of jelly to the wall.[9]

"Like trying to nail a glob of jelly. . . ." Though she relies on his arguments, Deborah Lipstadt is no Vidal-Naquet. She lacks his intellectual breadth, his clarity of thought and expression, and, most regrettably, his stature as a Jew who has never confined his political engagement to Jewish causes. And though she, too, opposes "legal restraints," Lipstadt seems to be setting aside the state's power to silence offending views on tactical grounds—"they transform the deniers into martyrs"—rather than as a matter of principle.

If Vidal-Naquet's remark that "In the Diaspora, Israel is frequently judged only in light of the Nazi experience, which is not a particularly lofty perspective for the state" would be inconceivable from Lipstadt, her book nonetheless sounds a warning about a phenomenon that Vidal-Naquet would be the first to agree deserves our attention.[10] Besides, Lipstadt's debt to Vidal-Naquet pales beside David Irving's debt to Faurisson.

Though he offered many times, David Irving told Robert Faurisson not to come to London to testify as a witness. Instead, Irving asked John Keegan and Donald Cameron Watt, two British historians who'd written favorably about his books, to repeat their comments in front of the judge. When they both declined, he subpoenaed them.

During the trial Irving often makes derogatory reference to "establishment historians" who, shunning the hard work of ferreting documents out of aging Nazis and their relicts, prefer to remain sequestered in their "book-lined caves." Like all caricatures this is a partial view, but when Donald Cameron Watt climbs to the witness box we can see what Irving had in mind. Professor of International History at the London School of Economics, where he has been for the past 39 years, Watt served in the British Army Intelligence Corps in Austria from 1947 to 1948, working on the captured archives of the German Foreign Ministry. He was also attached to the Foreign Office Research Department for many years.

In the late 1960s Watt wrote an introduction to one of Irving's books, a collection of documents from the German "research office"—the Nazi counterpart to the codebreakers at Bletchley Park. Irving, who has resumed his place at the counsel's table, asks Watt to describe the book. "I find it—invaluable is perhaps too strong a word," Watt replies, "but a very, very effective piece of historical scholarship, and it is one which does not deal with the issues on which Mr. Irving is complaining."

On those issues, Watt says, "I find your version of Hitler's personality and knowledge of the Holocaust, a knowledge of the mass murder of the Jews, a very difficult one to accept. That, of course, is a view that I have expressed in the reviews I wrote of your *Hitler's War*."

Rampton doesn't bother to cross-examine, leaving Mr. Justice Gray to satisfy his own curiosity. "Can I just ask this, as a military historian, and I underline the word 'military,' how do you rate Mr. Irving?"

"I think Mr. Irving is not in the top class," says Watt "but as a historian of Hitler's war seems to—"

"That is what I meant."

"I think his is a view which, even if one disagrees with it, has to be taken seriously. He is, after all, the only man of standing, on the basis of his other research, who puts the case for Hitler forward and it seems to me that it is mistaken to dismiss it. . . . I must say, I hope that I am never subjected to the kind of examination that Mr. Irving's books have been subjected to by the defense witnesses. I have a very strong feeling that there are other senior historical figures, including some to whom I owed a great deal of my own career, whose work would not stand up, or not all of whose work would stand up, to this kind of examination."

As if in penance for his earlier disavowal, Watt adds: "The challenge of putting forward the sort of views you [Irving] did and basing them on historical research, rather than ideological conviction, or at least seemingly so, has directly resulted in an enormous outburst of research into the—"

"Holocaust?" suggests Irving.

"—into the massacres of the Jews, into the Holocaust and so on, which is now so large an area of historical research that it can support journals, it can support conferences. I see that there are three scheduled in Britain this coming year and that I myself am appearing in one in America in March. This, I think, is a direct result of the challenge [of] Mr. Irving's work."

Irving's next witness is less helpful. On Day 11, Irving tells the court he reckons he'll need three days to question Kevin MacDonald, an American academic who is flying from California to testify on his behalf. But when MacDonald appears in court the following Monday, his testimony is over by lunchtime.

Tall and thin, wearing a grey pinstriped suit—in an American rather than English cut—and black wire-rimmed glasses, MacDonald is Professor of Psychology at California State University at Long Beach. MacDonald is an evolutionary psychologist, a field which grew out of sociobiologist E.O. Wilson's view that there is a genetic explanation for human behavior.

Wilson's theories are based on his research on ants. Evolutionary biologists like Randy Thornhill and Craig T. Palmer, authors of *A Natural History of Rape: Biological Bases of Sexual Coercion*, start by studying humans. Kevin MacDonald studies Jews.

In his book *A People that Shall Dwell Alone: Judaism as a Group Evolutionary Strategy*, MacDonald tells the court, "I'm just basically describing Judaism from the standpoint of my evolutionary biology, including the ideology of Judaism, the segregation of the Jewish gene pool from surrounding peoples, resource competition between groups, and so on, co-operation within the group and so on."

The second volume of MacDonald's Judaism trilogy, *Separation and Its Discontents: Toward an Evolutionary Theory of Anti-Semitism*, forms the basis for MacDonald's expert report, in which he writes: "While anti-Semitic attitudes and behavior have undoubtedly often been colored by myths and fantasies about Jews, there is a great deal of anti-Jewish writing that reflects the reality of between-group competition." MacDonald's view that Jews bring hatred on themselves is spelled out further in *The Culture of Critique: An Evolutionary Analysis of Jewish Involvement in Twentieth-Century Intellectual and Political Movements*. Here MacDonald concludes his trilogy by arguing that psychoanalysis, the Frankfurt School of German social criticism, and "New York intellectuals" are all part of a plot "to alter Western societies" for the benefit of the Jews.

Irving's apparent belief that MacDonald's grotesque parody of the social sciences can help his case is a gift to Rampton, who again doesn't bother to cross-examine. Even Irving's use of MacDonald to introduce into evidence his weighty "Bundle E"—the dossier of what has apparently been a long-term endeavor by Jewish organizations to discredit Irving's views, and which includes Lipstadt's correspondence with Yehuda Bauer—is of dubious benefit, since Irving's understandable irritation with this campaign is now associated with MacDonald's loony conspiracy theories.

MacDonald's testimony ends on an almost comic note, with Irving asking, "Do you consider me to be an anti-Semite from your knowledge of me?"

The absurdity of posing this question to this witness is lost on MacDonald,* who solemnly replies: "I do not consider you to be an anti-Semite. I have had quite a few discussions with you now and you have almost never even mentioned Jews and, when you have, never in a general negative way."

Irving's third witness is Peter Millar, whose apple-cheeks, affable manner, and curly blond hair give him a cherubic demeanor only slightly at odds with the lined face and red nose more typical of his profession. Millar is a reporter, and like MacDonald has appeared in court voluntarily. But there the similarity ends.

When the *Sunday Times* commissioned Irving to go to Moscow to bring back the Goebbels diaries, the paper sent Millar along to babysit. In her article "Spin Time for Hitler" Gitta Sereny charged that Irving, learning about the diaries' existence from Elke Fröhlich, a friend at the Institute for Historical Research in Munich, promptly "talked his way into the Moscow archives." Sereny said that Irving borrowed "a dozen" of the glass plates containing microfilmed diary pages, then "smuggled the plates out of the country." Finally, "knowing Dr. Fröhlich to be on holiday," Irving, Sereny wrote, had copies of the plates made at her Munich institute, then claimed credit for the whole discovery.[11]

The question of whether Irving took advantage of his relationship with Fröhlich, who once worked for him as a

* And on the British Press Association, whose report on MacDonald's testimony went out under the headline "Irving Not Anti-Semitic Judaism Expert Tells Court"!

researcher,* is central to Irving's suit against Gitta Sereny. But in Lipstadt's book the whole episode is literally reduced to a footnote. Lipstadt accused Irving of violating his agreement with the Russian archives when he "took many plates, transported them abroad, and had them copied without archival permission." There was, she wrote, "serious concern in archival circles that he may have significantly damaged the plates."[12] Fröhlich is never mentioned.

In court the defense claims merely that Irving risked damaging the plates, whose numbers are reduced from "many" to a few. In his diary Irving describes his behavior in Moscow as "illicit." Irving does not deny smuggling a set of glass plates out of the archive during a lunch break, wrapping them in cardboard and leaving them on some waste ground near the archive, to be retrieved that evening so that they could be shown to Andrew Neill, the *Sunday Times* editor who was in Moscow at the time. Nor does he deny, once these plates had been returned, removing two more and taking them first to Munich, where he had copies made, and then on to London so they could be subject to forensic tests—again without asking the Russians for permission.

A freelancer fluent in Russian and German, Millar confirms all this, and under cross-examination by Rampton makes clear his disapproval of Irving's conduct both at the time and afterwards. Irving himself says he is "deeply ashamed to have done that. You do not normally go into archives and remove materials, even though of course you are going to put them back the next day." This is exactly what Irving had done with Lord Cherwell's papers at Oxford thirty years earlier, and that hadn't turned out too badly.

Millar backs up Irving's contention that he made no written agreement with the Russians, whom he depicted as operating

* She later married the Institute's director, Martin Broszat, whose 1977 article attacking *Hitler's War* first raised questions about Irving's use of sources and documents.

on a cash-and-carry basis. He also says he knows of no reason to doubt Irving's claim that he first heard about the Moscow diaries from a friend at the Institute for Historical Research in Munich.

Millar adds that on his visits to Irving's flat he never saw the portrait of Adolf Hitler which Lipstadt said hung over Irving's desk.* "There was," he adds, "a water colour which I was extremely interested in, and [Irving] said that it had been painted by Adolf Hitler and I said it was rather better than my mother-in-law's."

"Your mother-in-law has got a picture by Hitler as well?" asks the judge incredulously.

"My mother-in-law does water colours, sir," Millar replies.

When Millar is dismissed there are still forty minutes before lunch. In the time remaining Rampton badgers Irving about the risk that the plates might have been damaged en route to London, asking too whether the Munich hotel safe they'd been left in was fireproof, but his heart isn't in it. He cheers up after noticing that Irving's account of the trip in his diary mentions a meeting with Ewald Althans, who has arranged for Irving to speak at a meeting also featuring Ernst Zündel. Who is Althans? Rampton asks.

"A young German hothead," says Irving. Asked to be more specific, he adds, "I think he was a revisionist. I think that is a fair word to pin on him."

"Certainly I would accept that he was a revisionist," says Rampton. But is Althans on the right? "By 'on the right' I mean somebody who would not approve of colored immigration into Germany or anywhere else in Europe."

"I do not think he would actively advocate it," Irving replies.

By that standard Irving's last witness might also be considered

---

* Though Lipstadt's description, which Irving protested bitterly at the trial, is clearly taken from *Selling Hitler* by Robert Harris (London, Arrow Books, 1996, p. 189), Irving has never sued Harris.

on the right. John Keegan is long-time defense editor of the *Daily Telegraph*, the broadsheet voice of respectable Conservative opinion in Britain, and the author of *The Face of Battle* and many other books on modern warfare. A few weeks earlier Keegan's name appeared on the Queen's New Year's Honours list: he was given a knighthood "for services to military history." This gives Irving the chance to address him as "Sir John." Writing in the *Times Literary Supplement* in 1980, Keegan had declared, "Two books in English stand out from the vast literature of the Second World War: Chester Wilmot's *Struggle for Europe*, published in 1952, and David Irving's *Hitler's War*."

As Keegan, who is disabled and walks with difficulty, sits in the witness box, Irving says he wants "first of all, to make it perfectly plain to the court, you are here pursuant to a witness summons, in other words, what used to be called a subpoena."

"I was subpoenaed by you," Keegan confirms. "I would also like to say that until this moment I have never met you, never spoken to you and never corresponded with you."

Irving asks Keegan if he has had cause to revise his high opinion of his work. "I often say you have to read *Hitler's War*," he says. But Keegan also reminds Irving of a sentence from his book *The Battle for History* that Irving hasn't read out in court: "Some controversies are entirely bogus, like David Irving's contention that Hitler's subordinates kept from him the fact of the Final Solution."

"That is, of course, still your opinion, is it not?" asks Irving. "That I am wrong on the Holocaust, or that my opinion on that is flawed?"

"That Hitler did not know," says Mr. Justice Gray.

"Well, I read *Hitler's War*, the appropriate passages, very carefully over the weekend," says Keegan, "and I continue to think it perverse of you to propose that Hitler could not have known until as late as October 1943 what was going on to the Jewish population of Europe, and indeed many other minority groups as well, not only minority groups."

In fact Keegan's asperity does Irving no harm. Though they differ on the question of Hitler's knowledge, they both share a view of history as basically "maps and chaps." To read Keegan's account in *The Second World War* is to enter a world of staff officers and battlefields in which the "ordinary men" whose complicity in genocide so exercises Daniel Goldhagen and Christopher Browning barely merit consideration. Indeed, in a 500-page book which takes pains to convey why, to the Germans who overran Poland, "*Blitzkrieg* seemed a magic which had taken over the army itself," and which allots an entire chapter to the invasion of Crete, and the better part of another chapter to Italian campaigns in Libya and Ethiopia, the Holocaust merits precisely two paragraphs.[13] In one of them, Keegan describes the killers as "German SS and securitymen and locally enlisted militias." That many thousands of Jews were killed by ordinary German soldiers is a point of agreement between Browning and Goldhagen,[14] yet the effect is almost as if Keegan is trying to preserve the honor of the *Wehrmacht*—as if the murder of the Jews had nothing to do with the war or the course of the fighting.

Military history may be a stunted discipline, the province of retired generals and armchair generals who actually take pride in their ignorance.* Asked by Irving to respond to a comment by Eberhard Jaeckel, Keegan says, "I never heard of him, but then I am a military historian of a rather technical sort and it is not necessary that I should have heard of him." It is Jaeckel, as much as anyone, who is responsible for bringing together the Holocaust and the battlefield. Still, attacking Keegan's public

---

* Michael Geyer, Professor of Contemporary European History at the University of Chicago, and a scholar whose own work integrates military and social history, suggested to me that this pugnaciously parochial worldview accounts for Irving's high reputation among military historians.

schoolboy's notion of history isn't going to score the defense any points with Wykehamist* Charles Gray.

Keegan, who has apparently never heard of Raul Hilberg either, does praise Gerald Reitlinger's *The Final Solution* (1953) "which I read as an undergraduate" and is "the source of everything substantial that I know about the Holocaust."† In his bibliography to *The Second World War* Keegan also praises Reitlinger—with these caveats: "though the historiography of the Holocaust has since been greatly elaborated, and while his book is largely concerned with the Jews, rather than the many other groups systematically massacred by the Nazi extermination apparatus."[15] The language here echoes the "many other minority groups" whose fate was equated with that of the Jews in Keegan's testimony. Apart from the Gypsies, who were indeed systematically slaughtered in much the same fashion as the Jews (and who don't merit even a single mention in his book), it is hard to know which "other groups" Keegan has in mind.

The appeal to Keegan of Reitlinger's long-outdated survey, however, is far easier to understand. *The Final Solution* offers what might be called a public schoolboy's view of the Holocaust. Reitlinger, the son of a prominent Jewish banker and himself educated at Westminster School and Christ Church, Oxford, describes the destruction of the Jews as an "attempt" which had not succeeded. But then how could it

---

* A alumnus of Winchester College, i.e. a former public schoolboy himself.

† Keegan's lack of familiarity with contemporary scholarship about the Holocaust hasn't kept him from making public pronouncements on the topic. In November 1996 he wrote an article for the *New York Times* intervening in the controversy over whether Britain could have done more to assist in the prosecution of war criminals, claiming that Soviet hostility prevented the handover of intelligence derived from German police decodes. But as Richard Breitman points out in *Official Secrets*, the Order Police decodes were not based on ENIGMA decrypts, and had in any case already been disclosed to the Russians during the war. (Breitman, pp. 241–244)

have when the perpetrators were, in Reitlinger's words, "puerile" and "ridiculous." He stressed Belsen, the only major camp liberated by British troops, in his narrative. Famous for his country-house parties in Kent and Sussex, which earned him the nickname "The Squire," Reitlinger's patriotism even led him to deny that Britain's Foreign Office had obstructed efforts to rescue Jews.[16]

On its own, Keegan's reluctant tribute to Irving's skills as a researcher posed no problem for Rampton, either. But even if it couldn't be attacked directly, the view of history he represented—and recognized in Reitlinger—would have to be overcome. It had been Reitlinger, after all, who, declaring his preference for research based on wartime German documents, warned that skepticism was "particularly necessary when approaching survivor accounts."[17] Yet, as the court was about to learn, without survivor accounts, the history of Auschwitz would still be a puzzle.

Mr. Death

Auschwitz wasn't built in a day. In their book *Auschwitz: 1270 to the Present* Debórah Dwork and Robert Jan van Pelt identify ten different stages in the camp's existence starting in 1940, when Auschwitz functioned as both a concentration camp to aid in subduing the area's Polish population and as the site of the German Earth and Stone Works, an SS-owned enterprise which turned sand and gravel from the Sola river into building materials for the Reich. The camp was also home to an experimental farm, intended to serve as the center of a vast agricultural empire providing food and employment for the ethnic German migrants Himmler planned to settle in the Lebensraum made available by the ethnic cleansing of the local population.

Another aspect of this same project—Himmler's development of the German east into a racial utopia—was the construction of the IG Farben "Buna" synthetic-rubber plant at Auschwitz–Monowitz. To lure Farben to his site, Himmler promised the company a slave-labor pool of 100,000 Soviet prisoners of war—a byproduct of the expected conquest of the Soviet Union—to build and work in the plant. These prisoners would also be used to construct an enormous company town, which could in turn house the other enterprises Himmler planned to bring to the area. In return, Farben agreed to finance and provide building materials for Himmler's Germanization project inside the SS's surrounding 15-mile-square "Zone of Interest."

By early 1942, when it was becoming clear that Soviet prisoners would not be in such plentiful supply, Himmler decided Jews would take their place. Although the mass murder of Jews by the *Einsatzgruppen* was well underway, Himmler was still committed to his racial utopia. His plans required laborers, and when, in January 1942, Hermann Goering directed that Soviet POWs be sent to work in German armament factories, Himmler used the powers given to Heydrich and himself by the recent conference on a "Final Solution to the Jewish Question," held in the lakeside resort of Wannsee, to order the transport of Jews to Auschwitz.[1]

As the crown jewel in Himmler's empire, Auschwitz was intended as a showpiece. And up to this point, say Dwork and van Pelt, "construction" predominated over "destruction." There had been executions at Auschwitz from the beginning, both of concentration-camp inmates and of other Poles condemned by the Gestapo Summary Court in Katowice. But the numbers were comparatively small: 3,000 from the court, fewer from the camp. The camp's high security and relative isolation, and the presence of crematoria for disposing of the bodies, made Auschwitz a convenient site for executions, and soon condemned Soviet POWs starting arriving as well.

Birkenau, an area several miles from the main camp, was originally intended to house Soviet POWs or, in their absence, healthy young slave laborers. But when the government of Jozef Tiso, the Catholic priest installed as dictator of Slovakia, arranged to furnish Slovak Jews to work at Auschwitz in the place of Slovaks who had been promised for labor in Germany, the Slovaks realized they would then be left with those Jews deemed unfit for work by the SS. The Slovaks complained to Adolf Eichmann, and eventually the SS agreed to take the other Jews off their hands for a fee of 500 *Reichsmark* per *Stück* (which the Slovaks more than made back by expropriating the property the deportees left behind). Anticipating their arrival, Himmler ordered a peasant cottage at Birkenau transformed into a gas chamber. And on July 4, 1942, the first transports of Slovak Jews were subject to selection on arrival, with those deemed fit for work admitted to the camp and the rest gassed.

Yet even then, say Dwork and van Pelt, "systematic extermination of Jews was still [merely] an auxiliary function of the camp," which throughout this period continued to serve as a pool of forced labor for various German factories located nearby, as well as a transit camp for those few Jews, mostly skilled laborers, selected for work in the Reich. Their history of the site traces a crooked path with many turnings before it arrives at Auschwitz as a synonym for mass death. (In doing so they offer the strongest possible rebuttal to Goldhagen's bizarre and unsupported assertion that "the road to Auschwitz was not twisted."[2])

In presenting his case, Rampton will have to re-trace that crooked path with the aid of van Pelt's report, while Irving, who offered no witness of his own on Auschwitz, attempts to detour the discussion. But before that process can begin, Rampton needs to establish certain premises.

The three balls Rampton must keep in the air are system, scale, and method. Its evolution may have been haphazard, but Auschwitz as an extermination camp emerged from an approach to the "Jewish Question" that was, whatever its origins, bureaucratic in its organization. Some of Rampton's stress on Hitler's knowledge, for example, may seem directed at Irving's contention that Hitler remained ignorant, and hence innocent, of the murder of the Jews. But no one claims the gas chambers were Hitler's idea.*

* Though Lucy Dawidowicz comes close. In *Mein Kampf*, Hitler wrote that if "twelve or fifteen thousand of these Hebrew corrupters of the people had been held under poison gas" during the First World War, "the sacrifice of

Scale is connected to system, indeed implies system, since not even David Irving believes that a bunch of disorganized thugs in uniform could manage to kill between five and six million people. Scale also implies method, and it is down this road that Rampton sets off for Auschwitz. He begins by tracing the consequences of Hitler's decision, in the fall of 1941, that the *Altreich* or Old Reich territory of pre-1939 Germany, and the annexed Czech territories, "be cleansed and rid of Jews."

Rampton reads out a letter from Himmler to Arthur Greiser, *Gauleiter* (governor) of the *Warthegau* (those portions of Poland which were to be incorporated into Germany), conveying the Führer's wish. Initially, the deported Jews would be housed in the ghetto at Lodz, which was in Greiser's territory. Irving, who quotes from the letter in *Hitler's War*, agrees: "Yes, Hitler has taken the initiative and has ordered the emptying out."

Rampton then produces a letter of May 1942 from Greiser to Himmler, informing him that "special treatment . . . of about 100,000 Jews in my district . . . could be completed within the next two to three months"; followed by a June 1942 message from the Gestapo in Lodz reporting "we have now generated enough space for about 55,000 Jews in the ghetto."

"That must mean that about 55,000 Jews more or less have been moved out somewhere?" asks Rampton.

---

millions at the front would not have been in vain." Dawidowicz wonders: "Did the idea of the Final Solution originate in this passage, germinating in Hitler's subconscious for some fifteen years before it was to sprout into practical reality?" Yet even she recognizes that "the idea of a mass annihilation of the Jews" had been around for some time. And of course you don't need gas chambers to kill 15,000 people. (*The War Against the Jews*, p. 27.) Goldhagen goes further, claiming that Auschwitz was "conceived by Hitler's apocalyptically bent mind as an urgent, though future, project, [but] its completion had to wait until conditions were right. The instant that they were, Hitler commissioned his architects, Himmler and Heydrich, to work from his vague blueprint in designing and engineering the road." (*Hitler's Willing Executioners: Ordinary Germans and the Holocaust*, London: Little, Brown, 1996, p. 425.) Even so, one has to assume he's speaking metaphorically.

"Yes," says Irving, "assuming that the ghetto had not been expanded at that time."

Rampton directs Irving to a heading in the same document: *Ausgesiedelt* ("out-settled" or taken away). "The first of the two columns in the middle says '*nach Kulmhof*,' does it not?"

"To Chelmno, yes."

"If you total up the figures in that column, they come, I can tell you, to 54,990."

"Yes."

"So that is where, using a reasonable degree of intelligence and interpretive wisdom, Mr. Irving, those 55,000 Jews in this Gestapo report have gone, is it not?"

"I will accept that as an interpretation, yes."

At which point Rampton asks: "Do you know anything about what was at Chelmno?"

"There were these gas trucks," Irving replies, "that were disposing of people at some time during the war, but whether they were operating in these five months, I do not know. I notice that Chelmno is on the border to the East, and an equally plausible interpretation would be that they had been sent there as the first stepping stage to go somewhere East. I am not saying this is what happened."

"Chelmno?" asks Rampton.

"Yes."

"No, no!" Rampton insists. "Chelmno—you are quite mistaken. Chelmno is in the *Warthegau*. It is about 40 kilometres west-north-west of [Lodz]."

Irving seems baffled, but Mr. Justice Gray, for whom this exercise is intended, immediately sees what Rampton is driving at. "The odd thing," says Gray, "is that they [the Lodz Jews] are going *West* rather than *East*."

"That point obviously does stand out," Irving says.

And then, with the air of a man not quite ready to lay down his last card, Rampton changes the subject. His manner changes as well, any notion of patience forgotten as Rampton badgers Irving to accept that, his many speeches on the subject notwithstanding, Belzec, Sobibór, and Treblinka—those "little villages in the middle of nowhere"—were indeed *Todesfabriken*, factories of death.

"Do you accept or do you not accept—because if you do we can go on to something else, Mr. Irving—that hundreds upon thousands of Jews were from, let us say, the spring of 1942 and in Chelmno earlier . . . deliberately killed in Sobibór, Treblinka and Belzec?"

"I think, on the balance of probabilities, the answer is yes," says Irving. "But I have to say 'on the balance of probabilities' because the evidentiary basis for that statement is extremely weak, even now, 55 years later. The Russians captured the camps, they captured the documentation of many of these camps, and we are still short of the actual smoking gun, shall I say."

Given Irving's many public statements casting doubt on the possibility that more than a handful of Jews were killed in gas chambers, this looks like a significant concession, wrung from Irving by his need to appear reasonable in front of the judge. But Irving also has his public to worry about—the young neo-Nazis who look to him for leadership and the elderly right-wingers in Britain and the United States who donate to his "Fighting Fund." So when Rampton rephrases it, referring to the three extermination camps as part of Operation Reinhard, Irving balks.

"No, I do not accept that," says Irving. "I say that Operation Reinhard was frequently . . . only a sub-operation. It was the looting part, the looting element, and the recycling element, which is where the name originally came from." Once again Irving has put his finger on a real, if inconsequential, disagreement among historians, some of whom say that *Aktion Reinhard* was named in memory of Reinhard Heydrich, assassinated by Czech patriots in May 1942, while others disagree. But Irving's pedantry about the name has a purpose, allowing him to step back from his apparent concession on what happened at those camps without formally resiling—a legal term for retracting.

In the ensuing confusion, Irving reiterates his position that the use of gas chambers to kill people was a British fabrication, not a German fact. "British propaganda," he says, "invented the story of the gas chambers or invented stories of gas chambers which were broadcast into Nazi Germany during the war years. There is any amount of evidence of this in the BBC monitoring reports, in the German radio monitoring reports, in the memoirs of people like Thomas Mann, the famous German novelist, who worked for British propaganda agencies, in their private diaries and so on."

Irving offers no evidence to support this assertion. (Later in the trial, "any amount" turns out to be a scant two pages of extracts from talks by Thomas Mann, with no indication on whose behalf the broadcasts were made. At the time, however, the effect of Irving's remarks is to distance him still further from his apparent concession.)

With Irving's semi-retraction perhaps in mind, the following day Rampton again takes up the fate of the Jews at Chelmno. He first asks Irving to identify Viktor Brack.

"Viktor Brack, I believe, was Number Two in the Führer Chancellery under Philipp Bouhler." As Irving has already told the court, Bouhler was in charge of the Nazi Euthanasia Program, known as T-4 from its address at Tiergartenstrasse No. 4, in Berlin.

Rampton continues: "One of the means used—I do not know whether it was the most frequently used—was carbon monoxide gas from bottles, was it not?"

"I believe that is correct, yes," Irving replies.

Rampton then shows Irving a letter from Eberhard Wetzel, Jewish Affairs expert at the Ministry for the Occupied Eastern Territories, conveying Brack's willingness "to aid in the construction of gassing apparatus" for use on Jews. "We have no misgivings," the letter adds, "if those Jews who are not capable of working are disposed of using Brack's methods."

Rampton next asks Irving to reflect on his remarks at the Leuchter report press conference, when he'd said: "I am prepared to accept that local Nazis tried bizarre methods of liquidating Jews. I am quite prepared to accept that, and that they may have experimented using gas trucks, because I have seen one or two documents in the archives implying that there was a roll over from the use of those methods of killing, the same people who created the euthanasia program."

"I think that is a very fair summary of the state of my knowledge at that time," says Irving. "Killing people in gas wagons is an extremely inefficient way of doing it."

At last, and with mounting irritation, Rampton returns to Chelmno, where, according to a report from the motor pool section of the RSHA (Main Office for Reich Security), they were having a minor problem with some trucks. The report proposed installing "a strongly protected light that would operate during the first minutes, so the 'cargo' would not make a bolting of the door difficult by pressing against the back door in panic when plunged into darkness." Even so, "since December 1941, for example, 97,000 were processed by three trucks in action, without any defects in the vehicles being encountered."

"Shall we go straight to the bottom line," Irving answers, "and say, yes, I fully accept the innuendo you are placing on that document."

"Innuendo?" Rampton demands.

"It is not stated clearly," says Irving, "but quite clearly 97,000 people have been liquidated in these trucks."

"In three trucks," Rampton practically shouts.

"Over the months concerned."

"No," Rampton corrects him, "it is actually just about a month and a week. Ninety-seven thousand people in three trucks in the course of five weeks?"

"It is a very substantial achievement," says Irving, "when you work it out with a pocket calculator."

At this, Mr. Justice Gray intervenes. "Is it very limited and experimental?"

"My Lord," says Irving, "I did not have this document at the time I said that. I had this document five or six months ago."

"Answer the question even so," Gray insists. "Would you describe it as very limited and experimental?"

"Not on this scale. This is systematic."

This time, Rampton leaves no room for ambiguity. "It is systematic, huge scale, using gas trucks to murder Jews?"

"Yes. No question at all."

Moving much more quickly through the documents, Rampton takes up an April 1942 letter from the head of the military administration in Serbia: "Already some months ago I had everything that could be got hold of in the way of Jews in this land shot, and had all the Jewish women and children concentrated in a camp and at the same time, with the help of the SD,* procured a 'delousing vehicle' that will now finally have carried out the clearing of the camp in some 14 days to 4 weeks."

Rampton looks up. "Well now," he says, "that is obviously code."

"Yes," says Irving.

"For some idiotic reason, he has put it in inverted commas, which rather gives the game away, does it not?"

"It does, yes."

"That is code for gassing truck, is it not?"

"Yes."

"Which camp is being referred to?" asks the judge.

"Semlin, outside Belgrade," Rampton answers.

"This is quite clearly a very sinister document," says Irving.

"Do you now accept therefore," asks Rampton, finally laying

---

* *Sicherheitsdienst* (Nazi Party Security Service).

down his last card, "that statements that you have made to the
effect that 'Oh, yes, they used gas trucks on a very limited
scale for experiments' were just plain wrong?"

"Yes." Irving has now conceded both system and scale.
Method will be harder. The gas trucks have given Rampton an
opening, but to fully make his point he'll need to get to
Auschwitz.

At the very end of the day, Rampton explains the defense
case on Auschwitz: "I am not here to prove that Auschwitz had
gas chambers, homicidal gas chambers. I do not need to do
that. If you . . . have an open mind and you look at the conver-
gence of evidence—eyewitness testimony from victims,
perpetrators, and the contemporaneous documentary evidence
and the archeological remains—you are going to conclude, as
a matter of probability at the very least, that indeed what
the eyewitnesses tell us is true. I am not here to persuade
your Lordship of that, save as a preliminary first step to
two things.

"Mr. Irving, on the back of a piece of so-called research
which is not worth the paper it is written on, jumped up and
said he was perfectly certain that there were never any gas
chambers at Auschwitz. And he has made that statement
repeatedly in circumstances where it is apt to excite the hostility towards Jews of people who are likely to be
anti-Semitic—which is the political side of this case which we
will get to later on. As an insight into Mr. Irving's credentials as
a so-called historian, it is extremely illuminating, and that is the
whole of my argument."

It is about 300 miles from Semlin to Auschwitz, 130 miles
from Chelmno to Auschwitz, but Rampton is on his way.

"Let me ask you this question," the judge says to Irving the
next morning. "If I were to come to the conclusion that there is
a whole range of formidable evidence of one kind and
another—camp officials, eyewitnesses, scientific evidence,

evidence of construction at the gas chambers and the like—all of which was there, but you paid no attention to it. Is that something you would accept? Is that the way you put your case? That you went for broke on the Leuchter report."

"It depends upon the degree of intensity which would have been appropriate," says Irving. "If I was intending to go on, for example, a BBC talk show, and I was likely to be asked about Auschwitz, should I therefore spend $5 million on sending researchers into archives around the world?"

Gray is still trying to keep history out of the court. "If your case is that Mr. Irving deliberately shut his eyes to that corpus of evidence," he says to Rampton, "and his case is, 'Well, I was not an Holocaust historian. Maybe I knew that some of that evidence was there, but I did not think it was any part of my function to go and trawl through it,' then—"

"Then he should have—" Rampton breaks in.

"Then we do not need to trawl through it in this trial, do we?" Gray asks hopefully.

"My Lord, [only] if he will accept that his denial is false," says Rampton.

"I am not sure," says Gray with a certain amount of petulance, "whether I see why you are now saying, rather contrary to what you have been saying before, that we have to make a finding of fact as to what happened in Auschwitz."

Rampton hastens to reassure him: "No, absolutely, I have never said that. I am not saying that." But he did. And he is.

So far as we know, Auschwitz was the only camp to use Zyklon-B to kill large numbers of people. Although it wasn't only a death camp, more people were killed at Auschwitz than at Majdanek* or Belzec or Sobibór or Treblinka or any other camp. Perhaps most importantly, Auschwitz–Birkenau is the only death camp with more than a tiny handful of survivors.

---

* Though there were gas chambers at Majdanek, captured more or less intact by the Russians, most of the camp's victims were killed by shooting, not gas.

Their accounts of what they saw and heard—confirmed by the confessions of perpetrators like camp commandant Rudolf Höss or Pery Broad, who worked in the camp's Political Department—are indeed at the core of our understanding of the Holocaust. So the question of whether those accounts are credible—not free of error, but credible—is an issue that is both at the center of this trial and, however uncomfortable it makes the judge, cannot be decided without reference to what actually happened.

Rampton knows this. In fact he put it as well as anyone a couple of days earlier. "Auschwitz," said Rampton, "in Mr. Irving's utterances and certainly in our eyes is at the center of Holocaust belief. It is therefore at the center of Holocaust denial." Pretending otherwise—pretending that this trial is only about historiography—is the defense's version of special pleading.

Irving, too, is well aware of what is at stake. On the one hand, he protests even more vociferously than Rampton that the court should restrict itself to the material actually consulted or cited by him in his books, and the question of whether or not he deliberately misrepresented that material. Indeed Irving goes so far as to ask the judge to rule that "any evidence regarding Auschwitz, with which he was unfamiliar" and may have studied only to prepare for the trial, be excluded both from his cross-examination and from being presented by the defense.

But when Rampton confronts Irving with the transcript of one of his speeches, in which he's claimed "The biggest lie of the lot, the blood libel on the German people (because people were hanged for this), as I call it, is the lie that the Germans had factories of death with gas chambers in which they liquidated millions of their opponents"—Irving doesn't plead ignorance. Nor does he try to pass off his comment as a purely rhetorical exaggeration. No, what Irving says is: "Truth is an absolute justification of that remark, of course."

This leaves Mr. Justice Gray little choice. In a formal, written ruling about what evidence will be allowed in relation to Auschwitz, he says, "It is, in my judgment, legitimate for Mr. Rampton to deploy evidence about what happened at Auschwitz, even if it is Mr. Irving's case that he was unaware of it at the time he made his various pronouncements."

On the morning that Robert Jan van Pelt appears in court as an expert witness for the defense Irving tries to show another video. In order to set up his cross-examination, Irving wants the court to hear van Pelt commenting on the ruins at Auschwitz, which in the clip Irving wants to show van Pelt describes as "like the Holy of Holies." As the camera dollies in, we are meant to see a grass- and dirt-covered mound, the remains of the subterranean gas chamber known as *Leichenkeller 1*, or Morgue 1, of *Krema 2* (Crematorium 2) at Auschwitz–Birkenau. The camera points down into an opening in the mound, and we are again meant to hear van Pelt's voice: "In the 2,500 square feet of this one room, more people lost their lives than in any other place on this planet. Five hundred thousand people were killed. If you would draw a map of human suffering, if you create a geography of atrocities, this would be the absolute center."

But someone has cued up the film to the wrong segment, and what we see instead is a nerdy-looking man in a parka scrambling over some snow-covered rubble, pausing every now and again to pick up a piece of brick or a fragment of concrete and put it in the kind of plastic bag you use for freezing leftovers. Van Pelt is a Dutchman, but the voice we hear is pure suburban Boston, with the flattened vowels of a man yelling "Beeaah heeaah!" in Fenway Park. The name of the film is *Mr. Death*, and though both van Pelt and Irving have supporting roles, the man we see and hear is Fred Leuchter, former expert witness for Ernst Zündel and author of the report which persuaded David Irving that the gas chambers were a hoax.

A pathetic character who seems to be fascinated with the mechanics of killing people, Fred Leuchter is the eponymous star of *Mr. Death*, the latest film by the investigative documentarian Errol Morris. In *The Thin Blue Line* Morris so thoroughly discredited a Dallas police investigation that a man wrongly jailed for murder had his conviction overturned. In *Mr. Death* Morris's camera casts an equally cold eye on Leuchter, revealed as the kind of man who takes his new bride to Auschwitz for their honeymoon. Morris shows that some of Leuchter's "samples" may have come from structures rebuilt after the war, and he tracks down the technician whose analysis of the samples supposedly turned David Irving into a "hardcore disbeliever." In the film, the technician explains that because he wasn't told what the material was for, he simply ground everything up—diluting many thousands of times any traces of cyanide that might have been on the surface. "I don't think the Leuchter results have any meaning," he told Morris.

In the United States, where *Mr. Death* was released over the summer of 2000, Fred Leuchter had become something of a sick joke. Indeed, viewers who saw David Irving interviewed on camera, and knew him only as the man who exposed the "Hitler diaries," might well have wondered how someone so adept at spotting forgeries could have been so easily gulled. Part of Irving's strategy in using the film may have been to neutralize it by giving it his own spin. And the clip he intended to show is also probably the handiest way for Irving to acquaint his audience—on the bench and in the press seats—with the terrain at the center of his claim about Auschwitz.

"My Lord, this is not the part I wanted," says Irving, who stops the film. Whether the columns of numbers at the end of the Leuchter report—which, as Rampton has established, Irving saw only the night before he announced his conversion at the Zündel trial—really were the reason Irving joined forces with Faurisson and Zündel, or whether the Leuchter report was merely the pretext for a move he had already decided to make, is impossible to say. Certainly, however, Irving has been Leuchter's most important publicist. Now that Leuchter has become a liability, Irving is in the delicate position of needing to distance himself without looking like a dupe.

He does this by suggesting he knew all along. "If you read the correspondence," he tells Rampton, "there are letters between me and Mr. Zündel and other people saying that engineers have now drawn attention to the serious flaws in the Leuchter report, and we have to address them."

So Rampton reads from the correspondence. He hands the judge two documents from Irving's discovery. One is a critique of the Leuchter report sent to Irving by a man named Colin Beer. Much of the critique is technical, a rebuttal of Leuchter's claim that the quantity of gas needed to kill human beings in the numbers attributed to the Auschwitz gas chambers would have poisoned the executioners as well as their victims—or required elaborate ventilation arrangements. But there are two points which, though stunningly simple, and totally devastating to Leuchter's credibility, had evidently escaped Irving's notice. One was that Leuchter had explicitly stated his calculations were based on the belief that it takes much more gas to kill human beings than lice (Zyklon-B was originally developed as an insecticide, and was indeed used by the Germans for delousing operations at some concentration camps). In fact the reverse is true, and though Leuchter had assumed a concentration of 3,200 parts per million of hydrogen cyanide—described by Beer as the "one-gulp-and-you're-dead" dose used in American prison gas chambers—a dose of 300 parts per million would be sufficient to be fatal. Indeed, said Beer, given the many eye-witness accounts of victims taking as long as 30 minutes to die, the concentration could have been as low as 100 parts per million—a concentration so low no ventilation at all was required. Making the victims undress allowed the gas to enter through the skin as well as the lungs—another factor suggesting lower concentrations were used.

At these low concentrations, Beer continued, "I would expect NO DETECTABLE CONCENTRATION" in any samples from sites exposed to weather, as those at Birkenau had been. Yet Leuchter had found small traces of cyanide in some samples. Far from proving these buildings had never been used as gas chambers, according to Beer the levels of cyanide residue shown in "the Leuchter report, when taken in the context of the times and in full consideration of all other evidence is consistent with that other evidence and together strongly supports both the fact and the scale of the massacres in the gas chambers of Birkenau."

The second document Rampton gives the judge is Irving's January 1990 letter to Beer. "I agree, in fact, with many of your . . . criticisms," wrote Irving, "and ascribe most of the shortcomings to the fact that engineers, like trade unionists, do not share the facility of expressing themselves in English that writers and poets have."

Except in his opening statement, Rampton never calls Irving a liar. Day after day he works at showing Irving distorting evidence, or quoting documents in a way designed to mislead his readers, but when Irving makes an improbable statement on the stand all Rampton says is "That is as may be." So it is perhaps significant that when Irving claims he has other studies which vindicate Leuchter's results, and that, in any case, "the whole purpose of the report was to put the ball in the court of the other side so they could come back and convince us," it is not Rampton, but Mr. Justice Gray who responds: "That is as may be, but I am interested to know what it was that emerged that told you that Leuchter was right, because at the moment it seems to me there is a fundamental problem with his report."

If Irving ever planned to "go for broke" on the Leuchter report he certainly knows better now. He does make a few references to a document he calls the "Rudolf Report"—a later attempt by the German chemist Germar Rudolf to duplicate Leuchter.

At one point he even hands the judge an English version, published by Irving's Focal Point imprint. Rampton protests this should have been exchanged in discovery; Irving claims it was. But when Rampton points out that the document Irving has produced is only 20 pages long, and itself offers for sale a German version which is 120 pages long, Irving admits this is not the full report, which he promises to produce later in the trial. He never does. Instead Irving goes into the forensic equivalent of four-wheel drift, sliding past Leuchter's limitations and once again bearing down on Auschwitz.

The first hazard in his path is yet another lab report, this one from Cracow and dated 1945. The objects under analysis were ventilator gratings taken from Morgue 1 of Crematorium 2—the same gas chamber described by van Pelt in the film.* The Poles found the gratings were covered with cyanide; they also found a January 1943 letter from Karl Bischoff, the camp's chief architect, referring to Morgue 1 as a *Vergasungskeller*—a gassing cellar. And they found orders for *gasdichte Türen*—gas-tight doors. These explicit references, or "slips," are extremely rare in the archival record. But in 1989 a French pharmacist, Jean-Claude Pressac, a one-time follower of Faurisson who'd gone to Auschwitz on a Leuchter-like mission but became convinced by what he found in the camp archives that Faurisson was mistaken, collated them in a book.[3] Irving knows he will have to account for them.

* The numbering of the various buildings at Auschwitz–Birkenau was a source of some confusion during the trial. In the interests of clarity I have generally followed van Pelt's practice of counting the crematorium inside the Auschwitz main camp, or *Stammlager*, as Crematorium 1, with the gas chamber/crematorium buildings at Birkenau numbered 2–5. Prisoner accounts often include only the installations at Birkenau, and when those are quoted I again follow van Pelt in using roman numerals (so that Crematorium 5, for example, becomes *Krema IV*. I have also followed van Pelt in referring to the gas chambers by the labels for those rooms on the architects' blueprints, namely as *Leichenkeller* or Morgue. These rooms were all located inside the crematorium buildings.

"I will concede," he says, "that they found in the ventilator grating taken from Morgue 1 of Crematorium 2 remains of cyanide."

"Yes," says Rampton. "How do you account for that, Mr. Irving?"

"Because that particular room was used as a *Vergasungskeller*, as a gassing cellar."

"Yes. Gassing what?"

"I think the evidence is clear that it was used as a gassing cellar for fumigating objects or cadavers."

"Fumigating cadavers?" Rampton asks.

"Yes."

Rampton's disbelief is obvious. "What makes you say that?"

"That is what that room was for," Irving replies blandly. "That is what mortuaries are for. In mortuaries you put cadavers."

"That is news to me, Mr. Irving. What is the evidence for that?"

"I beg your pardon?"

"What is the evidence that they used that [room] for gassing corpses?"

"That is what it was built for."

"I am sorry," Mr. Justice Gray interrupts, "this seems a crude question, but what is the point of gassing a corpse?"

"Because they came in heavily infested with the typhus-bearing lice that had killed them."

"So why," asks Rampton, "would it need a gas-tight door with a peep hole with double eight-millimeter-thick glass and a metal grill on it?"

Irving's answer launches a whole new hypothesis. "At this time in the war," he says, "most of Germany was coming under the—it was feeling the weight of Royal Air Force Bomber Command forays. We were bombing all over Eastern Europe. Our bombing raids were extending further and further into Central Europe. You will see from the Auschwitz construction department files an increasing concern about the need to build bomb-tight shelters and gas-tight shelters because of the danger of gas attack."

"Now it is an air raid shelter, is it?" Rampton asks sarcastically.

"I beg your pardon?"

"In early 1943, Mr. Irving? The first bombing raid anywhere near Auschwitz was not until late '44?"*

Once again Irving promises to provide documentation. "I will tomorrow produce to you an index of all the documents in the Auschwitz construction department files from late 1942 onwards dealing with the necessity to build air raid shelters, gas-tight air raid shelters and other similar constructions on the Auschwitz compound." And once again, the promised evidence never appears.

In the meantime Rampton is still trying to make sense of Irving's first suggestion: "If they were used for gassing corpses, I wonder if you can help me to understand the point, because shortly after they were in the mortuary they went to be incinerated?"

"Yes."

"What would be the point of gassing a corpse that was shortly going to be incinerated?"

"The corpses arrived . . . fully clothed. Before they were

* Auschwitz was out of range of Allied bombers until early 1944, when an air-base was established at Foggia in Italy. On April 4, 1944 an Allied photo-reconnaissance plane flew over Auschwitz to gather intelligence on the "Buna" synthetic-rubber factory at Monowitz. On August 20, a squadron of 127 B-17s from the American 15th Air Force dropped over 1,300 500-pound bombs on Monowitz. Three further raids in September and December dropped an additional 2,000 bombs. The Polish government-in-exile had been begging for Auschwitz itself to be bombed since August 1943; in the spring of 1944, British and American Jewish groups pleaded with their governments to bomb either the gas chambers or the railway lines leading to the camp (thus halting or slowing the deportations). Not a single bomb was ever intentionally dropped on either.

cremated they were undressed, and various other bestialities were performed on them. I believe the gold teeth were taken out and other functions were performed. As the corpses cooled, the lice that may have been on the body crawled off the body because lice were seeking heat."

"Where?" asks Rampton.

"I am not sure, saying this off the top of my head. Mr. Rampton, I have taken advice on this."

If a witness doesn't answer, repeat the question. Rampton repeats the question. "Where would the infestation problem arise, Mr. Irving?"

"Anywhere between the place of death and the *Leichenkeller.*"

"No. You were talking about gassing corpses in *Leichenkeller* 1, beside which is a lift straight up to the incineration chamber?"

"Yes."

"Think about it. Why would you gas a corpse that was going straight up to be cremated?"

"I thought I gave the explanation."

But Rampton doesn't think so. Unfortunately for Irving, neither does Mr. Justice Gray. "I do not understand the explanation," he says, "because, as I understood it, the undressing took place before the gassing."

Now Rampton is puzzled as well. "The undressing took place before the gassing?"

"That is not the evidence that I gave, my Lord," says Irving.

"I thought it was," says the judge. "Tell me if I am wrong."

Irving points out, "We have not had any evidence as to that, my Lord."

"No, but I have read the report," says the judge, meaning van Pelt's expert report on Auschwitz. "Am I wrong about that?"

"I shall certainly be questioning—"

Rampton can contain himself no longer. "You are absolutely

right, my Lord. On the evidence, if one can look at the evidence rather than at some bizarre version of it, the bigger room is the undressing room. They are then shepherded through into the smaller room where they are gassed. When they are dead, they are taken out through double doors that open outwards on to the lift and up into the crematorium, to put it crudely."

Irving protests: "I am having difficulty, my Lord. I have not been given a chance to comment on this rather global presentation of what Mr. Rampton alleges to have happened."

"Comment now," says the judge. "Now is your chance."

"Now is your chance," says Rampton.

Irving declines. "My Lord, we need to know what basis the evidence is put on. I apprehend that this is based on eyewitness evidence and I shall have something to say about each of the eyewitness reports on which Mr. van Pelt bases his statement. I think the proper place to do that is in the cross-examination of Professor van Pelt."

Van Pelt, who teaches at the University of Waterloo, in Ontario, will not arrive until the next day. In the remaining minutes of the afternoon, Rampton goes back to the gas-tight doors. These doors pose two problems for Irving. First, Leuchter claimed they didn't exist. "'There is no provision,'" says Rampton, reading from the Leuchter report, "'for gas-fitted doors windows or vents.' That as a matter of history is just wrong, is it not, Mr. Irving?"

"I do not know. I have never been to Auschwitz."

"No, the documents—" says Rampton. "There are repeated references . . . to the need for a gas-tight door with a peep hole."

"Yes. In the Auschwitz documents there are repeated references to this, yes."

"So that is a piece of Leuchter which has no foundation in history?"

"I think what he is saying," Irving replies, "is that nothing was to be seen when they inspected on-site."

Leuchter, who never saw the Auschwitz blueprints which are the foundation of Dwork and van Pelt's book, also claimed the doors had opened inwards. But as Rampton points out, the plans show the doors opening outwards. "All doors opened outwards," he says, "which is why they are not air raid shelters."

Irving doesn't even hesitate. "Air raid shelters' doors always open outwards."

"Why? What if the rest of the building tumbles down outside and you cannot get out?"

"The reason," says Irving confidently, "is because the blast from a bomb exploding outside will blow the door in if it opens inwards. Air raid doors always open outwards." This, too, will apparently have to wait for van Pelt. But before Rampton calls it a day, there is something else about Irving's air raid proposal that bothers him.

"Who were they for?" he asks.

"I have no idea," says Irving.

"For the inmates?"

"I have no idea."

"If this is for the SS, this air raid shelter, it is a terribly long way from the SS barracks, is it not? They would all be dead before they ever got there if there was a bombing raid. Have you thought about that? It is about two and a half miles?"

"I remember during the war," says Irving, "when we got air raid warnings half an hour, an hour, before the planes arrived."

"And you went down to the bottom of the garden, just as I did, and hid in your Anderson shelter, or whatever it was called?"

"We had a Morrison."

"We had one of those first and then we got grand and had an Anderson!"

"Well, that is enough reminiscing," says the judge, who was born in 1942 and may not remember his own wartime experiences. Rampton points out plans have been found for converting Crematorium 1, in the main camp, into an air raid shelter for the SS, whose barracks was nearby. He doesn't say, however, when these plans were drawn and if the shelters were ever built. Neither does Irving.

"Yes, well," says Irving, "I did not say this was for the SS."

"They could pop out of their living quarters into the air raid shelter," Rampton continues. "Do you really see a whole lot of heavily armed soldiers running two and a half or three miles from the SS barracks to these cellars at the far end of the Birkenau camp? I mean, Mr. Irving!"

It has been a long day, but Rampton is not quite finished. Every trial lawyer knows that the end of the day is the best time to spring a surprise. Your opponent is liable to be worn down, and the jury—or judge—are more likely to remember the details if they come just before the recess. Irving claims that the massive expansion in crematorium capacity at Auschwitz–Birkenau, far from evidence of genocidal intent, is explained by the typhus epidemic which ravaged the camp in the spring and summer of 1942. Rampton begins by trying to pin down the numbers, which he says were about 8,000 dead from the disease.

"Do you accept that?"

"Not necessarily."

Irving supplies no alternative figures, however, nor does he dispute the fact that the total prisoner population of Auschwitz–Birkenau (those actually living in the camp) never exceeded 150,000.

Rampton then produces a June 1943 letter from Bischoff, the camp architect, to Kammler, head of the Waffen SS supply department in Berlin, "setting out . . . the theoretical capacity of each of five crematoria at the time when he writes in a 24-hour period. Have I got it right?"

"Yes."

The judge does some quick calculation. "So that is 4,756 corpses in 24 hours?" he asks.

"That is 4,756 people—corpses," says Rampton. "I must not

suggest they were alive: 4,756 corpses to be incinerated by these five installations in a 24-hour period. If you multiply, Mr. Irving, 4,756 by 7 you get something like 33,000 in a week; and you if multiply that by 4 you get something like 130,000 a month; and if you multiply that by 12 you get about 1.6 million in a year. What, Mr. Irving, did they need that kind of capacity for?"

"Can we discuss the document first?"

"By all means."

"This is one of the few documents whose integrity I am going to challenge."

Auschwitz

Although his expert report runs to 767 pages, the examination-in-chief of Robert Jan van Pelt takes less than an hour. It starts with a misunderstanding. In every courtroom in Britain there is a printed card giving the "forms of oath" for the clerk to use when swearing in witnesses. Church of England members swear on the Revised Version of the New Testament, Catholics on the Douai Bible, Jews on the *Tanach* or Hebrew bible, Muslims on the Koran, and so forth. As van Pelt, a boyish-looking man with a brush of light-blond hair and wearing a boxy tan suit, walks to the front of the courtroom, Rampton says, "Professor van Pelt has a family bible which has been in his family since before the war. May he swear on that?"

"Of course," says the judge, who turns to van Pelt. "It is in English, is it? Or Dutch?"

"It is in German," says van Pelt, who is then duly sworn. Since no one enquires further, nothing emerges now or later during the trial to disturb the impression of a Dutch architectural historian whose interest in the Holocaust is purely academic. But van Pelt's family bible is the famous translation of the *Tanach* by Martin Buber and Franz Rosenzweig. Published in Germany three years after Hitler came to power, it is the monument of a culture, and a people, whose extinction is the subject of this trial.

The bible, van Pelt will tell me afterwards, belonged to his grandfather and had accompanied the family when they went into hiding from the Nazis. "What virtually no one knew," he added "was that when I was on the stand I had in my pocket my grandmother's yellow star, and right in front of me on the lectern the last two letters of her brother Robert Hanf, who was killed in Auschwitz in 1944. I was named after him."

Only an anti-Semite would argue that a Jew is somehow less qualified to give expert evidence on the Holocaust—or less capable of reporting to the court in the unprejudiced manner the law requires of expert witnesses—than a non-Jew.* Yet it had been widely remarked that, in a field where most of the prominent scholars are Jews—Hilberg, Martin Gilbert, Richard Breitman, Bernard Wasserstein, Yehuda Bauer—the defense had somehow assembled a team consisting of two Germans, a Dutchman, a Welshman, and an American Protestant. After the trial Richard Evans, the Cambridge professor who co-ordinated expert testimony for the defense, said this had been deliberate: "We didn't want to feed [Irving]'s anti-Semitic paranoia."†

In the report he prepared for this trial, van Pelt approaches the issue obliquely. Noting that he has opposed the criminal prosecution of "Holocaust deniers like Zündel in Canada, Faurisson in France, and Irving in Germany," he writes that "if Irving had been the defendant in this case, I would not have consented to" assist the prosecution. Where the other expert reports merely include the boilerplate pledge of impartiality required by law, van Pelt says: "While I wrote this report as an

* The notion that only Jews are somehow licensed to comment on such matters is, of course, equally bigoted.

† Evans made this observation at a public forum on the trial sponsored by the Wiener Library in London. The next morning I received a telephone call from Anthony Julius, who also spoke. Declaring his indifference to Irving's state of mind, Julius assured me that Evans was mistaken.

amicus curiae without prejudice for the defendant and against the plaintiff, I do declare my loyalty with the victims of Auschwitz and against their murderers."

Knowing van Pelt's history might have made some of his statements seem less melodramatic. Asked if he had been "deeply moved to visit the actual location where these atrocities had occurred?" he answers: "More than moved. I was frightened. I—"

"Ghosts of the dead were still all around?"

"No, I do not believe in ghosts," he replies, "and I have never seen ghosts in Auschwitz, but it is an awesome place in many ways, and it is also an awesome responsibility one takes upon oneself when one starts to engage with this place as a historian. For many years I felt I was not up to that task. It was only after very careful preparation that I finally decided to go there and to start work in Auschwitz."

Unfortunately, apart from the lawyers, the judge, and the principals, very few people have read van Pelt's report. For those of us who haven't, his cross-examination by Irving—the climax of the dispute over Auschwitz—is almost impossible to follow. And though perhaps no more deliberate than the confusion over van Pelt's choice of bible, this skewed perspective may have consequences that are far more serious.

In a jury trial, an expert like van Pelt would be taken by the hand by the lawyers who engaged him and led slowly through his evidence. Those who have seen him with students say van Pelt is a charismatic and effective teacher, and his professorial manner might have impressed a jury. But since it is presumed that the judge has already digested his report, van Pelt, like all the defense witnesses, is basically asked to confirm that he wrote it and believes it to be true before being turned over to cross-examination. Instead of a tutorial on Auschwitz, all the press and the public get from van Pelt is a sense of how he bears up under Irving's attack.

Unaware of van Pelt's family background, Irving begins

instead by accusing him of posing as an architect. He first softens his target with flattery: "What a great pleasure I had in reading your book on Auschwitz. For what it is worth, it is one of the few books that I have read from cover to cover." Then he asks about van Pelt's appointment, eliciting the following: "My appointment is kind of confusing. I am in the Department of Architecture and hence I am officially a Professor of Architecture. Your title as Professor depends on the department you are in. However, I teach in what we call the Cultural History stream, so normally, in order to prevent confusion in ordinary usage, I would call myself Professor of Cultural History because, both in my background, my Ph.D. and my teaching duties, I teach cultural history in the architectural school."

Noting that on his expert report van Pelt identifies himself as "Professor of Architecture," Irving asks, "Are you familiar with the fact that it is illegal in England to call yourself an architect unless you are registered with the Royal Institute of British Architects?"

Van Pelt replies that the same is true in Holland, but that he never had any reason to register, "since I never studied in an architectural school."

"In other words," says Irving, "your expertise, as an architect, is the same as Mr. Leuchter's expertise as an engineer?" Van Pelt replies defensively that he has taught design classes, and served on architectural juries, and advised architects. . . .

Irving cuts him off: "So if I am called a pseudo historian, then you are a pseudo architect, if I can put it like that?"

"Yes," says van Pelt, "except I have never claimed to be either an architect or a pseudo architect." Seemingly disconcerted by Irving's smiling insinuations, van Pelt concedes: "I agree that my formal qualifications are exactly the same as yours."

Irving's next question takes his campaign to suggest something shifty in van Pelt a step further: "Your report is unusual in one respect, and your Lordship may have noticed it, it has a copyright line on page 2. In other words, you claim copyright in this document. Now, remembering you are on oath, would you tell the court if you have any intention eventually of publishing this?"

Again, van Pelt's answer is defensive: "At the moment I do not have. I think it is an unpublishable document." This is unnecessary.* And as Irving manages shortly to establish, it isn't quite the whole truth.

"Very well," says Irving. "I will take your statement that you have no intention of publishing this ever, as you have now told the court. My Lord—"

As traps go, this was a small one. But van Pelt walks right into it: "May I just come back to this?" he interrupts. "I said 'in this form' . . . I did not write this with publication in mind *as such*."

Irving's misadventure with the video player follows, introduced by what the adherents of Sigmund Freud would doubtless consider a *lapsus linguae*, when Irving refers to Morris's film as "Mr. Truth— Mr. Death."

In order to make the point he'd hoped to make with the video, namely that if you want to deny the existence of homicidal gas chambers at Auschwitz, Crematorium 2 is the place to do it, Irving strides over to the easel on the right side of the courtroom. He takes down one of the large aerial photos of Auschwitz which have been stacked there since the first day of the trial, and, pointing to an indistinct shape, asks: "This [Crematorium 2] was the center of the atrocity?"

---

* In a criminal trial, a witness with a financial stake in the verdict—a contract to sell his story to a tabloid newspaper, for example, with the promise of a bonus upon conviction—can have his testimony set aside. But *Irving* v. *Lipstadt* was a civil case, and van Pelt testified as an expert witness, not a witness of facts. Richard Evans, Anthony Julius, Hajo Funke, and Deborah Lipstadt all planned to write books drawing on their experiences at the trial; doubtless Irving someday will follow suit.

"Yes," says van Pelt.

"So if I am to concentrate a large part of my investigation in this cross-examination on that one building and, in fact, on *Leichenkeller 1*—the one arm of the crematorium—this is not entirely unjustified if I am trying to establish that the factories of death did not exist *as such*?"

"No. I think that the obvious building to challenge would be Crematorium 2." For the next few days, at least, the pretense that this trial is about historiography alone is abandoned.

"You are familiar, no doubt," Irving asks, "with the book written by Professor Arno Mayer, *Why Did the Heavens Not Darken?*, in which this professor of Princeton University, who was himself Jewish, and who cannot be called a Holocaust denier presumably, said that most of the deaths at Auschwitz in his opinion were from what he called natural causes, and that a very small percentage had been criminally killed in the accepted sense."

Van Pelt says he thinks Irving's précis is wrong; he wants to see the text before he answers. Irving hasn't got it with him. What Mayer actually said cuts both ways. "There is a distinction," Mayer wrote, "between dying from 'natural' or 'normal' causes and being killed by shooting, hanging, phenol injection, or gassing. But quite apart from the vital importance of not allowing this distinction to be used to extenuate and normalize the mass murder at Auschwitz, it should not be pressed too far." Like Mayer's critics, Irving has conveniently forgotten this portion of Mayer's remarks.

But he—and they—have rightly focused attention on the sentences that followed: "The Nazis' leaders decided to transport frail and sick Jews, and Gypsies, to Auschwitz in full awareness of the perils they would face, and they continued to do so once there was no ignoring and denying the deadly conditions there, including the endemic danger of epidemics. Besides, from 1942 to 1945, certainly at Auschwitz, but probably overall, more Jews were killed by so-called 'natural' causes than by 'unnatural ones.'"

This was indefensible, as even Vidal-Naquet, who wrote the preface to the French edition of Mayer's book, pointed out. But Mayer attracted just as much criticism for another sentence: his claim that "sources for the study of the gas chambers are at once rare and unreliable."[1] Mayer may have been mistaken, but in 1988, when his book was published—before Western researchers gained access to Soviet archives, before Pressac, before Dwork and van Pelt—that sentence was at least defensible.

Van Pelt's task is to show that this is no longer the case, and hasn't been the case for some time. On the stand, though, the question hardly comes up. Instead Irving offers a series of hypotheses, most of them aimed at establishing not just that Auschwitz wasn't a place where roughly a million people were gassed to death and then incinerated, but that it couldn't have been.

Once again referring to his easel, Irving points to a coal bunker. "I have not got equipment here for measuring the size of that bunker, but it appears to be about 10 feet square, in other words a very small space."

"It seems to be a bit larger to me from what I remember," says van Pelt, "but, again, 10 feet, 13 feet square, whatever. It is not a very large bunker."

"Not a very large bunker for holding the fuel supplies for fueling a mass incineration program, I believe Mr. Rampton would have called it, for incinerating hundreds of thousands of bodies?"

"May I remind you, Mr. Irving, that also in the crematorium itself was a very large coke storage space right next to the incineration building."

"Yes, I am familiar with the position of that in the drawings of the building. Not very much larger than that little hut outside?"

"I think it will be probably possible to establish the size of that when we consult a plan, and I am happy to consult the plans in my trial bundle."

Though van Pelt appears disinclined to take it seriously, Irving's argument seems to have reached the judge, who asks: "Was there a coke bunker in each crematorium or just one?"

"Each crematorium has its own coke bunker, yes," says van Pelt, and there, for the moment, he leaves it.

Irving next turns to a blown-up photograph of Morgue 1 of Crematorium 2 "on which we have now zeroed in."

"Was this building destroyed by the Nazis," he asks, "or by the Russians?"

"The evidence," van Pelt says, "points to the fact that the Nazis destroyed this building in two phases, and specially Morgue 1. First of all, when the gassing ceased in late 1944 we have the testimony of *Sonderkommando** and others that the gas chambers were dismantled, which means that the actual installation within Morgue number 1 of Crematorium 2 and number 3,† which had been created to adapt this room into a gas chamber, was removed, and that later the shell of the room, so to speak, was destroyed by dynamiting. It was a very detailed account of one *Sonderkommando*, how they actually made holes in the columns. Dynamite is put in it and

---

* The *Sonderkommando* (special commandos) were prisoners assigned to work in the gas chambers and the crematoria. Periodically they would themselves be gassed, but some of those working at the end of the war survived. Two of them, Szlama Dragon and Henryk Tauber, escaped when the Nazis evacuated the camp in January 1945, but returned to give evidence to Soviet and Polish investigators. Dragon also remembered where his fellow *Sonderkommando* Salmen Gradowski had buried a journal, written in Yiddish, in an aluminum canteen. Though Gradowski had been killed, his canteen was dug up in the presence of the members of the Soviet prosecutor's office.
† Crematorium 3 was built from the same plans as Crematorium 2, but the plans were "flipped," making the buildings mirror images of one another. In both cases the room designated as Morgue 1 functioned as the gas chamber. Similarly, Crematorium 5 was the mirror image of Crematorium 4.

ultimately, in the case of Crematorium 2, all the columns collapsed, with the exception of one. In Crematorium 3 they were more successful and virtually everything collapsed there. So what you have now in Crematorium 2 is . . . the remains of a concrete roof, which is basically collapsed on the floor."

"It is pancaked downwards?"

"It is pancaked downwards. One column is still there and in some way it has folded over that one column."

"So there are reinforced steel bars inside the roof?"

"Reinforced steel bars in the roof, yes, and there is a hole right next to the column, and that is the hole through which Fred Leuchter climbed into that space at a certain moment. It is a very tiny space under that roof."

"Is it not extraordinary," says Irving, "that the Nazis in their ruthless efficiency would go round destroying buildings and removing incriminating equipment which might have helped us very much today in this courtroom otherwise, but at the same time they allowed the Red Army to capture the entire construction files without the slightest murmur?"

Van Pelt explains that when the Auschwitz construction office closed at the end of 1944 the architects were all "drafted back into the SS to fight on the Eastern Front." Also, the office was located some distance from the camp itself, and contained the architect's archive. A set of drawings kept in the camp had been destroyed, but the duplicate set, which formed the basis for van Pelt's book, had been overlooked.

"So the Nazis remembered to destroy the buildings and remembered to take out every nut and bolt which might have helped us today, but they allowed the Russians to capture all the incriminating paperwork, except that it is not very incriminating either?"

"Mr. Irving," says Mr. Justice Gray, "I have a feeling there is a suggestion lurking there and I want to try and put my finger on it. Are you suggesting that what the Russians captured were not authentic documents, or what the Russians had produced were not authentic documents?"

"No, my Lord, totally the opposite. I am sorry I am being so frightfully obtuse in my cross-examination."

"No, you are not," the judge reassures him. "You are doing very well but I want to understand the suggestion."

"I am indebted to my Lord. The reason I am asking this is for two reasons. I am laying a bit of a trap, if I may put it like that, which will be sprung either before or after lunch."

Irving's trap remains unsprung until the end of the day. Meanwhile, he suggests that the growth in the camp's crematorium capacity was a response to the typhus epidemic that killed about a third of the camp's inmates in the summer of 1942. Van Pelt responds that if this were true, one would expect at most a capacity of 50,000 bodies a month—a third of the camp's projected population. Instead, the Nazis built crematoria with a capacity of 120,000 bodies a month.

"If we are to believe these figures," Irving replies, "then the SS, or whoever, were planning to wipe out over three-quarters of the entire camp population and incinerate them—which seems a rather pointless exercise as this is a slave labor camp."

Van Pelt makes two points: first, that most of the Jews gassed at Auschwitz were never registered in the camp, and were never counted as part of the labor-camp population. When the trains halted at Birkenau, the SS first separated the men from the women and children, then "selected" those fit for work, who were marched to the camp, where they were registered and tattooed for identification. The rest were taken directly to the gas chambers.

His second point is that only two of the five gas chambers, those attached to Crematoria 4 and 5, were designed for this purpose. The others, and in particular the "morgue" in Crematorium 2, were converted from other intended uses during the construction process. The blueprints and planning records of this "adaptive re-use" are the basis of van Pelt's research. When he keeps to these, van Pelt is unshakable. But Irving has no intention of fighting him on his own ground.

Instead, he takes him back to the mortality numbers. Van Pelt argues that since the planned cremation capacity was "four-fifths of the total projected population of the camp" the "Germans would have had to ship 120,000 people to Auschwitz every month in order to keep ahead of—or even with—the typhus epidemic. It is absurd to use typhus as an excuse to explain the incineration capacity of the crematoria."

Irving doesn't repond directly. Instead he asks van Pelt if it is not equally absurd to imagine the camp capable of disposing of so many people in such a short time. "So we get an idea what we are talking about here, that is four times Wembley stadium, that is 12,000 tonnes of people, 12,000 tonnes of cadavers, that you are going to have to cremate with these very limited installations?"

"I do not think after you have you been in Auschwitz very long you weigh 100 kilograms," says van Pelt.

"OK. Say 12 people per tonne if you want to cavil," says Irving agreeably, "you are still going to end up with 10,000 tonnes of bodies to dispose of. This is bringing it home to you the size of the figures you are talking about there. That brings home to you the absurdity of the document you are relying on: 10,000 tonnes of bodies.

"If you will take it from me," Irving continues, "that it takes 30 kilograms of coke to incinerate, as you say, one body, can you work out how many tonnes of coke we are going to put into those tiny coal bunkers that you can see on the aerial photographs to destroy—to incinerate, to cremate—120,000 bodies? We are talking about train loads, if not ship loads of coke are going to have to go into Auschwitz, and there is no sign of the mountains of coke on the photographs, do you agree? There is no sign of the mountains—"

"We have two documents," says van Pelt. "One which talks

about incineration capacity, and one which talks about the coke use. It is about the same buildings. On the basis of that . . . we can calculate the amount of coke which is going to be used per corpse—which is not a happy calculation, I must say—but the bottom line is you come to three and a half kilos of coke per corpse."

At this, Irving picks up a clear plastic water bottle from the table in front of him. "Do you really, sincerely believe," he asks, holding the bottle aloft, "that you can burn one corpse with enough coke that you could fit in one of these water bottles? Is that what you are saying?"

"I would like to point out there are two documents which support this," van Pelt says gamely.

"Can you just pause for a second?" Irving's water bottle full of coke seems to have caught Mr. Justice Gray's imagination. "Three and a half kilos of coke per corpse," he says doubtfully, "one has to put it. . . ."

"That is when the—"

"That is assuming," says the judge, "a rate of incineration equivalent to that in the document of 28th June 1943 which Mr. Irving challenges?"

"Yes."

Irving turns next to the question of how the gas got into the gas chambers. "Did you rely on a woman called Bimko?" he asks van Pelt. "I mentioned Miss Bimko" in my report, says van Pelt, but "I did not rely on her to come to a conclusion about the incineration capacity in the crematoria."

After a few further exchanges designed to make van Pelt look evasive, Irving reads a portion of the deposition Bimko, a Polish-Jewish physician and prisoner at Auschwitz, gave to investigators, but which van Pelt did not quote in his report: "In a corner of the room were two large cylinders. The SS man told me the cylinders contained the gas which passed through the pipes into" the gas chamber.

As van Pelt observes, Dr. Bimko was describing a visit to the gas chamber at Crematorium 4. The SS man, he argues, was teasing Bimko, pretending that the ventilation pipes were used to introduce gas, when in reality the gas came in pellets of Zyklon-B, which were tossed through gas-tight shutters on the side of the building.* "How do you expect a person who has no technical education to distinguish one pipe from another pipe?" asks van Pelt.

But Irving isn't really interested in Bimko. He just wants to plant the idea in the judge's mind that van Pelt relies on eyewitnesses, and that eyewitnesses aren't to be trusted. Irving's real target is Henryk Tauber, a *Sonderkommando* who actually worked in Crematoria 2 and 4, and whose testimony before the 1945 Polish-Soviet joint commission to investigate Auchswitz offers a detailed account of the layout and operation of the gas chambers:

> In the undressing room, there were wooden benches and numbered clothes hooks along the walls. There were no windows and the lights were on all the time. . . . From the undressing room people went into the corridor through a door above which was hung a sign marked *Zum Bade* [to the baths] repeated in several languages. . . . From the corridor they went through the door on the right into the gas chamber. . . . At about head height for an average man this door had a round glass peephole. On the other side of the door, that is on the gas-chamber side, this opening was protected by a hemispherical grid. The grid was fitted because the people in the gas chamber, feeling they were going to die, used to break the glass of the peephole.

* In Crematorium 2 and Crematorium 3, where the gas chambers were located in underground buildings, the Zyklon pellets were inserted through holes in the roof. In Crematorium 4 and Crematorium 5, which were at grade level, they were tossed in through window-sized openings covered with metal shutters.

Van Pelt, who quotes Tauber at length in his report, reads from Tauber's description of the inside of the gas chambers: "The roof of the gas chamber was supported by concrete pillars running down the middle of its length. On either side of these pillars there were four others, two on each side. The sides of these pillars which went up through the roof were of heavy wire mesh."

Irving stops him. "What does it mean," he asks, "when it says 'the pillars went up through the roof'? Went up to the roof, presumably?"

"Yes, but they popped out above the roof," says van Pelt.

"The pillars popped out?"

"Yes, so the pillars went through a hole in the roof and then they went in through, basically, the earth which was assembled on top of the roof, and then there was a little kind of chimney on top of that."

"What was the purpose of that, architecturally speaking?"

"Because these were hollow pillars and these were the pillars where Zyklon-B was inserted into the gas chamber."

Irving asks a few more questions about these pillars. How big were they? What were they made of? How many layers of wire? Where exactly were they located? As van Pelt answers, he consults a large yellow plan of the crematorium.

"You have drawn in those wire mesh columns, have you not?" Irving asks.

"I mean the whole thing is a drawing by one of my students of the whole building."

"Yes, but the wire mesh is an addition," Irving says, rather than asks. "It is not based on any drawings or blueprints, is it?" It takes another couple of minutes before Irving gets the answer he wants. "When Tauber starts talking about, for example, either the gassing procedure or the incineration procedure," says van Pelt, "of course, then that is not in the blueprints—and very important, the wire mesh columns are not in the blueprints either."

Van Pelt has now sprung Irving's trap. But he is too deep in explanation to notice. The gas chamber in Crematorium 2, says van Pelt, was originally intended to be a morgue. But work on the roof didn't begin until December 1942, "by which time the modification of the building into a genocidal extermination machine had already been decided on. . . . The roof was not yet complete at the time."

The judge remarks on the lateness of the hour, and Irving says: "My Lord, you may apprehend that the trap is now sprung and it would be a pity to put the mouse back in its cage."

"The trap is what you have just asked?"

"Precisely it, my Lord. There are no holes in that roof. There were never any holes in that roof. All the eyewitnesses on whom he relies are therefore exposed as liars."

Irving asks van Pelt to read a passage from his report: "Today, these four small holes that connected the wire-mesh columns and the chimneys cannot be observed in the ruined remains of the concrete slab. Yet does this mean they were never there? We know that after the cessation of the gassings in the fall of 1944 all the gassing equipment was removed, which implies both the wire-mesh columns and the chimneys. What would have remained would have been the four narrow holes and the slab. While there is no certainty in this particular matter, it would have been logical to attach at the location where the columns had been some formwork at the bottom of the gas chamber ceiling, and pour some concrete in the hole and thus restore the slab."

"Hold it there," Irving says gleefully. "So what you are saying is with the Red Army just over the River Vistula ever since November 1944 and about to invade and (as we found out earlier this morning) the personnel of Auschwitz concentration camp in a blue funk and destroying their records and doing what they can, some SS *Rottenführer* has been given the rotten job of getting up there with a bucket and spade and cementing

in those four holes—in case after we have blown up the building they show?"

Irving's tirade continues for some time, and while van Pelt is
able to answer some of his points, he clearly wasn't expecting
this. "My Lord," says Irving, winding down, "it is four minutes
to four. Unless Mr. Rampton wishes to say something to repair
the damage at this point—"

"My Lord, may I respond to this?"

"Yes," says Mr. Justice Gray, "but not until 10:30 tomorrow
morning."

When van Pelt returns to the witness box he brings a set of
photographs of Crematorium 2 taken by a worker in the
Auschwitz construction office. One of them shows four objects
or projections on the building's still unfinished roof. Van Pelt
says these are the "chimneys" down which the gas pellets were
poured; Irving says the objects might just as easily be drums
full of water-proofing for the roof.

This is followed by a reprise of the previous day's argument
about holes. Irving again remarks on "the implausibility of the
story, that before putting in packs of dynamite beneath the
building to blow everything up so that the Red Army does not
find any criminal traces, they send in workmen with buckets of
cement and trowels and tell them to make good the holes in
the roof. This sounds, I must say, totally implausible to me, and
we know now that it never happened because the roof is there
and there is not the slightest trace of such patchwork having
been done on the concrete."

"My Lord," says van Pelt, "it is at the moment impossible
to see because of the state of the roof if there was patchwork
or not. The roof is fragmented. The roof has weathered very,
very badly over 50 years, and the color of concrete in the
roof is of a motley quality . . . and there is a lot of growth
[that] has been on the roof. It is impossible to tell one way or
another."

"It is impossible to tell." Van Pelt's answer is honest, but it does the defense little good. "Can we hear what other evidence you have," asks Irving, "that this building here, *Leichenkeller* No. 1, of Crematorium No. 2, was a homicidal gas chamber, apart from the eyewitnesses and apart from the smudges on the roof?"

"These are the two images which confirm the eyewitness reports, and then there are a number of drawings made by a survivor."

Van Pelt's two images are Allied reconnaissance photos taken in August 1944. In one of them a set of four box-shaped shadows is visible on the roof of Morgue 1 of Crematorium 3. The drawings were made by David Olère, a *Sonderkommando* who actually lived inside the crematorium, and who, before the war, had worked in Paris designing posters and film sets. Olère's artistic skills saved his life. The paintings he did for the SS guards kept him from being killed with the other *Sonderkommando*, and when he returned to Paris after the war he did a number of works based on what he'd seen, including a very detailed plan of the crematorium showing the hollow columns coming through the roof. Though the reconnaissance photos were classified for decades afterwards, the holes in Olère's drawings, said van Pelt, showed precisely the same alignment as those in the photo.

Irving's response is to treat Olère as simply another form of eyewitness (which he was), and to remind van Pelt (and the judge) of some of the more lurid claims made by eyewitnesses. With one eye firmly on the clock, Gray cuts him short: "Mr. Irving, will you just listen? We are taking Professor van Pelt through his evidence for saying that Crematorium No. 2 was used as a gas chamber, evidence apart from the eyewitnesses. We have seen the photographs. We have now seen the Olère drawings. Can we move on and see whether there is any other evidence he relies on; if not, you can move on." Though Irving pretends to look contrite, van Pelt does not look happy. The implication of Gray's "any other evidence" isn't lost on either of them.

Van Pelt has better luck later in the day, when Irving describes a trip to Lodz in September 1942 "for the purpose of inspecting the experimental station for field kitchens for Operation Reinhard."

"I think your translation is wrong, there, Mr. Irving."

"Yes. Tell—"

"The *Die Feldöfen* in this case," says van Pelt, "are 'field ovens,' and we know there is . . . quite an extensive documentation on this particular trip which was made by [Auschwitz] Commandant Höss and . . . they were going to Litzmanstadt [Lodz] to see the extermination site there, to actually look at the incineration grid, the incineration installation created . . . to get rid of corpses which had been buried as a result of the killings in Chelmno. So this has nothing to do with kitchens, these *Feldöfen*, but with incineration ovens to burn, to incinerate, corpses." It is a tiny reminder that under the Nazis even ordinary words took on sinister meanings.

Van Pelt then produces some material on Zyklon-B deliveries to Auschwitz, which Irving counters by drawing attention to the fact that deliveries of Zyklon were also made to the concentration camp at Oranienburg, where there was no large-scale gassing. The problem for the defense is that every inconclusive exchange favors Irving.

The same thing happens when Irving claims that the elevator from the gas chamber to the crematorium was too small and too slow for the number of bodies van Pelt says passed through it.

"You appreciate, do you not, that the lift shaft was the bottleneck," says Irving, using the 1940s slang for an obstacle in war production, "through which all the victims . . . had to go."

"The bottleneck in an hour glass is only a bottleneck if you want all the sand to go down simultaneously," says van Pelt. "If you want the sand to go down in an hour it is not a bottleneck." The point behind van Pelt's metaphor is simple: the crematoria could only handle a small fraction of the gas chamber's capacity at any one time. In his report, he wrote: "Incineration capacity and not gassing capacity was the bottleneck." But on the stand, he seems flustered by Irving's request for a "back of an envelope" calculation. "It is going a little fast for me, my Lord, right now. I am happy to come back to this on Friday.

"I would of course be quite pleased," van Pelt adds almost plaintively, "if somebody who knows—if we got some more specific data about, you know, how long it would take for this elevator to come up, because obviously if we are 50 percent wrong, then we suddenly have the bottleneck."

Van Pelt's last day is his best. In order to make sense of the architectural evidence, he has temporarily transformed the courtroom into a lecture theater, and as he stands in front of a portable screen, the remote control from the slide projector in his hand, van Pelt regains some of the authority he seemed to lose under Irving's barrage.

"I am first going to actually walk you through the building, around the building [Morgue 1 of Crematorium 2], in a reconstruction made on the basis of the blueprints.

"Here is the grade level. We have here the underground morgue and we see actually the staircase going down. Basically, the soil has been cut away with the entrance right here going into this little vestibule." As van Pelt flips through his slides, it is almost as if he is the project architect, and we are his clients. This bizarre sensation is heightened when, "walking us" into the undressing room, he says: "I am very sorry for the way the lighting has been depicted. This has been, basically, standard 1999 kind of light fixtures, and this is certainly not how . . . these light fixtures would have looked, but one gets a sense of how much light would have been in this room."

Most of van Pelt's points have already been made in his responses to Irving's questions. But he does use the drawings to good effect in showing that while in the original design the doors in Morgue 1 opened inwards, at the last minute they were altered to open out. And he shows that a ramp for carrying bodies down into the morgue, included in the original plan, has also been deleted.

"A convenient system for bringing in people who died outside the building [the ramp] has been removed," he explains, "and a new convenient system [staircase] has been installed in order to bring down people who have not yet died."

When the lights come up Irving asks: "Professor van Pelt, you have been to Auschwitz in connection with your researches how many times? Once or twice?"

"No. I have been there yearly since 1990. Sometimes twice or three times yearly."

"Have you frequently visited this roof of the alleged factory of death, the mortuary—?"

"Yes, I have been there, yes."

"Have you never felt the urge to go and start scraping just where you know those holes would have been because you know approximately where, like a two or three foot patch of gravel to scrape away?"

Van Pelt is appalled. "I have authored a report already in 1993 for the Poles in which I actually argued that they needed very, very strict preservation standards, and the last thing I would ever have done is start scraping away at the roof without any general plan of archeological investigations."

"You do accept, do you not, that if you were to go to Auschwitz the day after tomorrow with a trowel and clean away the gravel and find a reinforced concrete hole where we anticipate it would be from your drawings, this would make an open and shut case and I would happily abandon my action immediately?"

Irving repeats the offer at the end of the day, before wishing van Pelt "a pleasant flight home."

In his re-examination, Rampton takes up the question of

coke consumption, referring to patent application T 58240 for a "Continuous Operation Corpse Incineration Furnace for Intensive Use," filed by Topf on November 5, 1942. He asks van Pelt to read from an engineering report on the application prepared for the Auschwitz Museum:

> After . . . pre-heating the oven will not need any more fuel due to the heat produced by the corpses. It will be able to maintain its necessary high temperature through self-heating. But to allow it to maintain a constant temperature, it would have become necessary to introduce at the same time so-called well-fed and so-called emaciated corpses, because one can only guarantee continuous high temperatures through the emission of human fat.

Rampton also takes van Pelt through numerous calculations regarding the capacity of the gas-chamber elevator. This time, van Pelt makes his point. "Certainly," he says, "I think the elevator could keep up with the ovens."

"Yes," says Rampton. "That is much more neatly put than I could have put it. Thank you."

Some of the damage has been repaired. But as court adjourns, the correspondent for *Time* magazine, who has been sitting next to me, turns and says: "It seems like this business of the holes ought to be easy to get to the bottom of—one way or the other."

The truth is that nothing about Auschwitz is easy, even today. The sheer scale of killing is difficult for the mind to grasp. The site of that killing is, as Dwork and van Pelt make clear, a palimpsest of intentions, actions, adaptations, and evasions. Thanks to their careful peeling back of all these layers we now have a good understanding of the Nazis' methods. But since those victims gassed on arrival were never counted, we will probably never know their exact number. While the post-war

Soviet estimate of four million has long been discarded, the gap between Dr. Franciszek Piper, chief historian of the Auschwitz Museum, who gives a figure of 900,000 Jews gassed, and Jean-Claude Pressac's estimate of about 800,000 may never be closed.

Auschwitz is the scene of an enormous crime, yet many of the criminals were never punished. As Irving reminded van Pelt, Walther Dejaco, the SS lieutenant who drew the designs for the gas chambers—and who accompanied Höss on his trip to inspect the "field ovens" at Lodz—was never convicted of any crime. Neither was his fellow architect Fritz Ertl. Raul Hilberg observed that at Auschwitz, history was destroyed at the same time as history was made. And if one effect of this destruction was to diffuse responsibility for the crime, this, says Pierre Vidal-Naquet, is no accident.

"Who is the murderer?" he asks. "The doctor who carries out the selections? The *Häftling* who directs the crowd of those condemned to die? The SS who take the Zyklon-B to the gas chamber?"[2] The crime can be denied, says Vidal-Naquet, because it is anonymous.

In his testimony, David Irving sometimes describes Hitler as operating via a "Richard Nixon kind of complex," making known his intentions while carefully preserving his own deniability. The history of Auschwitz poses another Nixonian question, a variation on the Watergate prosecutor's query: What did we know, and when did we know it?

To respond adequately to the interpretive and evidentiary problems posed by Auschwitz in the space of a few days' testimony was a doomed venture; to try and do so under hostile cross-examination was quixotic in the extreme. "To remain human in the exercise," as van Pelt told the court, is certainly a necessary condition for any investigator. But the complexity of Auschwitz demands not merely a presentation of evidence, but an archeology of evidence. Any genuine expertise must be based not just on a body of knowledge, but on a whole

sociology of knowledge. The absence of these deeper structures of understanding during van Pelt's cross-examination
meant that too often the discussion seemed reduced to dueling
assertions, a stichomythia whose outcome rested entirely on
the judge's whim.

Unlike his testimony, van Pelt's expert report more than
meets this demanding brief. The report is divided into chapters, with an epigraph before each chapter. Van Pelt's
self-consciously literary style can sometimes grate, and in the
light of how much sheer cognitive effort went into the task, at
least one of his quotations seems spectacularly ill-chosen:
*"There is something no less in the reality of the death camps that
denies the attentions of thought. Thinking and the death camps are
incommensurable."*[3] Van Pelt's scrupulous interrogation of facts
and interpretations, his admirably lucid account of how the raw
materials of history have been turned into myth as well as
history, and his patient picking apart of the one from the other,
quickly put paid to such reservations.

He begins with a robust statement of what is known about
Crematorium 2:

> Today we know who designed the building: Georg
> Werkmann, Karl Bischoff and Walther Dejaco. We know who
> constructed the furnaces: the Topf and Sons Company in
> Erfurt. We know the power of the forced-air system (over 4
> million cubic feet per hour) to fan the flames. We know the
> official cremation capacity (32 corpses) per muffle* per day.
> We know that it was Bischoff who took the decision to
> change the larger morgue into an undressing room, and the
> smaller one into a gas chamber. We know that Dejaco drafted
> the plan that transformed a mortuary into a death chamber.
> We know the specifications of the ventilation system that

---

* A muffle is a chamber in an oven. Crematorium 2 (and 3) had five triple-
muffle ovens; Crematorium 4 (and 5) had two four-muffle ovens. In each
muffle an average of five bodies could be incinerated at one time.

made the room operable as a site for mass extermination: seven horsepower is required to extract the Zyklon-B from the gas chamber in 20 minutes. We know that the building was brought into operation on 13 March 1943 and 1,492 women, children and old people were gassed. We know about the difficulties the Germans had getting everything just the way they wanted. We know who paid the bills and how much was paid.

"We know all of that," his report continues. "But we understand very little about many issues central to this machinery of death." This is not false modesty. Nor is this purely a consequence of distance—either temporal or professional—from the events described.

"If I now take my own experience," writes Vidal-Naquet, "as the son of two French Jews who died in Auschwitz, I would say that for several years I did not make a real distinction between concentration camps and extermination camps." Yet as the distance increased, so did the difficulty in understanding what was happening. In 1943 the *New York Times* correspondent Bill Lawrence filed a story on the disappearance of 50,000 Jews from Kiev two years previously. This occurred during an *Einsatzgruppen* action, but van Pelt cites Lawrence's inconclusive report as emblematic of one factor that influenced the news from Auschwitz:

On the basis of what we saw, it is impossible for this correspondent to judge the truth or falsity of the story told to us. It is the contention of the authorities in Kiev that the Germans, with characteristic thoroughness, not only burned the bodies and clothing, but also crumbled the bones, and shot and burned the bodies of all prisoners of war participating in the burning, except for the handful that escaped, so that the evidence of their atrocity could not be available for the outside world. If this was the Germans' intent, they succeeded well, for there is little evidence in the ravine to prove or disprove the story.[4]

And if Lawrence's skepticism—too early in the war to be a product of anti-Communism—is probably just a wised-up newsman's reluctance to believe what he's told, van Pelt doesn't shy away from darker explanations: "In April 1940, [when] the British Foreign Office received a fully corroborated account of Jewish life in German-occupied Poland, Assistant Under-Secretary Reginald Leeper dismissed the report. "As a general rule Jews are inclined to magnify their persecutions," Leeper commented.[5]

Van Pelt's description of mass murder at Auschwitz is suitably restrained, almost austere. His quotes from survivor accounts are vivid, even graphic, but never descend into the lurid or sensational. Nonetheless these sections make extremely uncomfortable reading.

Yet so, in a different way, does van Pelt's account of the contemporary evidence for the genocide. Set alongside the latest work of scholars like Richard Breitman, van Pelt's narrative of clues neglected, testimony ignored, and pleas unanswered makes it clear that anyone who remained ignorant about the fate of Jews sent to Auschwitz did so because they didn't want to know. In November 1941—before the conversion of Crematoria 2 and 3, when the number of Jews and Soviet POWs gassed at Auschwitz could still be counted in hundreds— "the *Polish Fortnightly Review*, an English-language newspaper published by the Polish government-in-exile, carried a . . . long article entitled 'Oswiecim Concentration Camp.' It described the camp as the largest concentration camp in Poland, and provided much detail about its extraordinarily violent regime."

By the following July, the *Polish Fortnightly Review* reported gassings of Poles and Russian POWs; in December the paper carried Polish underground fighter Jan Karski's account of his visit to Belzec disguised as a Latvian policeman. Up to this point, says van Pelt, Auschwitz did not play a significant role in the destruction of Polish Jewry, who were more likely to be shot by *Einsatzgruppen* or killed at an Action Reinhard camp.

Karski never went to Auschwitz, but in November 1942 he did reach London, where he met with Foreign Secretary Anthony Eden. Eden listened to Karski's report on the situation in Poland, but when Karski recommended dropping leaflets to warn Jews, and asked the Allies to threaten the Germans with retaliatory bombing, Eden cut him off.[6] Karski also met Arthur Koestler, who published an account of Karski's experiences in *Horizon*, and H.G. Wells, who was moved to wonder "why anti-Semitism emerges in every country the Jew resides in."[7]

In July 1943 Karski went to Washington, where Supreme Court Justice Felix Frankfurter refused to believe him.[8] He also spoke with President Roosevelt. If nothing else, Karski's travels should have prepared the ground for the reports by a Polish prisoner, Jerzy Tabeau, and two young Slovak Jews, Rudolf Vrba and Alfred Wetzler, who had escaped from Auschwitz. Their accounts, which reached London and Washington in the summer of 1944—as the Nazis were shipping hundreds of thousands of Hungarian Jews to Auschwitz—were vouched for by Roswell McClelland, a representative of the War Refugee Board in Berne. By then, says Breitman, the British, who had been reading German army, police, and railway codes, had no shortage of information about Auschwitz.[9]

Vrba and Wetzler's report did not generate immediate headlines in the United States; the *New York Times* ran a 22-line story entitled "Czechs Report Massacre," reporting the death of 7,000 Czech Jews. Two weeks later the paper ran a longer story, "Inquiry Confirms Nazi Death Camps," and two weeks after that the soldiers of the Soviet Eighth Guards Army reached the Lublin suburb of Majdanek. This time Bill

Lawrence could see for himself, and his description of the gas chambers and furnaces as "a veritable River Rouge for the production of death," made the paper's front page. But Lawrence was the exception. And by then it was too late to make a difference to the fate of Europe's Jews.

The story of how the world learned about Auschwitz is complex, and riddled with paradox, and van Pelt tells it superbly. But he is even better on the not quite identical subject of what we now know about the camp, and how we came to know it. On January 27, 1945 the Red Army liberated Auschwitz. At Monowitz, they found 600 sick prisoners from the IG Farben rubber plant. In the main camp, 1,200 prisoners had been too ill to join the 60,000 sent on the death march to the west; at Birkenau, 5,800 inmates remained. Hoping to avoid the propaganda disaster that followed the discoveries at Majdanek—where in addition to the gas chambers the Russians found 820,000 shoes—the Nazis had dismantled the gas chambers, blown up the crematoria, and burned 32 storage huts to the ground.*

"All that was left," writes van Pelt, "in the four storage barracks that were not completely destroyed at Birkenau were a mere 5,525 pairs of women's shoes and 38,000 pairs of men's shoes—and 348,820 men's suits, 836,255 women's garments, 13,964 carpets, 69,848 dishes, huge quantities of toothbrushes, shaving brushes, glasses, crutches, false teeth, and seven tons of hair."

Van Pelt shows how mistrust of the Russians kept the story off Western front pages; he reports the lack of interest shown in the Auschwitz trial, held in Cracow in 1947. But he also shows how well the work of Jan Sehn, the Polish judge who led a year-long forensic and historical investigation leading up to the

---

* Though Majdanek was largely ignored by the West, this was far from the case in Eastern Europe, and in the Soviet zone of influence generally.

trial, has stood the test of time. Johann Paul Kremer, an SS doctor at the camp, was one of the defendants. An avid diarist, Kremer's record of his descent into horror meets every test for contemporary documentary evidence. On September 2, 1942, he writes: "Was present for the first time at a special action at 3 a.m. By comparison Dante's *Inferno* seems almost a comedy. Auschwitz is justly called an extermination camp!"

At the trial he explained: "These mass murders took place in small cottages situated outside the Birkenau camp in a wood. The cottages were called 'bunkers' in the SS-men's slang. All SS physicians on duty in the camp took turns to participate in the gassings, which were called *Sonderaktion* [special action]."

Kremer's diary also showed that the typhus epidemic made little impact on the pace of the genocide:

October 12, 1942. (Hössler!) The second inoculation against typhus; strong reaction in the evening (fever). In spite of this was present at night at another special action with a draft from Holland (1,600 persons). Horrible scene in front of the last bunker! This was the 10th special action.

If Kremer's diary reflected little knowledge of the gassing process, that was remedied by the testimony of SS-*Unterscharführer* Pery Broad, an officer in the camp's Political Department. In June 1945 Broad, who was in British captivity, wrote an account of what he'd seen at Auschwitz for his employers in the British counter-intelligence unit, where he worked as a translator. Broad's office was adjacent to Crematorium 1, and he witnessed the first gassings there. In a way, though, his testimony about the limits to what can be known was just as important:

Nobody could learn anything in Auschwitz about the fate of a given person. The person asked for "is not and never has been detained in camp," or "he is not in the files"—these were the usual formulas given in reply. At present, after the evacuation of Auschwitz and the burning of all papers and records, the fate of millions of people is completely obscure. No transport or arrival lists are in existence any more.

Though Broad himself did not testify at the Cracow trial, his deposition was made available to the Polish judge Sehn. And in May 1946, a month after his confession at Nuremberg, Rudolf Höss was extradited to Poland. Knowing he had no chance of acquittal, Höss decided to co-operate, and wrote 34 separate statements about "The Final Solution of the Jewish Question in Concentration Camp Auschwitz"—as he titled the first of these essays.

The detailed picture that emerged from these perpetrator witnesses was then supplemented and revised in light of testimony from the victims. Among them were the escaped *Sonderkommando* Henryk Tauber and Szlama Dragon, and Alter Feinsilber (alias Stanislaw Jankowski), a veteran of the Spanish Civil War who'd been deported from France, and had worked in Crematoria 1 and 5. All of their accounts were tested against the mass of evidence Sehn had already accumulated.

"The only piece [of Henryk Tauber's deposition] for which there is no corroboration in the archives," writes van Pelt, "are the metal columns in the gas chamber of Crematorium 2 [which] . . . allowed for the introduction of the Zyklon." As van Pelt testified, these columns do not appear on the blueprints. But his report points out, with much greater clarity than emerged at the trial, that Tauber's account of these wire-mesh columns was confirmed for Sehn by Michael Kula, a Roman Catholic mechanic imprisoned in Auschwitz since August 1940 and the man who actually made them. Kula and his colleagues in the camp metal shop also made the trucks for inserting the corpses into the ovens, as well as all the hooks, shovels, and utensils to run the crematoria. It was Kula who alerted Sehn to the zinc ventilator covers, which were retrieved from the rubble of Crematorium 2 and found to be covered with cyanide.

Despite his protestations at the trial, van Pelt's report is worth reading for this digest of the evidence alone. For the first time, the facts about Auschwitz are presented not only in the order they emerged, and in the contexts they emerged, but divested of the various filters—ideological, institutional, national—that prevent or impede their proper interpretation.

Van Pelt begins his report with an account of the death of two Hungarian Jews, a small girl and her grandmother, as told by the girl's aunt, Sara Grossman-Weil, who is also the aunt of Debórah Dwork, the co-author of van Pelt's book on Auschwitz, and who witnessed the events described. Noting her interchangeable use of "gas chambers" and "crematoria," van Pelt comments: "Half a century later, Sara Grossman was not precise." Nor is her testimony the sole source for van Pelt's account. Here, and in the pages that follow, van Pelt's fidelity to the witnesses never overpowers his commitment to the facts. His presentation of what can be known about Auschwitz fills his first six chapters. But it is in the five chapters that follow that he earns his expert's fee.

Here van Pelt's subject is Holocaust denial. And here he offers not just an explanation of why Auschwitz is the principal target—the "Battleship Auschwitz" in Irving's phrase—of Holocaust denial. And not just a devastating demolition of the Leuchter report. And not just a patient and persuasive exposé of Butz, Faurisson, and their epigones as intellectual bankrupts. Though it accomplishes all these things, van Pelt's report goes further, beyond the mere refutation of Holocaust denial to what might be called a hermeneutics of Holocaust denial.

What he finds is a kind of crazed positivism. "The assumption that the discovery of one little crack will bring the whole building down," he writes, "is the fundamental fallacy of Holocaust Denial."

Van Pelt compares the fake revisionism of the deniers with

the genuinely subversive aim of the late French critic Michel Foucault's *Discipline and Punish* (1976), a history of penal reform which argued "that the Enlightenment ascent from the world of explicit judicial violence enacted on the body had been, in fact, a descent into a closed universe of total surveillance and unrelenting discipline, a world ruled by some cunning, shadowy and ultimately sinister power." Note that this contrast is independent of whether Foucault was right. In other words, by proposing a genuine "revision," a comprehensive explanation of events that seeks to overturn received wisdom, Foucault changes the way we see the events he writes about even if he doesn't persuade us to see them his way. This, says van Pelt, is precisely what the so-called "Holocaust revisionists" signally fail to achieve—or even attempt.

"We read *Discipline and Punish* today more . . . as a representative of the intellectual climate of the 1970s than for its value as history of the Enlightenment," says van Pelt. "Yet the fact remains that in its time it offered a revisionist interpretation of the history of punishment that was plausible and therefore was taken seriously.

"Up to today," he writes, "Holocaust deniers have been unable to produce, in forty years of effort, a counter-narrative to the inherited history of Auschwitz. The deniers claim to be revisionist historians, but they have yet to produce a history that offers a plausible, 'revised' explanation of the events in question."

What they have produced instead, says van Pelt, is a series of excuses, variations on a nihilist theme. Since all of these excuses surface at one point or another as part of David Irving's argument, their deconstruction—to call the process by its proper name—by van Pelt is a great service to Deborah Lipstadt's case. It must also be said, however, that the catholicity of reference and interpretive flair he brings to the task are something of a rebuke to Deborah Lipstadt's book.

Irving's insistence that Auschwitz was merely a labor camp,

for example, comes from Thies Christopherson, a soldier at one of the satellite camps near Auschwitz and author of a pamphlet entitled *The Auschwitz Lie*. Though the killing installations were off limits to anyone not assigned there, as an SS officer Christopherson was able to visit the rest of Birkenau, where he said, "I also saw families with children. It hurt to see them, but I was told that the authorities felt it kinder not to separate children from their parents when the latter were interned."[10]

Manfred Roeder, a lawyer who wrote the introduction to Christopherson's book, is the source of the argument that there was not enough fuel "in the entire sphere of German influence to burn just a fraction of so many human bodies." Another former soldier, Wilhelm Stäglich, a Hamburg judge who'd served with an anti-aircraft battery near Auschwitz, came up with the idea that the *Vergasungskeller* in Bischoff's letter "was intended for the fumigation of clothing and other personal effects, a common practice in all concentration camps."[11] This explanation, van Pelt notes in passing, displays "a total ignorance of the circumstances. The rooms designed for fumigation of clothing and other objects were always constructed in such a way that they had two doors: one entrance and one exit. The entrance door opened to the *unreine* (unclean) side, the exit door opened to the *reine* (clean) side. This arrangement conformed not only to common sense, but also to specific SS regulations."

Stäglich also originated the notion that the gas-tight door on Morgue 1 was evidence, not of a gas chamber, but of an air raid shelter. In his report van Pelt is briskly dismissive: "Stäglich's speculation is nonsensical. First of all if, as he assumed, Morgue 1 was used as a mortuary, then the problem arises about the protocol during an air raid. Would the living join the putrefying dead for the duration of the alarm?"

Finally, says van Pelt, Irving's claim that reports of gas chambers originated as the figment of Allied atrocity propaganda, or psychological warfare, is itself not the fruit of Irving's own research, but originated in the brain of Dr. William Lindsey.[12] A former DuPont chemist and witness at the first Zündel trial, Lindsey is a frequent contributor to "revisionist" journals, where he is given to fevered pronouncements on "Franklin D. Roosevelt and his proto-United Nations conspirators." When Zündel recruited witnesses for his second trial, says van Pelt, Lindsey was not asked to return.

Oddly enough, Irving's only argument whose provenance van Pelt doesn't trace and demolish is the "no holes, no Holocaust" which seemed to give him so much trouble at the trial. Yet this is just as second-hand as the rest of Irving's case, originating with Faurisson and like many of the Frenchman's conjectures offered in complete disregard of the facts (even if Morgue 1 was intended for gassing clothing or cadavers, the gas had to get in somehow) or the record (testimony by Tauber, Kula, and Broad; Olère's drawings).

Van Pelt does provide an excellent account of the ways in which the Auschwitz of history—complicated, ambiguous, overdetermined—becomes the Auschwitz of memory, the Auschwitz that we think we know.

> By the late 1970s, other genres of knowledge had been grafted on the original evidence: memoirs of survivors, interpretation of writers, evocations by filmmakers, symbolic monuments designed by architects and sculptors, public rituals of commemoration, theological speculation, and so on. In other words, by the late 1970s, knowledge of "Auschwitz" became transmitted as a mixture of learning and second-hand memory, shaped by public political discourse and private anxiety.

The refashioning of "Auschwitz" by all these actors is, to van Pelt, the byproduct of an inevitable process of appropriation. The resulting artifact—an "Auschwitz" at once different from the Auschwitz of history and yet dependent on it—can be used

for any number of ends: as a spur to conscience, an icon of suffering, a challenge to theodicy, a lever for Zionism, a stick with
which to beat Germans or Poles. Like many of us, the deniers
confuse this "Auschwitz" for the Auschwitz of history. And
though he has had much to say about their means, regarding
their ends, the possible uses of their anti-Auschwitz—this
question van Pelt leaves for others.

Massive confrontation

"I am considered to be a danger to something, and the word 'danger' is what puzzles me. I am not a member of the IRA. I do not go round blowing up cars. So what am I a danger to?"

Ostensibly addressed to van Pelt, this question, like many of Irving's sallies, is rhetorical, and really intended for the judge. Hanging in the air long after van Pelt leaves the witness box, it can be unpacked in many different ways: a claim that he is harmless, and in any case bears no malicious intent; an insistence that the defendants have over-reacted; an insinuation that they act to protect some illegitimate or shadowy interest; a reminder that historians who take only a peripheral interest in the Holocaust—in Irving's eyes more dispassionate observers than his accusers—have welcomed his researches.

It was the *Economist*, after all, that dubbed Irving "the forensic pathologist of modern military history"; William Casey, the Wall Street lawyer turned CIA director, once wrote him a fan letter. What makes Irving dangerous is precisely that he has been able to keep what Michael Naumann, the German Minister of Culture and a former publisher, called Irving's "brown underwear" carefully hidden from public view beneath his banker's pinstripes.

Van Pelt's report—especially his excavation of Irving's

various "revisionist" borrowings—hints at this. But in the courtroom Irving's intellectual antecedents have gone largely unmentioned. And if van Pelt's report effected a thorough demolition of Irving's various postures in relation to Auschwitz, the van Pelt we heard on the stand was far more diffident. Irving's cross-examination fought that van Pelt more or less to a standstill, leaving it to the judge to decide which van Pelt to credit: the unprepossessing witness or the prodigious scholar.

When Rampton resumes his cross-examination of Irving he sets about tipping this balance in the defense's favor. He starts with Irving's account of a two-day meeting between Hitler and the Hungarian Regent, Admiral Horthy, in April 1943. "Horthy apologetically noted," Irving had written, "that he had done all that he decently could against the Jews: 'But they can hardly be murdered or otherwise eliminated,' he protested. Hitler reassured him: 'There is no need for that.'" In *Hitler's War*, Irving puts Hitler's soothing remarks at the end of the second day. Yet in the source he cites, says Rampton, they come at the end of the first day.

"I got the date wrong by one day," says Irving. So what?

Rampton replies that what really happened on the second day was that in response to Horthy's query, "What should he do with the Jews then, after he had pretty well taken all means of living from them—he surely couldn't beat them to death?" Ribbentrop, who accompanied Hitler to the meeting, responded: "The Jews must either be annihilated or taken to concentration camps. There was no other way."

Hitler, says Rampton, then explained: "If they couldn't work, they had to perish. They had to be treated like tuberculosis bacilli, from which a healthy body could be infected. That was not cruel, if one remembered that even innocent natural creatures like hares and deer had to be killed so that no harm was caused."

It was his desire to conceal this openly murderous Hitler from his readers that led Irving to his "mistake," Rampton says. "Hitler jumps in with an analogy which is based on the justification for killing wild animals—killing wild animals!—in case they should cause damage. Now, that left the matter as plain as a pikestaff!" he barks.

Rampton turns next to Irving's Goering biography, reading out his account of Hitler's trial following the 1923 *putsch* attempt. "Learning that one Nazi squad had ransacked a kosher grocery store during the night, he [Hitler] sent for the ex-army lieutenant who had led the raid. 'We took off our Nazi insignia first!' expostulated the officer—to no avail, as Hitler dismissed him from the party on the spot. . . . Goering goggled at this exchange."

"How do you know Goering was there?" asked Rampton.

"Have you ever heard of author's license?"

"Are you criticizing 'Goering goggling' or being there?" asks Mr. Justice Gray.

"I am asking both questions, I think, am I not, Mr. Irving? Do you know that Goering was there?"

"Yes," Irving replies. "It is—he was there because it is evident from the timetable. . . ."

"And how do you know that Goering goggled?"

"That was author's license."

"You mean it was an invention?"

"Yes."

Rampton's questions lack any apparent sequence, having no discernible purpose beyond pointing up some mistake or distortion of Irving's. Likewise, the impression he gives when producing a document is of an immense disorder, restrained, like his temper, only by the heroic diligence and saintly character of his junior counsel, Heather Rogers. By the middle of the trial Rampton's choleric outbursts, his muttering about papers he can't find—or can't read, being either in German or in print too small for his glasses—and the inevitable resolution of these outbursts when Miss Rogers manages to unearth the desired document, have assumed an almost Punch and Judy character.

So on Day 12, when Rampton hands up a disorderly sheaf of papers, Mr. Justice Gray asks, "Mr. Rampton, I am just a little puzzled by great stacks of documents in German being handed up. . . . What am I meant to do with all this?" Irving, sitting in the witness box awaiting cross-examination, says nothing.

"If the witness has translated them in the witness box," says Rampton, "and I have not contested his translation, then one can take it—his German is very good—that what he said is accurate." Again Irving says nothing.

And when Rampton, who for some reason can't seem to find his own translation, asks Irving to translate the text of a telegram sent by Hitler's deputy, Rudolf Hess, in the early hours of November 10, 1938, as the pogrom known as *Kristallnacht* raged through Germany, Irving is delighted to oblige.

"I know the text of that telegram off by heart. I have quoted it so often in speeches," says Irving.

"I bet you do," says Rampton. "Now tell us what it says, would you?"

" 'On express orders from the very highest level,' which is always—"

"That is Hitler."

"—which is always a reference to Hitler."

"I agree."

" 'Acts of arson against Jewish shops or the like are under no circumstances and under no conditions whatsoever to take place.' "

"Good."

Unlike Irving, Rampton is a professional. When he sets a trap, as he has just done, he makes no announcements. His gratitude for Irving's assistance seems as genuine as his previous befuddlement. Irving has no way of knowing that his opponent actually possesses a photographic memory. Nor does he suspect that each of Rampton's tiny points— "pin-pricks," Irving calls them derisively—is laying the ground for an onslaught that will reveal Irving's entire career and reputation as little more than a house of cards. But he is about to find out.

Rampton's next piece of stage business involves Hans Aumeier. For about a year—from early 1942 to the spring of 1943—Aumeier was Höss's deputy at Auschwitz. Arrested after the German surrender, Aumeier wrote a series of confessions for his British interrogators. According to Höss, the events Aumeier witnessed at Auschwitz led to a drinking problem, and eventually, to the edge of mental collapse. Höss had him transferred to Estonia. In his report, van Pelt enumerates the various inaccuracies and inconsistencies which mar Aumeier's confessions. Nonetheless, he concludes, they provide crucial detail on both the gassing process and the conversion of Crematoria 2 and 3 into killing installations. They are also independent corroboration of Höss and Broad's confessions, and of the *Sonderkommando* testimony.

Van Pelt never mentioned Aumeier's name in court—because David Irving never asked. Yet as van Pelt says in his report, it was David Irving who first discovered Aumeier's hand-written confession in the Public Record Office files in London.

"Mr. Irving," Rampton begins, "Hans Aumeier, I think you first discovered him in June 1992? Your diary entry reads—you can see it if you like, we have it here— 'Later at PRO all day. Finished reading file of interrogations and manuscript by one SS officer, Hans Aumeier, a high Auschwitz official. . . . His reports grow more lurid as the months progress. I wonder why? Beaten like Höss or was he finally telling the truth? A disturbing two hours anyway.' Do you remember that entry?"

"Very clearly, yes."

Irving did not publish his discovery. Instead, he wrote a

letter to Mark Weber at the Institute for Historical Review
which Rampton proceeds to read into the record:

> Working in the Public Record Office yesterday, I came across
> the 200 page handwritten memoirs . . . of an SS officer,
> Aumeier, who was virtually Höss's deputy. They have just
> been opened for research. He was held in a most brutal
> British prison camp, the London Cage (the notorious
> Lieutenant Colonel A Scotland). These manuscripts are
> going to be a problem for revisionists and need analysing
> now in advance of our enemies and answering. I attach my
> transcript of a few pages and you will see why. It becomes
> more lurid with each subsequent version. At first no gassings,
> then 50, then 15,000 total. Brute force by interrogators per-
> haps.

"Why," asks Rampton, "are the manuscript notes, or whatever they are, memoirs of Aumeier, going to be a problem for
revisionists?"

"I think because they refute a number of the tenets of the
revisionist bible, if I can put it like that."

"What is the revisionist bible?"

"Well, the revisionist credo."

"Which is?"

"Oh, at its most extreme, it is that not a hair was harmed on
the head of the Jews—which was the most extreme and indefensible position."

With uncharacteristic reticence, Irving sat on his scoop until
1996, when, writes van Pelt, "seeking to make the best from a
very bad situation, he buried a reference to Aumeier's statement in a footnote in his 1996 book on the Nuremberg Trials."
In the footnote, Irving implies that Aumeier's confession had
been beaten out of him by Colonel Scotland.

Rampton is indignant: "Mr. Irving, you have made a suggestion . . . that this man gave a fallacious account because he

was tortured or threatened with torture by the Brits. You have absolutely no basis for that whatsoever."

"Mr. Rampton, when the time comes to cross-examine your expert witnesses, I shall be putting to them documents which show very clearly what methods were used to extract information from witnesses. . . . I shall invite them to state whether they consider this kind of evidence is dependable."

"Mr. Irving, I am tempted myself to resort to such methods to get a straight answer to my question, I have to say. You have no evidential—"

"It included, for example, crushing the testicles of 165 out of 167 witnesses. Is that what you are proposing to do to me?"

What Rampton proposes to do to Irving—indeed, has just done to Irving—is to show that he is a man who will invent evidence, distort evidence, and even suppress evidence when it suits his purpose. He has also neatly managed to tip the balance away from van Pelt's cross-examination and in the direction of his report. What he hasn't done, yet, is to more than suggest what Irving's purpose might be.

Months earlier, in the discovery hearings, Anthony Julius set out one of the legal authorities for the obligation to provide the other side with materials that might damage your own case. This, said Julius, referring to the decision by name, "is *Peruvian Guano*." In the next few days, as Richard Rampton dumps the more fetid contents of his discovery over David Irving's head, the citation seems particularly well named.

Though his family comes from the administrative, rather than patrician class, Irving, like many a public schoolboy before and since, has learned the manners of his betters. Indeed part of his courtroom strategy has been to use those manners—and the innate institutional decorum of the courts—as insulation between himself and his unsavory ideas and associates. In order to get past that barrier—and under Irving's skin—Rampton deploys a variety of means. One is his own manner, which without warning can swoop from slightly pompous barrister-speak to the depths of demotic when he wants to emphasize a point. Another is insult.

"When I asked you about this document before," he says to Irving, "it was ages ago, you denied ever having seen it."

"Now I am seeing it for the first time, yes."

Rampton all but shakes his head. "So you say."

"I beg your pardon," says Irving, drawing himself up like a stage dandy who's just been called a cad. "I am on oath and, if I say I am seeing this for the first time, then I am seeing it for the first time."

"Mr. Irving," says Rampton, "you have said many things on oath which I simply do not accept, so we can get past that childish stage of this interrogation."

"I think this is probably the time to have it out," says Irving, taking off his metaphorical gloves. "Where you think I am lying on oath, then you should say so."

"He is saying so," explains the judge.

A few minutes later, when Rampton hands the judge a pair of thick loose-leaf binders containing "Mr. Irving's utterances on the subject of Jews, blacks, etc." and a short catalogue of Irving's more *farouche* pronouncements, Irving, still smarting from Rampton's accusation, protests.

"These little catalogues of excerpts that they are presenting your Lordship with, appear . . . to me not so much like case management as case manipulation," says Irving, making his own accusation.

But Irving's indignation is no match for Rampton's hauteur.

"Mr. Irving," he says, "can I suggest that every time you think we have tried to distort the record—"

"'Manipulate' is the word I used."

"Yes, great, 'manipulate the record'—I must remember that—for the purposes of presenting a skewed picture to the court, please mark beside whichever quote I refer to [a] 'check' because then when you re-examine yourself you can show his Lordship how bad our manipulation has been."

Branding someone a bigot has an etiquette all its own. Britons pride themselves on not being hobbled by American-style "political correctness," so it is important that Rampton not appear over-fastidious or prissy. Rampton can display a manly disdain for Irving. Scorn is fine, even sarcasm, as long as it's not supercilious. The object is to hammer home the point that Irving is a nasty piece of work and not deserving of common courtesy.

Rampton begins his exhibition of David Irving's underside with a reading from Irving's on-line newsletter: "Why are they [the Jews] so blind that they cannot see the linkage between cause and effect? They protest, 'What, us?' when people accuse them of international conspiracy. They clamor, 'Ours, ours, ours' when hoards of gold are uncovered and then when anti-Semitism increases and the inevitable mindless pogroms occur, they ask with genuine surprise, 'Why us?'"

Irving protests that the quote is partial, and himself reads out the previous paragraphs discussing efforts to have him barred from Australia: "'The Prime Minister of Australia this morning has criticized me. This kind of thing generates the anti-Semitism in countries,' and this is precisely what this is about."

"You do not see anything in what I have just read," asks Rampton, "which might account for the Australians' unwillingness to have you on their shores?"

"On the contrary," says Irving, "this is saying cause and effect. Why is there increasing anti-Semitism in Switzerland today when it is going down everywhere else in the world? Answer, we know why.* Why is there anti-Semitism in Australia today? Answer, we know why."*

* Presumably because Jewish groups have demanded restitution for gold and other monies retained in Swiss banks after their owners perished in the Holocaust. But you don't have to be an anti-Semite to feel profound disquiet at the vigor with which massive sums in compensation have been pursued on

"But you are adopting it, are you not? You are saying the anti-Semitism is justified on account of the fact that the Jews are greedy?"

"Did I say justified or explicable? Is there a subtle difference there, do you think?"

In Rampton's next example, the difference between justifying hatred and explaining it is perhaps even subtler. "You people," Irving tells an imaginary Jewish interlocutor, "are disliked on a global scale. You have been disliked for 3,000 years and yet you never seem to ask what is at the root. . . . I am just looking at this as an outsider; I come from Mars and I would say they are clever people. I am a racist, I would say they are a clever race. I would say that, as a race, they are better at making money than I am."

After lunch Rampton plays a video of Irving speaking to a National Alliance meeting in Tampa, Florida. Irving tells the group about an encounter he had a few days earlier, in Shreveport, when a heckler, a British Jew, interrupted his speech to demand: "'Are you trying to say that we are responsible for Auschwitz ourselves?' and I said, 'Well, the short answer is, yes!'" His audience in Tampa roars with laughter.

This is the audience to whom Irving explains: "If you [Jews] had behaved differently over the intervening 3,000 years, the Germans would have gone about their business and would not have found it necessary to go around doing whatever they did to them, nor would the Russians, the Ukrainians, the Lithuanians, Estonians, Latvians and all the other countries where you have had a rough time."

"Your thesis," says Rampton, "is that the Jews have deserved

behalf of an ever-dwindling number of survivors—most of whom never dreamed of opening a Swiss bank account.

* Presumably because David Irving has been barred from the country. This kind of false analogy is indicative of what happens to Irving's powers of reason when the subject is anti-Semitism.

everything that has been coming to them." Irving shakes his head.

The climax of the day, though, is Rampton's recital of Irving's doggerel verse "I am a Baby Aryan."

"Racist, Mr. Irving? Anti-Semitic, Mr. Irving, yes?"

"I do not think so."

"Teaching your little child this kind of poison?"

"Do you think that a nine month old can understand words spoken in English or any other language?"

"I will tell you something, Mr. Irving. When I was six months old, I said, 'Pussy sits in the apple tree until she thinks it's time for tea.'"

The weeks of trainspotting debate have taken their toll on the press corps, but Irving's poem makes the front page of the *Times*, and the next morning the court is once again full to bursting. It is to this packed house that Rampton opens the second act of his morality play. In 1993 Irving told an Australian radio interviewer that black men on the English cricket team made him feel queasy.

"Why does it make you feel queasy," asks Rampton, "that black Englishmen should play cricket for England?"

"My reply to him on air," Irving answers, "was, 'What a pity it is that we have to have blacks on the team and that they are better than our whites.'"

"Why is that a pity?"

"It is a pity because I am English."

"Are they not English too?"

"Well, English or British, are you saying?"

"I am saying that they are English. Most of them are born here, just as all the Jews in England were born here—most of them."

"Are we talking about blacks or Jews now?"

"It does not matter. They are all English."

Actually, they are not all English. Certainly not in the eyes of

the law, since—as Rampton must surely know—under
Margaret Thatcher's 1981 Nationality Act being born here
doesn't even make you British, let alone English. Rampton's
performance of outraged liberalism contains no acknowledgment of this contemporary reality: that he speaks his lines in
a country that changed its very definition of citizenship to
keep out the Hong Kong Chinese who thought their British
passports would save them, yet somehow manages to find room
for whites fleeing Zimbabwe. It is also devoid of any sense
of history.

England is the home of the "blood libel," the accusation,
first recorded in Norwich in the year 1144, that Jews required
the blood of freshly killed Christian children to celebrate the
Passover. By the time Geoffrey Chaucer repeated it in the four-
teenth century, in "The Prioress's Tale," there were no Jews
left in England—they had been expelled in 1290, centuries
before Spain or Germany. When Shylock made his London
debut three centuries later, he did so in a country that still had
no legal Jewish residents, though a handful of illegal immigrants had begun to slip back in during the reign of Henry
VIII. It was the middle of the nineteenth century before a Jew
was allowed to sit in the House of Commons—long after the
emancipation of French Jews. It might have taken even longer
if the Jew in question hadn't been Lionel de Rothschild.

Jews were barred from Oxford and Cambridge, and excluded
from those professions—such as law or medicine—that
required their members to take an oath "upon the true faith of
a Christian." It was Matthew Arnold, bard of "sweetness and
light" who campaigned against removing these restrictions,
finding Jews an "unamiable people" and declaring: "England is
the land of Englishmen, not Jews."[1] The influx of Jewish
refugees from the pogroms of Tsarist Russia led to the passage
of the 1905 Nationality Act—the first in Britain's century-long
history of efforts to bar the doors against foreigners.

Many Britons of Irving's generation take pride in the

country's generosity toward the *Kindertransporte*—the 7,500 Jewish children admitted as refugees from Hitler. The fate of their parents—the hundreds of thousands of adults refused admission, and condemned thereby to certain death—is seldom mentioned. In this respect, of course, America's record is little better. We have our own history of racism, our "gentleman's agreements" and segregated South, our immigration quotas and Ku Klux Klan, to live down. And of course these days many of David Irving's most energetic supporters live in the United States.

Yet to American ears there is still something shocking about British prejudice, and that is its unabashed quality. Modern Britain may be developing a multi-cultural society, but the dominant culture is still dominant—and homogeneous—in a way that is no longer possible in the United States. The National Curriculum requires every schoolchild to learn the tenets of the Christian faith in Religious Education, and though there are neighborhoods in London or Manchester that are every bit as Jewish as their counterparts in Philadelphia or Los Angeles, the Jews who live in them live very different lives.

"English anti-Semitism was, and remains, an affair of social exclusion," wrote Anthony Julius in his critique of T.S. Eliot. "Jews have not been harried, but kept at a distance. The dominant note since their readmission in the seventeenth century has been one of fraught accommodation."[2] And if fraught accommodation is the lot of some Jews, surely a corresponding level of discomfort is to be expected on the part of at least some Englishmen. So why does the defense pretend that Irving's nostalgia for the England of his childhood is a sign of his monstrous character—or even particularly unusual for a man of his age and background?

"I regret what has happened to our country now," Irving tells the judge. "Sometimes I wish I could go to Heathrow Airport and get on a 747 and take a ten hour flight and land back in England as it was, as it used to be . . . the England of the blue lamp and Jack Warner and when there was no chewing gum on the pavements, and all the rest of it." Whatever these references mean, there is no doubting the intensity of his sentiment—or that these tokens of lost Empire and innocence seem to move Irving far more than his many objects of hatred.

Of course, as Anthony Julius points out, when we judge racism we must take the perspective of the victim. Whether Irving really "meant it" or not doesn't mitigate the harm he causes. Even so, it was hard not to feel queasy listening to Rampton quiz Irving about his attitude to "intermarriage between the races"—on behalf of a defendant who has written, "We know what we fight against: anti-Semitism and assimilation, intermarriage and Israel-bashing," but who uttered not one word of public protest when her American publisher issued Charles Murray's neo-eugenicist tract *The Bell Curve*.[3]

Coming as it does in the wake of the court's consideration of the high tragedy of Auschwitz and the low farce of Irving's social views, the arrival of Christopher Browning in the courtroom brings a moment of relief. Browning's firm grasp of the Holocaust in history—as neither a Jewish sideshow nor a theological "Tremendum"—is immediately evident, and in sharp contrast to John Keegan, that morning's previous witness.

Taller than Irving, with an open face and a tight, slightly nervous smile, Browning gazes at Irving through square aviator glasses waiting for his cross-examination to begin. Browning's expert report is on the "Evidence for the Implementation of the Final Solution." He is the author of five books on the subject, including *The Path to Genocide* and *Nazi Policy, Jewish Workers, German Killers*. A professor of history at the University of North Carolina, Browning has been an expert witness in a number of war-crimes trials. He also testified in the trial of Ernst Zündel, where like all the prosecution witnesses he was abused by Zündel's attorney.

Browning's testimony in these cases has made him a hate

figure among "revisionists," and as he sits clenching and unclenching his fingers he may be expecting Irving to give him a rough time. What happens instead is more like a colloquium or a tutorial than an inquisition.

"Am I correct in saying," Irving asks, "that there has been one school of thought . . . that the Operation Reinhard had been named after the late lamented or unlamented chief of the security police, Reinhard Heydrich?"

"That is one suggestion," says Browning, "made because the files on personnel in Berlin spell it with just a 'D' ["Reinhard" as opposed to the more common "Reinhardt"] which is the way he spelt his name, so that was one suggestion that has been made which I do not endorse."

Like a butterfly collector with a rare species, Irving wants to show Browning a security classification "AR" he's just noticed on some Nazi documents produced as evidence in this trial.

"Is there any significance you would attach to the fact that that had the initials 'AR' on it?" Irving wonders.

"It could indicate that a copy of this was to be filed in some file called Aktion Reinhard," says Browning, confirming Irving's hunch.

"So we are constantly discovering new things, is this correct?"

"Yes."

"So that the last chapter on the Holocaust really still has to be written?"

"We are still discovering things about the Roman Empire. There is no last chapter in history."

Irving's evident eagerness for some kind of recognition from Browning lowers the courtroom temperature considerably. Even so, after several days of Peruvian Guano, it is almost shocking to hear Browning say to Irving: "What had not been studied before you published was a particular focus on decision-making process and Hitler's role. That is one part and, in so far as we can confine ourselves to that, indeed, your publication of *Hitler's War* was the impetus for the research in that area."

Irving, delighted by this, asks, "What was the reason for this 20 year, 22 year, lack of interest in examining whether the decision had been given or how the decision had been given for the Holocaust?"

"I think probably several things," says Browning. "One, the person who had focused mainly on the German documents, Raul Hilberg, was very interested in the bureaucratic structure, but not terribly interested in dating decisions. This happened to be his focus."

"Have you discussed this matter personally with Raul Hilberg?"

"Yes and he is more interested in bureaucratic structure than he is in linear or chronological decision-making process. I am more interested in chronological process than bureaucratic structure."

"Do you know what his opinion is on whether Adolf Hitler actually issued an order or not?"

"I think his feeling is," says Browning, "if you are looking for an order in a formal sense, that such a thing probably was not given. If you are looking at it in the way that you described earlier, calling it the 'Richard Nixon complex'—that Hitler made very clear to Himmler and Heydrich what he expected, and they understood what was expected of them— I cannot speak for him, but I believe he would not have been uncomfortable with that formulation."

The following day, Irving asks Browning, "How realistic was the Madagascar plan?"—a scheme to ship Europe's Jews to this French island off the coast of Africa.

"Do I think they took it seriously?" An experienced witness, Browning rephrases the question he wants to answer. "Yes, I do think they took it seriously. It is fantastic but of course Auschwitz is fantastic, too."

"In what way is Madagascar a fantastic plan?" asks Irving.

"Fantastic in the sense that it is bizarre, the notion that you could take four million Jews and put them on ships and send them to Madagascar, and that anything other than the vast bulk of them would die under the conditions of being dumped into the jungle of Madagascar."

But when Irving pushes his luck, calling the plan Hitler's "pipe dream," Browning balks.

"I would not call it a pipe dream," he says, "because I think, if England had surrendered, they would have tried to do it. They would have tried to implement it just as they tried to implement the Lublin reservation plan* and just as they tried and succeeded in implementing the death camp plans."

Still, on the question of whether Irving's doubts that Hitler gave an explicit order for the extermination of the Jews are tantamount to Holocaust denial, Browning is equally forthright: "[Hans] Mommsen and [Martin] Broszat have argued for a long time, as you have, they do not think that Hitler gave an explicit or formal order."

"It would be a grave injustice to call either of those two professors Holocaust deniers, would it not?" asks Irving.

"Yes. The argument over whether Hitler gave an order or not is not commonly part of the issue of Holocaust denial."

"Thank you very much for saying that."

Not all of Browning's testimony is so welcome to Irving. His confident reading of the Himmler telephone log's reference to *Keine Liquidierung*— "No liquidation"—as clearly indicating an exception to a standing policy in favor of liquidation is unshakable by Irving. And though he may himself be agnostic on the question of a formal Hitler order, Browning points to Hitler's December 12, 1941 speech to the Gauleiters as "the point at which Hitler makes clear . . . they will proceed with the extermination. Up until that point they used two phrases 'after the

---

* A 1939 scheme whereby Czech Jews and Jewish prisoners of war were deported to the region around Lublin, where they were forced to build a camp for themselves.

war' and 'next spring' [to refer to the timing of the extermina-
tion]. After Pearl Harbor, one has to clarify which of those two
it will be and, in my opinion, this is the point at which Hitler
says it will be next spring even though it will no longer be after
the war."

Nor does Irving find any comfort in Browning's account of
what we know of the scale of the Holocaust. "Is it not right,
Professor," asks Irving, "that our statistical database for arriving
at any kind of conclusions for the numbers of people who have
been killed in the Holocaust—by whatever means—we are
really floundering around in the dark, are we not? Is that
correct?"

Browning's response is both blunt and comprehensive: "No.
I would not express it that way. I would say we have a very
accurate list of the deportation trains from Germany. In many
cases we have the entire roster name by name and we are not
floundering. We can tell you, as we have seen in the intercepts,
974 on one train. . . . In terms again of France, the
Netherlands—the countries from which there were deportations from Western Europe—we can do a very close
approximation by trains, the number of people per train.

"In the area of Poland," Browning continues, "there were at
least statistics in terms of ghetto populations and these ghettos
were liquidated completely, so we can come to a fairly good
rough figure of Polish Jews. We also have a fairly reliable
prewar census and postwar calculations so that one can do a
subtraction. So, in terms of Holocaust victims from Poland
westward, we are not floundering. We are coming to a fairly
close approximation. Where historians differ and where you
get this figure of between five and six [million] is because we
do not have those figures for the Soviet Union."

And when Irving attempts to recruit Browning to his view
that eyewitnesses are under no circumstances to be trusted—
"Rather like Rommel, I am coming round from the rear and
attacking . . . the eyewitnesses"—Browning again declines.

"Did he [Adolf Eichmann] once testify," asks Irving, "or write in his papers—in fact, in my collection of papers too—did he write that he got so close to one shooting that bits of babies' brain were splattered across his nice leather coat?"

"He complained that at Minsk that happened and, of course—"

"Is that credible in your view?"

"I have written on Police Battalion 101 where the men came [back] routinely with their uniforms saturated in blood. When you shoot people at point blank range, you get bloody."

It is Browning's pioneering work on Battalion 101 of the German "Order" Police[4] that attracted such hostility from Daniel Goldhagen, whose book *Hitler's Willing Executioners* is in part an extended polemic against Browning's view that a complex interplay of peer pressure, careerism, and socialized conformity were to blame for the fact that so many ordinary Germans participated willingly in mass murder. In his book, and in an attack in the *New Republic* accusing Browning of fabricating his evidence "out of thin air," Goldhagen advances instead a monocausal theory of German "eliminationist anti-Semitism."

With regard to "the crucial motivational element which moved the German men and women . . . to devote their bodies, souls and ingenuity to the enterprise," writes Goldhagen, "for the vast majority of perpetrators, a monocausal explanation does suffice."[5] What is this explanation? The belief, supposedly shared by all Germans, "that Jewish influence, by nature destructive, must be eliminated irrevocably from society."[6]

There are so many flaws in Goldhagen's account it is difficult to know where to begin. His simple-minded theory of the cultural transmission of anti-Semitism (a kind of dumbed-down version of Chomsky's account of how we learn grammar)? His promotion of an "explanation" that accounts neither for those Germans who never hated Jews, nor for the eagerness of many Lithuanians, Latvians, Romanians, and others reared outside the eliminationist umbrella of German culture to participate in the genocide? A supposedly unique eliminationist ideology that (substituting Arabs for Jews) applies to Meir Kahane's *Kach* party and others on the far right of Zionism as readily as it does to the Nazis? His pornographic reveries about the sex lives of camp guards? Or his assertion that "contrary to both scholarly and popular treatments of the Holocaust, gassing was really epiphenomenal to the Germans' slaughter of Jews. It was a more convenient means, but not an essential development."[7] David Irving could hardly have put it better himself.

As Raul Hilberg points out, in place of complexity, "Goldhagen has left us with the image of a medieval-like incubus, a demon latent in the German mind . . . waiting for the opportunity to strike out."[8] Irving's gloss on Goldhagen is his view that if Jews provoke this demon, they have only them-selves to blame.

Browning's very presence on the roster of Lipstadt's wit-nesses is itself testimony to the wide range of views within the bounds of legitimate scholarly debate on the Holocaust. As is the presence of Peter Longerich, who testifies later in the trial, and who disagrees sharply with Browning's stress on a sudden change at the time of Operation Barbarossa, putting the deci-sion for genocide back to the fall of 1939. These men's work is a rebuke to any reductionist explanation of the Holocaust; their prominence in the defense's case is a refutation of those who accuse Lipstadt, or her lawyers, of enforcing a rigid or parochially Jewish orthodoxy of interpretation.

Browning's easy American manners make Irving's slightly sheepish effort to discredit him for accepting a commission by Yad Vashem look ridiculous. "I have contracted to write a book for them and that has not been completed," says Browning cheerfully.

"They paid you $35,000?" asks Irving.

"No, they have paid me, I believe, $27,000."

"Yes. Yad Vashem is an institution of the State of Israel, is it not?" asks Irving.

"Yes."

"So you are, in that respect, a paid agent I suppose of the State of Israel—using the word 'agent' in its purely legal sense?"

"If that was the case," Browning replies, "then since I had been at the [US] Holocaust Museum, I would also have been an agent of the American government, and since I have received scholarships in Germany, I would be an agent of the German government, so I must be a very duplicitous fellow to be able to follow these regimes."

While Irving is unable to damage Browning, it is far from clear how much damage Browning has done to Irving. On all their areas of disagreement the judge might well trust Browning's greater expertise. Irving agrees with Browning that while all historians make mistakes, it would be suspicious if the pattern of mistakes all went in the same direction. "You mean . . . like a waiter who always gives the wrong change in his own favor?" says Irving helpfully, articulating a standard he will have cause to regret. But all this collegial goodwill also sends a message: if Irving's views on the Holocaust are acceptable in the Senior Common Room, then even if he is a bigot that doesn't make him a Holocaust denier.

> The most powerful weapon which can be used to destroy false evidence is the technique of massive confrontation. This technique, at its best, may be compared to a creeping artillery barrage, driving back the enemy foot by foot. For this purpose it is essential to have ammunition, consisting of damaging facts and documents which cannot be denied. The ammunition should not be fired all at once, but by degrees.
>
> John Munkman, *The Technique of Advocacy* (1991)

It was Chekhov who famously said that if you put a pistol on the table in the first act, one of the characters must pick it up and fire it by the end of the play. On Day 18—in trial terms at about the beginning of Act IV—David Irving walks into the courtroom with a desktop calculator, an old tan model with rubber feet and a little roll of paper tape, and puts it on the desk in front of him. Given Irving's enthusiasm for back-of-the-envelope figuring—he's already done crematorium capacity, coke consumption, and gas-van through-put—it is hard to imagine what calculation he deems so important as to require mechanical precision.

When Richard Evans takes the stand the bonhomie of the previous few days disappears almost immediately. A short, squat man with beetle brows and an expression of faint disgust, Evans is not an ingratiating witness. Irving first asks him about his political views.

"I am a member of the Labour Party," he replies. "I do not suppose that means that one is left wing these days."

Irving also asks Evans, who has taught courses on the Third Reich, if he ever thought of putting *Hitler's War* on the reading list.

"Not really," says Evans. "I think it is more concerned with military history than anything else." Though this slight may be unintentional, Evans is a man spoiling for a fight. His opening comes in just a few moments.

"Professor Evans," says Irving, "you expressed the opinion in your report that my diaries may have been written for some ulterior motive."

"Could you point to the page in my report where I say that, please?" Evans's report is over 700 pages long.

"That sounded to me as though it was a rehearsed remark," says Irving, who may be right. "Is it true that it is your opinion that I may have written the diaries for some reason other than one would normally write a diary? What are your suspicions about why I wrote that?"

"Would you like to point me to the page where I—you see, I have a problem, Mr. Irving, which is that, having been through your work, I cannot really accept your version of any document, including passages in my own report, without actually having it in front of me, so I think this may be a problem for us." And with that, the hostilities commence.

Since he was first approached by Anthony Julius in the fall of 1997 Evans and his young assistants have had access to videotapes and audiocassettes of Irving's speeches, tens of thousands of pages of documents, his complete private diaries, thousands of letters, and a great deal of other material. Though he began his research with Irving's "chain of documents"—the material Irving cites to support his claim that Adolf Hitler was "probably the biggest friend the Jews had in the Third Reich"—Evans looked at the totality of Irving's career, from the Dresden book to the Goebbels biography. What he found shocked him deeply:

> Penetrating beneath the confident surface of his prose quickly revealed a mass of distortion and manipulation . . . so tangled that detailing it sometimes took up many more words than . . . Irving's original account. Unpicking the eleven-page narrative of the anti-Jewish pogrom of the so-called *Reichskristallnacht* in Irving's book *Goebbels: Mastermind of the Third Reich* and tracing back every part of it to the documentation on which it purports to rest takes up over seventy pages of the present report. A similar knotted web of distortions, suppressions and manipulations became evident in every single instance which we examined.
>
> I was not prepared for the sheer depths of duplicity which I encountered in Irving's treatment of the historical sources, nor for the way in which this dishonesty permeated his entire written and spoken output. It is as all-pervasive in his early work as it is in his later publications. . . . It is clear . . . that Irving's claim to have a very good and thorough knowledge of the evidence on the basis of which the history of Nazi Germany has to be written is completely justified. His numerous mistakes and egregious errors are not, therefore,

due to mere ignorance or sloppiness; on the contrary, it is obvious that they are calculated and deliberate. That is precisely why they are so shocking.

If Evans's verdict on Irving's methods is unequivocal, he is equally hard on Irving's defenders in journalism and the academy: "Irving has relied in the past, and continues to rely in the present, on the fact that his readers and listeners, reviewers and interviewers lack either the time, or the expertise, to probe deeply enough into the sources he uses for his work to uncover the distortions, suppressions and manipulations to which he has subjected them."

Evans's very recalcitrance on the stand underlines the gravity of his findings. A pedant's pedant, there is not an ounce of banter in the man. And however apparently obstructionist he may seem, Evans's obvious unwillingness to take anything Irving says on faith, no matter how innocuous, serves to reinforce the scathing conclusion of his report: that Irving is simply not a man who can be trusted.

"In your expert report," says Irving, "you said that I was obliged to turn over my diaries to the defense. What did you mean by that?"

"Could you point to me the page where I say that?"

"Oh, dear!"

Even the judge seems exasperated. "Well, do we really need to go to that?" he appeals to Evans. "I expect you probably did say that."

"Well, I really, my Lord, would ask I be pointed to where I say that."

"All right," says Gray resignedly, "if you really want it?"

"I am afraid I do, yes."

Although his cantankerous attitude risks alienating the judge, it also shows Evans has understood (or been told) the most important lesson a witness can learn: You are not there to be agreeable. Irving's chances depend on his rolling back the juggernaut Evans has aimed at his reputation. Evans's job on the stand is to make him sweat for every inch.

So when Irving turns on his calculator, he gets no help from Evans. "You have had all these diaries which go very clearly to my state of mind, my private state of mind, and you have found at the end of this enormous mountainous task: one ditty?"

"That is not my report."

"To prove that I am racist?"

"I am sorry, that is not quoted in my report." Evans is right. The now infamous ditty is quoted only by Brian Levin, a former New York City Police Officer who teaches at Stockton College in Pomona, New Jersey, where he is Director of the Center on Hate and Extremism. Levin isn't coming to London, so Gray suggests Irving ask Evans if, having read the diaries himself, he finds the poem unrepresentative.

"It was 19 words out of 30 million," says Irving.

"It is not quoted in my report, Mr. Irving. I am here to answer questions on my report. You may ask other witnesses on their reports."

"Do you know what percentage of me is therefore racist?" says Irving, hellbent on firing up his calculator with or without Evans's co-operation. Irving squints down at the keys through half-glasses perched on the end of his nose. "Point 00016 percent of me is racist," he says.

"Is that a question?" says Evans.

"Which means," Irving announces triumphantly, "that 99.9984 percent of me is not, according to the diaries."

Evans is supposed to testify for three and a half days. For the first two of those days the central allegation of his report—that Irving repeatedly, consciously, and wittingly distorted or misrepresented the sources he used in writing his books—barely comes up. Instead Irving hands around photos of the "colored people" he has employed on his staff over the years.

"Would you accept from me that they were all my personal

assistants over the years concerned, and that they received a proper salary from me?"

"Have you got documentary proof of that?" says Evans.

"Yes."

"Could I have a look at it, please?"

"Well, let us take it as read," says an exasperated Mr. Justice Gray, "that these ladies were all employed by Mr. Irving."

Irving asks Evans about the affidavit that got him expelled from Canada. Evans protests: "I mean, I do find it very difficult to answer questions on other people's reports." And again, the judge intervenes.

"Mr. Irving is representing himself. I am, therefore, giving him what I hope is an appropriate but quite a wide degree of latitude. He is accused of various things, like racism and anti-Semitism. He has been cross-examined vigorously on that topic. The Defendants had experts who produced great long reports, as you know, dealing with those topics and the Defendants have decided not to call them.

"Mr. Irving is, therefore," Gray continues, "in the position of being the subject of the criticisms that they make of him, albeit no longer part of the Defendants' formal case, and he wishes to put one or two points to you as being somebody who is there to be shot at, as it were. I have decided that it is proper that he should do so."

Given leave to fire at will, Irving engages Evans in a war of attrition over the initial sections of his report, where Evans summarizes Irving's reputation and treatment by other historians. With one exception, all of Irving's questions aim at minor points. Indeed, he seems to be trying to turn Evans's pedantry—his reluctance to let the smallest error pass without comment—against him. If he can make the court choke on minutiae, and then convince the judge that all of Evans's criticisms are equally petty—and some of them mistaken—Irving may just manage to deflect the heavy artillery in Evans's report.

More a siege than an attack, Irving's strategy of massive resistance quickly empties out the press section. Yet the stakes couldn't be higher. Five weeks into the trial Irving is still standing. Van Pelt and Browning have come and gone, and though the two men offered accounts of the Holocaust that were both more coherent and more plausible than Irving's version, neither delivered a knockout blow to Irving's credibility. Van Pelt may have persuaded the judge that Irving's views were mistaken, but, at least in the witness box, he hadn't quite managed to show they were perverse or dishonestly maintained. Everything now hinges on Evans.

Though excruciating to sit through, Irving's strategy appears to be paying off. When Rampton rises to protest— "We have done 45 pages in a day and a half. At that rate Professor Evans will be in the box for another three weeks!"—the judge verbally slaps him down.

"The difficulty, Mr. Rampton, if I may explain, is that Professor Evans has made reference to these other historians and their views. That does rather open up cross-examination."

Rampton persists: "It does seem to me that this is a rather futile game of ping pong that is going on at the moment, and far better to get on to the detailed criticisms."

"In that case," says Irving, "it would have been well if Professor Evans had not written the initial 100 pages in his report."

"I think I said that myself," Gray pronounces, "and I do rather take that view. He did. You know my view of it."

The defense does get one lucky break. Early on, Irving asks Evans if he was "shown at any time any law report that had been produced by Penguin books in this country, any libel reading [or] report on [Lipstadt's] book." When Evans, quite truthfully, answers "No," Irving drops the matter. He never asks—and Evans never volunteers—any information about the book's American libel reading. If he had, and if Evans had seen the American publisher's report, the resulting disclosure of the inevitable list of cautious lawyer's reservations could have seriously embarrassed the defense.

Irving also makes one major tactical mistake. The judge may have thrown the first 100 pages of Evans out the window. But the 600-plus pages that remain are a catalogue of misrepresentation, mistranslation, misleading phrasing, and imperfectly varnished deceit. Persuading Mr. Justice Gray to disregard the balance of Evans's report—the heart of the defense case—will take every ounce of credibility and evident reasonableness Irving can muster. Yet when, at the very end of Evans's second day, Gray refers to Irving's position on the use of gas to kill Jews as having "evolved" in the course of the trial, Irving demurs: "My recollection of the matter is that in order to speed the trial along we have streamlined a lot of the arguments and concentrated on certain institutions and centers, and left it like that."

The first problem with this formulation is that it isn't true. Irving had indeed conceded ground during cross-examination. The second problem is that Irving's attempt to resile or step back from his concessions looks slippery and casuistic precisely when he needs to appear ingenuous and reliable. Whether motivated by his own vanity or the need to keep his revisionist backers—who may hold to their credo more fiercely than he does—on board, Irving's attempt to save face will prove costly.

On Tuesday, Evans returns to the witness box, and though the pace of Irving's cross-examination has, if anything, slowed down, an electric current of loathing now arcs and crackles between the two men. An eternity ago—the previous Thursday—Irving had asked "You don't like me, do you?" and received a laconic "I have no personal feelings about you at all."

To a casual observer, the two antagonists have much in common. Evans grew up in Theydon Bois, three stops into London on the Central Line from Ongar, Irving's childhood home. He, too, had been a scholarship boy, first at the local grammar school, then at Jesus College, Oxford. Both men had achieved success at least in part by simply working harder than anyone else around them; Evans was every bit as much of a "documents hound" as his adversary. And of course they had both been drawn to Germany at a time when the country was profoundly unfashionable, both within the academy and in Britain generally.

Look closer, however, and you see two lives whose trajectories point in opposite directions. Evans's father, a clerk, and his mother, a schoolteacher, were both Welsh-speaking. And though his parents trekked to a Methodist chapel in the East End every Sunday, they raised their son to speak English as his native tongue. Evans is not a particularly modest man—his letterhead proclaims his fellowship in the British Academy, and he clearly enjoys his status as a member of the country's intellectual establishment—yet for all his laurels he seems ill at ease, retaining the coiled tension and "chippy" truculence characteristic of the British outsider. Irving's nostalgic yearning for Britain's past glory finds no echo in Evans.

As for Irving, his contempt for Evans combines the traditional scorn of the déclassé for the rising man with his self-definition as a "shirtsleeves historian" who can beat the academics at their own game. Plus of course the Englishman's boundless condescension toward the inhabitants of the country's Celtic fringe. In his diary, Irving refers to Evans as "that horrid little Welshman."[9] At the trial he confines himself to the observation that "the Welsh are famous for their loquacity—and I hope that this will not be taken by Mr. Rampton as yet another example of my racist predilections when I say that—but your answers sometimes do tend to run overboard." At one point, when Evans asks to see a document whose translation is in dispute, Irving walks up to the witness box, turns away from Evans so that he is neither facing him nor looking at him, picks up a loose-leaf binder from beside Evans's chair, drops it in front of Evans and says "The original German is here."

Personalities aside the two men have every reason to be wary of one another. In his report, Evans lays out the roadmap for the defense case. Though he is not a specialist in either the Holocaust or the Second World War, Evans devotes nearly a hundred pages to a consideration of what "Holocaust denial" might mean and whether Irving's writings and speeches meet that definition. The meat of his report, though, and the pillars of the defense case against Irving, are two sets of case studies. The first examines the nine links in Irving's "chain of documents." The second set, which takes up over 200 pages of the report, looks at Irving's use of evidence at three different stages of his career: his first book on the firebombing of Dresden, his treatment of the testimony of Hitler's adjutants in his book *Hitler's War*, and the explanation Irving gives for Nazi anti-Semitism, taken mostly from his Goebbels biography. In every single case Evans finds the historical equivalent of fraud.

The Destruction of Dresden launched Irving's career; first published in 1963, it is still probably the most widely read of his books, and certainly the most widely admired. Yet Evans reveals that Irving (1) fabricated a strafing attack on German civilians and refugees by British and American pilots, rearranging dates and misattributing testimony to bolster his account, (2) knowingly took an account of a bombing run on Prague and pretended the events happened over Dresden, (3) derived his own initial estimate of 135,000 dead from the testimony of a lone source who supplied no documentary evidence of any kind to back up his figure, (4) raised the count to 202,040 on the basis of a typed copy of a document which later turned out to be a forgery, (5) refused to modify the figure even when the man who supplied the document wrote Irving to complain that he had been wrongly identified as Dresden's Deputy Chief Medical Officer when he was merely a urologist at the local hospital and "only heard of the numbers third-hand," (6) suppressed internal evidence suggesting the document was a fake, and (7) also suppressed testimony—a letter to Irving—from a man whose job had been to tally the dead, and who put the number at just over 30,000, (8) grudgingly acknowledged the discovery of an official "Final Report" that estimated the death toll at 25,000, but later discounted it, and finally (9) ignored the discovery of the genuine document whose forged copy was referred to in (4) above. The authentic total was 20,204—the forgers had simply added an extra zero!

Evans's dissection of *The Destruction of Dresden* runs to over sixty pages; his analysis of the way Irving "uncritically accepts the testimony of members of Hitler's entourage when it is suitable to his arguments, but ignores it, suppresses it, manipulates it, or attempts to discredit it when it is not" goes on for more than a hundred pages. Neither gets more than a glancing mention at the trial.

What does get discussed—at almost unendurable length—is a passing remark that Evans made casting aspersions on the 1938 German plebiscite in which Hitler received 99.8 percent of the vote. Irving, bizarrely, seeks to defend the fairness of the vote, asking Evans if he had any "proof" that voters were intimidated. This is too much for Mr. Justice Gray: "Mr. Irving, will you listen to me for a moment, because I think we probably have spent long enough on the 99.8 percent. There is a danger I think, and this is designed to help you, that we are missing the wood for the trees."

"My method, my Lord," Irving replies, ". . . has been to graze through this passage and come across these occasionally indigestible rocks where he picks on something where I know I am right and where your Lordship probably does not appreciate that I am right."

"If that is what you are planning to do for the next 550 pages of this report," Gray warns, "I am not going to find that helpful."

*

Evans began his testimony standing in the witness box, hands thrust deep in his pockets. By the fourth day he appears slumped over in his seat. Mr. Justice Gray has been trying desperately, but without much success, to get Irving to engage with the substance of Evans's charges against him. He has, however, managed to elicit Irving's views on his associates at the Institute for Historical Review.

"So your case is—I want to be clear about this—you do regard the IHR as an organization consisting of cracked anti-Semites, is that your case?"

"I think that the correct thing to say there," Irving replies, "is that it consists of some elements which are cracked anti-Semites. I do not think I would wish to brand an entire organization. As far as I know, some of the officers of that organization, I would regard them as cracked anti-Semites."

In his report, Evans spends over 80 pages tracing the various misrepresentations and distortions in Irving's account of the *Kristallnacht* pogrom of November 9–10, 1938. Wearily, Gray tries one more time to get Irving to answer these criticisms: "This cross-examination does not appear to me to be grasping the nettle of the criticisms against you. You are finding tiny little points on which you hope, and sometimes succeed, in tripping up Professor Evans, but you are not grappling with what the criticisms are of your account of *Kristallnacht*. . . . There is no point in, if I may put it this way, pussyfooting around the borders of the issue because that is not going to help me, is it, really?"

But when he finally does begin to deal with *Kristallnacht* Irving immediately finds himself in the trap Rampton had set nearly a week before, when he'd asked Irving to translate Rudolf Hess's telegram. In *Goebbels: Mastermind of the Third Reich* Irving had written: "At 2:56 a.m. Rudolf Hess's staff also began cabling, telephoning and radioing instructions to Gauleiters and police authorities around the nation to halt the madness." Hess was Deputy Führer, and the document Irving cites in the book to support this passage is a cable indicating that the order comes from "the highest level," i.e. Hitler. The relevant passage is read out: "*Brandlegungen an jüdischen Geschäften oder dergleichen . . .*" which Evans translates as "acts of arson on Jewish shops and the like." Irving argues that the phrase *oder dergleichen*— "and the like"—modifies "acts of arson," and thus justifies his interpretation of the order as calling for a general halt to the violence. At which point Evans reminds Irving that when he had so helpfully translated this very document for the seemingly befuddled Rampton, he'd given the meaning as "acts of arson against Jewish shops or the like."

Since the Jewish shops "and the like" were often in German-owned buildings, far from being, as Irving would have it, an indication of Hitler's outrage at the pogrom, the order indicates at best a desire to limit collateral damage. Yet Irving, entirely unabashed, merely asks Evans if his interpretation is "based on your superior knowledge of the German language?"

"I am not claiming my knowledge is superior to yours," Evans replies. "You also have a very good knowledge of the German language. That is why I say this is a shameless manipulation of the text. It is not due to mere ignorance."

"A historical fact," Evans writes in his book *In Defence of History*, "is something that happened in history and can be verified as such through the traces history has left behind." As rough-and-ready definitions go this is not bad, but as a guide to conduct it begs all kinds of questions. Who decides whether the thing "happened" in the first place? What are the procedures for verifying these facts and who sets them? How do we select our facts? What do we do when the "traces" admit more than one explanation? Can there be events that happen outside of history?

The philosopher Hayden White thought there could. White distinguished between "events"—things that happened in the past—and "facts"—things made by historians or found in a document or a record. As a self-styled defender of "objectivity in history" Evans has limited sympathy for White, and quotes with disapproval his claim that "when it comes to the historical record, there are no grounds to be found in the record itself for preferring one way of construing its meaning rather than another. . . . We can tell equally plausible, alternative, and even contradictory stories . . . without violating rules of evidence or critical standards."[10]

Evans seems to read this as a conflation of history and fiction, and to be fair, a lot of White's acolytes have made precisely that argument. But if we amend the claim to "there are *often* no grounds," and we attend to White's insistence that historians still need to respect the rules of evidence—not to mention "critical standards"—we come pretty close to what it must mean to do history in an epistemologically reflective way.

The odd thing is that Evans's own books offer as good an example as any of what this might look like in practice. Indeed his focus on subjects like disease, capital punishment, and the history of feminism shows not only an acute awareness of "facts" that wouldn't even be visible to a "maps and chaps" historian, but a sophisticated understanding of the factors, cognitive and institutional as well as social, which turn one historian's background noise into fundamental data for someone else.

But like the proverbial man on the bicycle who falls off when he contemplates the underlying physics, Evans's theoretical pronouncements can be a bit wobbly. At one point in *In Defence of History* Evans argues that historians ultimately stand or fall "on the extent to which their historical arguments conform to the rules of evidence and the facts on which they rest. . . . In other words, they have to be objective." A few pages later he is far more modest: "Through the sources we use, and the methods with which we handle them, we can, if we are very careful and thorough, approach a reconstruction of past reality that may be partial and provisional, and certainly will not be objective, but is nevertheless true."[11]

Given the choice between Evans the scourge of postmodernism and Evans the "careful and thorough" advocate for the "partial and provisional" I prefer the latter. Unfortunately, at the trial we saw mostly the former. This might not have been entirely his fault.

Something about the Holocaust as a subject seems to rein in the critical impulse. Indeed Evans relates with satisfaction that Hayden White himself "retreated from his earlier position to defend himself against the accusation that his hyper-relativism gave countenance to . . . 'Holocaust denial.'"[12] Though the Holocaust can present a kind of boundary marker for theoretical speculation, its use as a chain on the limits of discussion strikes me as unfortunate. "Auschwitz was not a discourse," writes Evans. Fair enough. But that doesn't mean Auschwitz is outside discourse either. Anything which acts to remove the Holocaust from history, or to insulate it from the kind of speculation and skepticism that ought to be brought to bear on all historical narratives, only serves to bring it that much closer to the realm of myth.

The more tentative, more reflective, more theoretically heterodox Evans might have just as much reason to be outraged at the kind of fraud and deceit he found pervading Irving's work. And though there would be no professional obligation to disapprove of Irving's bigotry or its political expression, such a historian would be as free as anyone else to do so for his own reasons, whether as a matter of political engagement or from common humanity. And as an added bonus, he would be far less likely than the Richard Evans we saw in court to be flummoxed by a document which, shorn of its context, appeared to mean precisely what, given its context, it couldn't mean.

The "Schlegelberger Memorandum," as Irving called it, is a short typewritten text on unheaded paper. There is no date, no signature, no security classification and no clear indication of the recipient. The text, in full, states:

> Reich Minister Lammers informed me that the Führer had repeatedly explained to him that he wanted the solution of the Jewish Question put back until after the war. Accordingly the present discussions possess a merely theoretical value in the opinion of Reich Minister Lammers. But he will be in all cases concerned that fundamental decisions are not reached by a surprise intervention from another agency without his knowledge.

The document was first discovered—not by Irving, but by Eberhard Jaeckel—in a collection put together after 1945. Within this collection, it appears to also belong to a file of five documents gathered by the Allies in preparation for the Nuremberg prosecutions. A staff analysis by the US war-crimes prosecutor's office lists these five documents as coming from Ministry of Justice archives. Using these indications, in his report Evans outlines three possible interpretations: first, that the document might have been written in 1940 or 1941, in which case the reference to postponing the Final Solution might mean just what it says (but Hitler must have changed his mind). Alternatively, the document might be linked to one of the other four in the file, dating from November 1941 and dealing with the right of Jews to appear in courts of law, in which case it also means what it says (suggesting that Hitler decided on extermination rather late). Finally the memo might be linked with the three remaining documents in the prosecution file, all of which were concerned with the treatment to be accorded *Mischlinge*—"half-Jews"—or Jews in mixed marriages. This topic was the subject of a number of meetings in the spring of 1942, all of which were held under the rubric *Endlösung der Judenfrage*—Final Solution to the Jewish Question.

In his report, Evans opts for this last interpretation, which as he says is also the view of both Jaeckel and Irving himself. But in the witness box he stumbles, not so much over the interpretation itself as over the fact that the other two alternative explanations can't be eliminated. His discomfort is obviously increased by the circumstance that, having dated the memo to 1942, Evans must then argue *against* Irving's claim that when it says Hitler wanted to postpone the "solution of the Jewish Question" until after the war, that is exactly what it meant. Instead, says Evans, the words "solution of the Jewish Question" really refer to the *Mischlinge* question.

Evans points out that by the spring of 1942 the mass murder was well underway. He also points out that, by the criteria Irving used to attack some of the Auschwitz documents—that a document is not found in its original file, there is no clear indication of when it was sent or why, and it has no security classification—the "Schlegelberger Memorandum" should be a highly suspect document. Yet because it suits his purpose, Irving embraces it without reservation. Still, Evans doesn't propose to reject it either. Faced with exactly the kind of ambiguous situation suggested by Hayden White, and forced to make an interpretation at least partly on the basis of external factors, all Evans can say is "It is not entirely implausible whether he [Hitler] was giving this kind of meaning to the *Mischlinge*." As grounds for rejecting Irving's interpretation, "not entirely implausible" is not a very strong claim.

As Irving seems to understand, our very desire for certainty, for comprehensiveness—for historical neatness—operate to his advantage. "It is a terrible problem, is it not," he asks Evans later in the day, "that we are faced with this tantalizing plate of crumbs and morsels of what should have provided the final smoking gun proof, and nowhere the whole way through the archives do we find even one item that we do not have to interpret or read between the lines of, but we do have in the same chain of evidence documents which . . . quite clearly specifically show Hitler intervening in the other sense?"

This time Evans responds more robustly: "No, I do not accept that at all. It is because you want to interpret euphemisms as being literal and that is what the whole problem is. Every time there is a euphemism, Mr. Irving . . . or a camouflage piece of statement or language about Madagascar, you want to treat it as being the literal truth, because it serves your purpose of trying to exculpate Hitler. That is part of . . . the way in which you manipulate and distort the documents." Still, this has been Irving's best day since Evans was sworn in—and he knows it. Agreeing to the judge's suggestion to adjourn, Irving says: "I think we have broken through the barbed wire. We are right through the mine field now and we are out in the open desert and our guns are blazing."

With a weekend to recover, both sides return to court refreshed. Irving has a new haircut. Evans has regained his early form.

"Can you accept," Irving asks, "that Dr. Goebbels, in the year 1942, saw Adolf Hitler about ten times all told? I mean in private."

"I do find it difficult," Evans replies, "to accept anything you say, Mr. Irving, without looking at the documentary basis for it." Perhaps because this is his last day, he even shows flashes of dry wit. When Irving, referring to a comment by Hitler invoking the Madagascar option in May 1942, suggests "either Hitler is totally in the dark as to what is going on, or he is the biggest hypocrite there has been?" Evans responds: "I would go for the second of those two alternatives, Mr. Irving."

There are also signs that Mr. Justice Gray has gotten over his initial irritation at Evans. When Evans yet again refuses to answer a question without having the relevant document in front of him, Irving chides him: "I am not going to keep on falling for this game throughout the day, Professor Evans, because we have to get through a great deal today." This time, though, when Evans says his reluctance to take Irving's word for the content is "perfectly reasonable," the judge agrees.

"I am afraid it is," he tells Irving. "It does slow things down but I think, if you put a proposition to the witness, and he is not inclined to agree to it unless he sees the document you rely on, then he is entitled to ask you to look at it."

Later in the day, when Irving yet again asks Evans to comment on whether Hitler's remark proposing the Jews be sent "to Siberia" was merely a euphemism for murder, the judge cuts him off: "I know what you say about it, I know what Professor Evans says about it and, in the end, I have to decide what a sensible, objective historian would make of it."

When I first read the Evans report I sent Irving an e-mail saying I frankly found it a convincing "demolition" of his scholarship, but presumed he disagreed. A few weeks later he replied: "I have now begun reading the Evans report. I am eagerly looking forward to the cross-examination. If he ventures into the box, I shall tear him to shreds." This did not happen. Instead, Irving attempted to grind Evans down, using the historian's own abrasive personality and pedantic manner as his instruments. Yet here, too, he seems to have failed, and when Irving concludes his cross-examination at the agreed time Rampton has very little damage to repair. He does produce a Nazi court report in which the Hess telegram that trapped Irving is summarized as simply forbidding "arson on Jewish shops." With this slight twist of the knife, Evans is dismissed.

Germans

After so many weeks arguing about the meaning of German words, and German deeds, the court is finally about to hear from a real live German. Perhaps as a cautionary gesture, perhaps as a sort of amulet, on the morning Peter Longerich testifies for the defense David Irving sets down a leather-bound volume in the same spot to the right side of his table briefly occupied by his calculator. The title, embossed in gold gothic letters on the cover, is unmistakable: *Mein Kampf.*

Compactly built, with sloping shoulders and a mop of thick black hair falling over thick eyebrows, Longerich looks more like a Black Forest woodcutter than one of the most accomplished German historians of the Holocaust in the generation born after the war. His books—which include a history of the Nazi stormtroopers, a history of Hitler's Party Chancellery, and an analysis of the Nazi propaganda machine, as well as a comprehensive history of Nazi persecution of the Jews—are at present available only in German, and as Longerich walks to the witness box he is shadowed by a primly dressed woman who is sworn in at the same time. She is the translator. For the past six years Longerich has been on the faculty of London's Royal Holloway College, and although his syntax is occasionally Germanic to the point of incomprehension, the translator is rarely needed.

Indeed the first topic Irving raises in cross-examination is Longerich's "Glossary of some terms used by the NS regime in connection with the murder of European Jews." A short dictionary of Nazi euphemism, the document, prepared for the defense and offered in evidence after the trial began, contains entries such as:

> **Umsiedeln, aussiedeln** (noun: *Umsiedlung, Aussiedlung*), English: resettle. This term was first used from summer 1941 onwards in the occupied Soviet territories to refer to the systematic murder of the Jews. . . . On 5.2.43 the commander of the security police . . . in White Ruthenia issued a command ordering the "resettlement" (*Umsiedlung)* of the Jews living in the city of Sluzk. The order continued: "At the resettlement site are two pits. A group of ten leaders and men work at each pit, relieving each other every two hours."

Longerich quickly demonstrates that he is not only perfectly comfortable in English, but also perfectly at ease with the kind of hermeneutic considerations Evans found so troublesome. "What a historian has to do," he tells Irving, "[is] . . . look at each document and . . . look at the context and then try to reconstruct from the context what actually the meaning of this—of this passage might be."

"But is not the danger there," asks Irving, "that you then come back using *a priori* methods, that you extrapolate backwards from your knowledge and assign a meaning to the word rather than using the word to help you itself?"

"That is the problem with all interpretations," Longerich replies. "You have to come back. Of course, you cannot analyze the word completely, you know, outside. You have to look at the meaning of the word, but always in a historical context. I am not a linguist, so I prefer to actually, as I said, to look at the context."

And as Longerich observes, though the Nazis almost always

cloaked their murderous intent in various euphemisms, there were significant exceptions. In October 1943 Heinrich Himmler addressed a meeting of senior SS officers in Poznan, Poland:

I also want to talk to you quite frankly about a very grave matter, we can talk about it quite openly among ourselves, but nevertheless we can never speak of it publicly...just as we did not hesitate on the 30th June 1934* to do our duty as we were bidden and to stand comrades who had lapsed up against the wall and shoot them, so we have never spoken about it and will never speak of it.

It was a natural assumption, an assumption which, thank God, is inherent in us, that we never discussed it among ourselves and never spoke of it. Each of us shuddered, and yet each of us knew clearly that the next time he would do it again if it were an order, and if it were necessary. I am referring here to the evacuation of the Jews, the extermination of the Jewish people. This is one of the things that is easily said: "The Jewish people are going to be exterminated," that's what every Party member says, "sure, it's in our program, elimination of the Jews, extermination—it'll be done." And then they all come along, the eighty million worthy Germans, and each one has his one decent Jew. Of course, the others are all swine, but this one, he is a first-rate Jew. Of all those who talk like that, not one has seen it happen, not one has had to go through with it. Most of you men know what it is like to see a hundred corpses side by side, or five hundred, or a thousand.

We have been through this and, disregarding exceptional cases of human weakness, have remained decent. That is what has made us tough. This is a glorious page in our

* The Night of the Long Knives, when Hitler ordered the murder of the SA brownshirt leadership in order to consolidate his own grip on the Nazi movement.

history, one that has never been written and can never be written.[1]

"Of course," says Longerich, looking up from his reading, "the last sentence is a kind of challenge for historians, I think."

At the very beginning of the trial Irving produced a British decrypt of a coded German railway message concerning a train load of 944 Jews that left Berlin for Kovno in Lithuania in November 1941. The report noted that the train also carried 3,000 kilograms of bread, 2,700 kilograms of flour, 200 kilograms of peas, 300 kilograms of cornflakes, 18 bottles of soup spices, 47,000 *Reichsmark* in credit and various "appliances." When Rampton asked him, in cross-examination, what all this might mean, Irving's answer was succinct: "It shows that these trains were actually well provisioned." Irving offered the document as an explicit challenge both to "the image we have from the literature . . . of coal trucks and cattle trucks" and also to the defense experts, who he said ignored it "because of course it does not fit into the perception they are trying to create."

A lawyer would have left it at that. Instead, Irving now re-introduces the decrypt to illustrate what he thinks is an innocent use of the word *Evakuierung*—evacuation. With no more than his own mental agility to go on, Rampton had done his best to cast doubt on Irving's interpretation. But Longerich knows all about this particular evacuation, pointing out that the tools and provisions would have come from the Jewish community in Berlin, and can hardly be taken as evidence of Nazi benevolence. "Do you think," he asks Irving, "this is money from the Gestapo . . . to buy food for the Jews?"

What makes Longerich so sure? Because although Irving's document is silent on their fate, Longerich also knows that the Jews on this particular train "were all killed in Kovno" immediately upon arrival. The provisions furnished by the community to aid their resettlement, he now tells the court, would have been confiscated by the SS. This is clearly news to Irving, who utters a mumbled "Thank you for telling us. That is very interesting to know that" and then drops the subject as soon as he can.

Yet perhaps because—unlike Irving or Evans—the Holocaust is very much Longerich's patch, he seems far more tolerant of uncertainty. Irving asks him about a 1942 conversation in Hitler's "Table Talk"—a record of the Führer's mealtime utterances as preserved by his faithful adjutants*—where, with Goebbels present, Hitler still talks of sending the Jews to Siberia or Central Africa. As Longerich points out, the killings at Semlin, Chelmno, and Belzec have been underway for some time. "I have difficulties, I have to say, to find, you know, an easy answer to this document because, I mean, they are in the middle of mass extermination and Goebbels is quite aware of that, and they are still talking about the idea that they could force the Jews out of Europe. I find this really difficult to explain."

In an odd way, Longerich's modesty, his ready willingness to admit he can't always make sense of the evidence, seems to encourage Irving to come out of his defensive crouch. What we see is not only the biographer who regards Adolf Hitler as a familiar presence—at one point Irving asks Longerich if a particular document "is a very shaky kind of testimony, is it not, so far as Adolf's responsibility is concerned?"—but whose identification with his subject is far stronger than he seems to realize. Irving wants to use the *Mein Kampf* on his desk to support his claim that Hitler, though an anti-Semite, had no genocidal intentions toward the Jews when he wrote it. This particular *coup de théâtre* is foiled when Longerich declines to disagree, again saying the evidence is inconclusive. Instead Irving wonders "whether he [Hitler] was a cynical anti-Semite and used it in the same way that an Enoch Powell might use

* Hugh Trevor-Roper edited the English edition, which was published in 1953.

immigration—as a means of establishing a political position—
or whether he was profoundly viscerally anti-Semitic."

"Which option are you going for?" asks Mr. Justice Gray.

"I am going for the cynical version, my Lord."

"So he was not really an anti-Semite, it was just a political
gambit?"

"He was when it served his purpose. He was a beer-table
anti-Semite. He used it to whip up support, but in private—
and this is what counts—his state of mind was slightly
different."

Irving's assumption that cynical anti-Semites are somehow
less offensive, or less dangerous, than sincere bigots is debat-
able. While a cynical anti-Semite might abandon his prejudice
once it has served its purpose, he might also cleave to it long
after the visceral anti-Semite's hatred has burned out, so long as
there is some advantage in doing so. But what really makes
this exchange remarkable is the unconscious self-revelation
that comes from the way Irving framed his question: as a man
clearly fascinated by the political vistas opened by the resort to
prejudice.

Though Longerich's testimony marks the climax of the
trial's historical phase—Evans was the climax of the historiography section—as a foreigner and a non-celebrity his
appearance has been largely ignored by the press. One morning
Greville Janner, the Jewish MP who spearheaded the campaign
to get the statute of limitations lifted for war crimes—and who
has called for laws criminalizing Holocaust denial in Britain—
sits unnoticed behind Anthony Julius. The next day half the
press seats are filled by French Explorer Scouts—boys and
girls in blue uniform, with neckerchiefs, and patches that say
"*Union des Etudiants Juifs de France*." They are on the *March
des Vivants*—March of the Living—a pilgrimage organized by
various Zionist organizations that sends young people to Israel
by way of Auschwitz.

Ironically, many of these scouts also belong to Betar, the

youth wing of Revisionist Zionism, whose founder Vladimir Jabotinsky was an avowed admirer of Fascism (he preferred Mussolini to Hitler). Though they sit radiating both sectarian contempt and hormonal restlessness, few of them seem able to follow Longerich's testimony, which is perhaps just as well, especially when Irving asks him if the infamous "Commissar Order" calling for the elimination of "the Jewish Bolshevik intelligentsia" was motivated primarily by racism or ideology.

"Both," Longerich replies. "You cannot separate that. You cannot separate anti-Semitism from the anti-Communism. This is one thing." An acknowledgment which says nothing about any relationship between Jews and Communism, but which would nonetheless have distressed Jabotinsky as much as Lucy Dawidowicz or Daniel Goldhagen—and which probably doesn't make Lipstadt's backers in the Anti-Defamation League too happy, either.

Longerich's views are at wide variance with the kind of simple-minded demonology found in Dawidowicz and Goldhagen, and he is very much in the mainstream of Holocaust scholarship. His presence in court, like Christopher Browning's, seems calculated to reassure Mr. Justice Gray that there is nothing parochial about the case against Irving.

How much the judge is paying attention is another matter. Despite numerous exchanges on this topic, at the end of Longerich's testimony the judge interrupts:

"I am sorry to ask you this (and I think I have asked you before and I have forgotten the answer). The Hungarian Jews were not in the end handed over, were they?"

"They were handed," says Longerich. "In 1944 they were handed over."

"Is the evidence there," asks the judge, "that they were killed at Auschwitz, that they were gassed?"

"Yes, the evidence is there." Perhaps out of tact, Longerich says no more. But Rampton wants to make sure the judge remembers this time.

"It was called the Hungarian action," he says, "and 450,000 Hungarian Jews . . . were gassed at Auschwitz."

When Rampton re-examines Longerich, his voice bounces on certain words: "Can we compare for a moment what *Himmler* wrote in *that* letter about the very difficult order that the Führer had laid on his shoulders with what Mr. *Irving* relies on as evidence of the truth?" Partly he seems to be winding up to his closing argument, and briskly takes Longerich through some of the themes he stressed in his opening: the movement of Jews from east to west, the chronology of which death camps became operational when, the absurdity of Irving's claim that the deported Jews might have simply been resettled "in White Ruthenia."

But Rampton also seems to be trying to rouse the court—and himself—from the profound lethargy of a long trial. He has one more witness to call, one more leg to his case: Irving's political extremism. He's only going to go through this material once, and this time he needs to be sure everyone is paying attention. Whether by design or coincidence, he is immensely aided by a story in that morning's Israeli newspapers reporting that, in response to a request by Lipstadt's lawyers, the Israeli government is considering releasing Adolf Eichmann's prison notebooks, which have been locked away in the Israeli archives for over 30 years.

The prospect of a direct link to the most celebrated Holocaust trial in history—-the chance that, speaking from beyond the grave, Adolf Eichmann himself would provide the evidence that sends David Irving down to defeat—is a scenario as irresistible as it is unlikely. And since getting this particular *deus*—or *diabolus*—*ex machina* out of the machine takes several days (the notebooks were sent to the defense lawyers from Israel as an e-mail, and there is some difficulty opening the file) only on the very last day of the trial does it become clear that while of immense potential interest to historians, from the point of view of both claimant and defendants the Israeli material is completely irrelevant.

Once again the court is packed with reporters—who each afternoon, having sat through the day's testimony in vain hopes of an Eichmann scoop, instead file stories about Irving's connections with German extremists. Some of these stories make it into print—a circumstance which, even allowing for the high level of interest in the trial and the long-standing fondness of the press for "guilt-by-association" stories, is still probably attributable to the elusive Eichmann connection. Because if ever a man seemed destined to be overshadowed by an e-mail, Hajo Funke, a professor of political science at the Free University of Berlin and author of an expert report on Irving and "neo-National Socialism in Germany" is that man.

Dressed in a fashionably cut grey suit, grey shirt, and grey tie, Funke at first appears determined not to be outdone by Evans in the wariness of his replies, asking to see the text of the oath before he agrees to be sworn in. But as Funke begins his testimony, another basis for his caution emerges. Though he, too, declines the services of the translator, Funke's English is much more unpredictable—in his case the result of translating not just from another language, but from the peculiar dialect of German social science.

When the judge, trying very hard to follow Funke's rambling commentary, larded with compound nouns and with vast stretches between verbs, asks him "Can you explain what you mean by [Irving's] interactions or contacts?" Funke replies:

It is all sorts of interactions: to prepare things, to take sides, to be invited. So, for example, at the 3rd March of '90 David Irving was invited to the group. He especially had, I have to say, in Hamburg, the so-called nationalist, this is a bunch of little tiny groups. So he was invited to give one of David Irving's speeches there, and there were, of course, the Nationalists, so part of this neo-Nazi camp, in that region, that is to say in Hamburg, and, on the other hand, new invited East Germans around the new built other group like the *Deutsche* Alternative. So just to say the minimum that groups of the neo-Nazi camp around Hamburg and groups of the new organized groupings of East Germany came together to hear David Irving at the 3rd March of '90. This kind of interaction, preparing speeches, tours and the like. . . .

Fortunately for the defense, Funke comes prepared to show as well as tell the court what he means. The five videos that accompany his testimony show Irving speaking in a variety of settings. In Hagenau, a town in Alsace, he is shown telling the joke about the one-man gas chamber. The German-speaking crowd laughs appreciatively. At the same meeting the tape also shows Ernst Zündel referring to their opponents as a "*Judenpack*."

At an outdoor rally in the east German town of Halle, a trenchcoat-clad Irving is shown addressing a crowd of young skinheads. This particular tape has been the subject of vociferous objections by Irving, who was inadvertently given a copy of it when the defense returned his discovery material—and it is easy to see why. As the ranks of skinheads march in front of him stamping their Doc Martens and waving the red and black *Reichskriegsflagge*—Reich battle flag, emblem of German irredentism since the turn of the century, and a stand-in for the banned Nazi swastika—the image is every bit as eerily evocative as it was doubtless intended to be. Then, in response to a burst of German rhetoric from Irving, they begin chanting: *Sieg Heil! Sieg Heil! Sieg Heil!*

"I should never have started public speaking in Germany," Irving told me the summer before the trial. "It is very easy to rouse a rabble in German."

Funke's videos link Irving with, in Irving's phrase, "a rogue's gallery" of German right-wingers. Wilhelm Stäglich, author of *The Auschwitz Myth*, is seen in the audience at one speech; Thies Christopherson, author of *The Auschwitz Lie*, helped to organize the Hagenau rally.

Some of the connections seem tenuous. Otto Ernst Remer, who played a key role in crushing the July 1944 attempt to depose Hitler, was a leader in post-war attempts to revive the Nazi philosophy. Irving offered readers of his Action Reports a "magnificent souvenir color photo of Remer in full uniform," and wrote a warm eulogy after his death in 1997, but seems to have only met the man once, when he interviewed him for the Goebbels book.

Others, like his long-standing association with Gerhard Frey, leader of the right-wing (and virulently anti-foreigner) German People's Union (DVU), or his close collaboration with Gunter Deckert, of the German National Party (NPD), are more substantial. According to Funke, under Deckert the NPD, still a legal party in Germany, functioned as a front for various banned groups united by a hatred of asylum-seekers and migrant workers and a shared language of Holocaust denial. Irving himself used the example of "Gunter Deckert, who is admittedly a friend of mine," and currently in jail for Holocaust denial, to demonstrate Germany's supposed lack of intellectual freedom.

The aim of Funke's testimony is twofold: to show that Irving is not just a harmless crank who likes to sound off about the Jews, but a calculating political operator who sounds off about the Jews in front of groups who not only share his prejudices but may be inclined to act on them (if not against Jews, whose numbers in contemporary Germany are somewhat diminished, then against Turks or other foreigners). By demonstrating the role of Holocaust denial as both a shibboleth and a crucial element in the repackaging of Fascism, Funke is also supposed to flesh out the motive that unites Irving's personal prejudice with his perverse interpretation of history.

Or as Funke tells the judge: "By denying, by relativizing, by blaming the Jews as those who made it up or who did it or who let it do, so by all various kinds of rhetorics, agitations, to downplay this Nazi period, to restore, you know, the kind of proud of the extreme Aryan racist anti-Semitic nation."

This is not a particularly subtle point, yet once again Irving declines to meet it head on. He first argues that "non-violent extremism is not defamatory, if I can put it that way round. If I were to associate with somebody who held extremist views, this would not be in the least bit reprehensible." Though his language is confusing, Irving's argument isn't really about extremism. This is neither Barry Goldwater's famous "In defense of liberty, extremism is no vice,"—in other words that extremist views are often vindicated by history—nor an appeal to relativism, but a narrow legalistic argument: if calling someone an "extremist" isn't defamatory, then testimony about extremism should be inadmissible. In other words, he wants Funke thrown out.

Mr. Justice Gray disagrees. "I think it may be defamatory of somebody to say that he or she consorts or associates with what you might call extreme extremists," he says, perhaps in unconscious homage to Funke.

Irving's second front is to claim that the Halle video has been deceptively edited, and that though it couldn't be seen on the tape, when he realized the marchers were chanting *Sieg Heil!* he told them to stop. Irving walked the fine line between provocation and prudence for a long time in Germany (before he was officially banned from the country in 1993) and this claim may be true. But Irving would have an easier time convincing the judge that he not only voiced disapproval, but actually meant it, if he hadn't adopted the same pose of outraged innocence over the slogan of a 1990 conference in Munich: *Wahrheit Macht Frei* (The Truth Makes [or Sets] Free).

Does this phrase, Rampton asked Funke, "have any resonance with some language used during the Nazi period?"

Mr. Justice Gray answered for him: "I think we all know."

Indeed, one of the many true things "everybody knows" about the Holocaust is that the gates to Auschwitz were decorated with the phrase *Arbeit Macht Frei* (Work Makes [or Sets] Free). Yet in his cross-examination of Funke, Irving claims the Munich conference organizers—who scheduled Irving back-to-back with Wilhelm Stäglich, author of *The Auschwitz Myth*—were merely quoting from John 8:32, and that Auschwitz was the furthest thing from their minds. "It had nothing to do," he insists, "with whatever private obsessions Mr. Rampton may have with that phrase."

Rampton says nothing at the time, but when Irving returns to this theme the next day, Rampton is ready for him. "In Mr. Irving's diary for October 3rd 1989 when he was in West Berlin, he writes this: 'At 11 a.m., a well attended press conference at the Kampinski, around 20 writers, six or seven genuine journalists . . . closed with my new slogan *Wahrheit Macht Frei*. The lefty journalists got the allusions.'"

The good-humored reference to "lefty journalists"—the opposing team in some great game—is typical Irving. So, too, as we have seen, is a tendency to play fast and loose with historical evidence. But until this point in the trial, Irving has managed to avoid getting caught actually lying to the judge.

The timing is particularly unfortunate for Irving, since he seems to be arriving simultaneously at the end of the trial and at the end of Mr. Justice Gray's enormous forbearance. His patience already worn by Irving's foot-dragging with Evans, Gray has stopped dropping hints— "it is really the big picture you must tackle, not whether particular footnotes are accurate"—and bluntly asked Irving to state his case. Finally his patience snaps.

"Mr. Irving, I think you have been cross-examining for nearly a day now. I have to tell you that I am not much the wiser as to what your case is in regard to what this witness has said, namely that there are these individuals with whom you have a close association and they are all on the extreme right-wing fringe. I cannot let the cross-examination go on. I keep asking you to focus on what matters."

"On individuals," Irving suggests.

"And you are continuing to go through footnotes and trivial points. I think the point has come where, unless Mr. Rampton discourages me, I must say to you: 'You must at 2 o'clock put your case in relation to these individuals and the organizations so that I understand what it is,' because I do not think it is right for me to let the court's time be taken up with cross-examination which seems to me to be achieving virtually nothing." Rampton does not discourage him.

At 10:45 a.m. on Thursday, March 2—Day 29 of the trial—David Irving returns to the witness box for the last time. Having established Irving's unreliability as a historian, and his aggravated unreliability as a historian of the Holocaust, Rampton devotes his final cross-examination to establishing that the errors and distortions in Irving's books and speeches were deliberate. Rampton has suggested as much all through the trial, but proving it is far more difficult. He needs to show not just that Irving is capable of lying—most of us are—but that he does so habitually, without hesitation, almost as a reflex. *Wahrheit Macht Frei* is a start, but Rampton will need more than that.

He begins by playing a tape of Irving speaking in Milton, Ontario, telling an expanded version of the one-man gas-chamber story. "Where did the telephone box come from?" asks Rampton. "Where does that little anecdote come from? How many sources?"

"The phone ringing is an embellishment," Irving admits. "But the [gas chamber] disguised as a telephone box is in the eyewitness account."

How many eyewitnesses? "Certainly one," says Irving, who cannot produce it.

Rampton plays a bit more of the same tape:

Ridicule alone is not enough. You have got to be tasteless about it. You have to say things like more women died on the back seat of Senator Edward Kennedy's car at Chappaquiddick than died in the gas chambers of Auschwitz.

As the audience on the tape clap appreciatively, Irving addresses the judge: "The applause drowned the rest of the sentence, unfortunately, which is 'in the gas chambers of Auschwitz which are shown to the tourists.' I always say exactly the same thing."

"Oh, no you do not," says Rampton.

"Is it on the video?" asks the judge.

And so the video is rewound and replayed, and indeed, as Irving is forced to admit, "In that particular one I did not put in the rider" about the tourists.

"Frequently you have not," says Rampton. "Not only have you not put in the rider, you have added other gas chambers elsewhere: Treblinka, Belzec. . . . I have put the question already. You made a statement not more than a couple of minutes ago that you never make reference to the non-existence of gas chambers except in relation to what you call the fake gas chamber at Auschwitz 1. That statement was false, was it not?"

Irving reads from a transcript of one of his speeches: "'The dummies were still standing in Auschwitz . . . and probably in Majdanek, Treblinka and in the other so-called extermination camps.' I think the word 'probably' therefore has to be looked at and emphasized."

Entertaining as they are, Rampton's fireworks have so far been relatively small-caliber. But he begins to pick up the pace, quoting from Irving's response to a written interrogatory (the equivalent of sworn testimony) denying any association with the American white-supremacist group the National Alliance and specifically denying that he has ever spoken at an Alliance meeting. Rampton produces an invitation to an

Alliance meeting from Irving's discovery (the note is on Alliance letterhead), then reads out Irving's diary entry describing the same meeting.

"There is not the slightest reference either in that diary entry or in any other diary entry to the NA or the National Alliance," says Irving, ". . . which confirms what I said about having had no knowledge of them."

"I asked you to be patient," says Rampton, picking up the diary again. "Five days later: 'Drove all day to Tampa, phoned Key West, etc. etc. etc. Arrived at the Hotel Best Western at 4:00 p.m. Sinister gent with pony tail was the organizer. Turned out the meeting here is also organized by the National Alliance and National Vanguard Bookshop. Well attended.' Now, Mr. Irving, do you want to revise the answers you have just been giving me?"

Throughout the trial Mr. Justice Gray has maintained a perfect poker face and impassive demeanor. But when Rampton confronts Irving with his own diary, the judge looks at Irving dubiously, under hooded lids.

"What do you know about the British National Party, Mr. Irving?" Rampton continues.

"I know more about them than I know about the National Alliance."

"You speak to them, do you not?"

"No."

"Or you have done?"

"No."

There is nothing equivocal about Irving's answers. At least not until Rampton produces a letter, again from Irving's discovery, from one "Geoffrey D Brown. British National Party, Yorkshire region. 'Dear Mr. Irving, further to our telephone conversation today, I am writing to confirm that we would be very happy for you to come up to Leeds on Friday 14th September to address a special northern regional meeting.'"

"It is very similar to the functions in America," says Irving, "where somebody who is a local functionary of some political group is inviting me to come and address an umbrella body . . ."

The judge cuts him off: "Mr. Irving, come on, that letter is on the stationery of the British National Party!"

There is a brief interval of light relief, when Rampton asks Irving about the political beliefs of his printer, British National Party activist Tony Hancock.

"I think he is a right-winger," says Irving.

"What do you mean by a right-winger? Free market?"

"Somebody who is to the right-wing of me, shall I say. If I describe him as being right-wing, then he is right-wing."

But Irving's credibility with the judge is badly shredded, and when, in response to yet another of Rampton's little blasts, Irving claims his answer of "Yes," now shown to be false, was merely meant "to say, 'Yes, I hear what you are saying,' right? This should not be taken as being, 'Yes, I agree with what you are saying,' but, 'Yes, I hear what you are saying,'" Gray comments acidly: "I hope we are not going to treat all your answers in that light."

Like any good pyrotechnician, Rampton saves his best display for last. And for this trick, he'll need the co-operation of David Irving. The preparation is technical, revolving around Adolf Hitler's December 12, 1941 speech to the Nazi leadership. Goebbels quotes the speech in his diaries for that date: "The world war is there, the annihilation of Jewry must be the necessary consequence." Yet in his Goebbels biography, though Irving cites the speech, he leaves out Hitler's reference to the Jews. Why?

Earlier in the trial Irving claimed that when he'd gone to Moscow to read the Goebbels diaries for the *Sunday Times* he had a "shopping list" of specific topics, such as Pearl Harbor or the invasion of Russia, and that this speech wasn't on the list. First Rampton shows that Irving's notes indicate he did read the entry for December 12. Irving replies that he only read part of that day's entry, stopping four lines down on the glass plate that held the remainder of the day's entry. So Rampton produces a photocopy of the plate in question, from the Russian State Archives, showing that Irving quoted from material much further down on the glass plate—well into Goebbels's account of the speech.

Irving admits he appears to have read on further than he'd thought, but repeats his claim to have stopped well before the reference to the Jews.

Rampton raises his voice. "Are you seriously telling me that you resisted the temptation to read this important speech of the Führer from end to end, start to finish?"

Irving says he just didn't have time. Besides, how was he to know there was anything special about this occasion?

Rampton responds: "Why was Hitler speaking to the Gauleiters [the Nazi Party leadership] on 12th December? The reason is that he declared war on the United States the day before. . . . This is the date, is it not, Mr. Irving, on which in effect Hitler, having declared war on the United States and thus having brought about a world war, declares war on the Jews?"

"No."

"He says to them, does he not: 'Right, mates, you brought about the first war, I told you that you would be for it if there was a second war. Now this is it. Face the music.'"

"Actually," says Irving, "the declaration of war was the next day."

"What, the 13th?" asks Rampton.

"That is right. Hitler declared war on the United States on 13th December, and the speech is on the 12th." And with that, Richard Rampton stops dead in his tracks.

"Just pause a moment," says Mr. Justice Gray superfluously. The courtroom has suddenly become so quiet you can almost hear the whispers of the two graduate students, who flip feverishly through Irving's books. Rampton, Heather Rogers, and

Irving himself all do the same. Some of the trial regulars turn to the last row of spectators, where on most days Sir Martin Gilbert sits in the middle seat, but Gilbert, biographer of Winston Churchill and author of numerous books on the Holocaust and the Second World War, is not in court today.

"I think it is a 'Who wants to be a millionaire?' question, is it not?" says Irving dismissively.

Finally Rampton speaks. "This is Professor Irving writing his Goering book . . . page 337: 'It is probably only now that he'—that is probably Hitler, might be Goering—'learned that the Japanese had attacked Pearl Harbor. At the Reichstag session on December 11th Hitler declared war on the United States.'"

"I found it at the same time, yes," says Irving.

"Well, who is right," asks Rampton, "you or you?"

"Luckily I haven't lost a million quid," Irving says in a voice too quiet for the transcriber to hear.

To which Rampton, in a louder stage whisper, replies: "Yet."

The next day is very brief, taken up mostly with scheduling. Both sides will be given a week to write their final arguments. "I shall reserve to myself the right to pick out major points," Irving says, noting that since "the onus is on the defense to justify" they will have to address every item on the lengthy list of points at issue handed out by the judge.

Irving prefaces his remarks "by expressing words of my appreciation for the work put in by the defending firms of solicitors. They have had an extra burden put upon them by the fact that I am a litigant in person and I deeply appreciate their efficiency in this matter. I appreciate their help in this matter." Despite this flourish of manners, Irving launches almost immediately into a furious attack on Mishcon de Reya's handling of the Halle video. This last-ditch effort fails, but not before prompting Anthony Julius to rise to his feet for the first and only time in the course of the trial to defend his firm's conduct.

Normally in a case tried by a judge alone both sides would

submit written statements to the judge; in this case it is agreed that in addition each side will be allotted court time to make "statements for public consumption" as well. And though the only jury he will be addressing will be the jury of public opinion, as the claimant, David Irving will have the last word.

Closing arguments

When Richard Rampton rises to begin his closing argument we have finally reached the last act in the case of *David Irving* v. *Penguin Books Ltd. and Deborah Lipstadt.* By now the court has heard from nine witnesses and sat through one and a half million words of testimony. The judge has read thousands of pages of expert reports, and tens of thousands of pages of documentation. All through the trial he has been making daily notes toward his judgment, and may well have formed a view of the evidence, yet at this moment the judge's mind should still be open to argument from either side.

Today, as usual, Charles Gray sits at the dais with pursed lips and a slightly abstracted expression. The judge has given very little indication of how he sees the case. But as those of us who were present the previous morning know, at the moment Gray's imperturbable exterior masks considerable irritation. The judge wanted both sides to exchange their written statements, then to spend a day in court answering his questions and explicitly addressing the points made by their opponents. That session would be open to the public, but intended primarily for his—Gray's—benefit. This final session was supposed to be reserved for "public statements."

As an exercise in forensics Gray's plan has much to

recommend it—and if it meant the final day's speeches are anti-climactic, so much the better. But as the date for exchanging statements approached, neither side was ready. Gray himself didn't receive the material until just before yesterday's session, which led the judge to pointedly wonder, "why we have all turned up."

Though both sides attempted to assuage the judge, neither seemed eager to blunt the impact of this final performance. And so yesterday, after a short display of judicial pique—"I had expected to get a little bit of assistance really from both sides. But if you are both saying that you stand by what you submitted to me in writing and you make your public statements tomorrow, which I do not think will help me particularly in the task that I have, well, so be it"—court was adjourned.

Now the court is indeed jammed, with reporters standing in the aisles and behind every pillar. Some sit cross-legged on the floor. The line of spectators waiting to get in overflows the vestibule and stretches down one long corridor, around a corner, and down most of the next corridor as well.

As he has for the past several days, Irving gives the press copies of his documents—this time his 104-page closing statement. Today, however, the defense team does the same, distributing copies of Rampton's 24-page text throughout the courtroom. There is a brief scramble when it becomes clear there are far fewer copies of the defense's written statement— many hundreds of pages long and held in a thick ring binder—but the promise of extra copies after the lunch break, and the urgent pleas of the court usher, sends the reporters back to their seats. The "Court Full" signs once again on the doors, Rampton gets to his feet.

In a trial, nine weeks is an eternity. This is Rampton's last chance to pick up points made by his witnesses, or in his cross-examination of Irving, and fashion them into a coherent narrative. It is also his last chance to plug holes in his case. He begins by reminding the court how this action came about, giving a brief publication history of *Denying the Holocaust* followed by an even briefer summary of what the book said about David Irving.

"My Lord," Rampton continues, "those were undoubtedly serious charges and, had they been untrue, Mr. Irving would clearly have been entitled to a large sum of money and an order of the court preventing the Defendants from repeating their accusations. But, as it turns out on the evidence before this court, the accusations are true, in every significant respect."

Brandishing his written submission, Rampton says that the defense experts found "in relation to Hitler alone, as many as 25 major falsifications of history, as well as numerous subsidiary inventions, suppressions, manipulations and mistranslations employed to support the major falsifications. If those relating to Auschwitz, Dresden and other matters are added in, the number goes well over 30."

Turning to the question of Irving's treatment of the Holocaust, Rampton offers a history lesson: "The Holocaust—that is the systematic mass murder of millions of Jews, Gypsies and others—took place in stages. The first stage, beginning in the autumn of 1941, after Hitler's invasion of the Soviet Union, consisted of mass shootings carried out by specially formed SS groups and their local allies. This continued through into 1942 and resulted in the deaths of up to 1.5 million Jews living in Russia and the Baltic states.

"The second stage, which began in December 1941 and continued through into 1943 or later, consisted of the gassing of the Jews of the Warthegau and Poland. This resulted in the deaths of probably as many as 2.6 million Jews (300,000 in the Warthegau and 2.3 million in Poland).

"The third stage, beginning with mass deportations to the East in the autumn of 1941, culminated in the deaths by gassing, mostly at Auschwitz, of Jews from Central, Western and Southern Europe. This stage lasted until late 1944. Reliable recent estimates of the numbers gassed at

Auschwitz–Birkenau give a figure of about 1.12 million. Thus the total achievement of this horrendous exercise in systematic mass murder was probably somewhere between five and six million innocent lives."

And so to Auschwitz. Once again Rampton is juggling, telling the story of what happened in the war while both pointing out the gaps in Irving's account and tying up any loose ends in the defense case. It is an exhausting performance and for the most part an impressive one, touching down briefly on matters like the gas-tight doors with their glass spyholes—"Why, it was asked of Mr. Irving, should these be required for the observation of the gassing of lice-infested 'objects' and corpses?"—and the matchup between the Olère drawings and the aerial photos. He even addresses the infamous "no holes, no Holocaust" argument.

"In the first place, Professor van Pelt, who has subjected the remains of the roof of *Leichenkeller 1* at Crematorium 2 to careful examination (which Mr. Irving has never done), told the court that the remains are so fragmentary that they do not allow any firm conclusions to be drawn as to the existence or non-existence of the holes. Second, if, as Mr. Irving accepts, *Leichenkeller 1* was a gas chamber (for whatever purpose) it would always have needed apertures for inserting the Zyklon-B, since it never had any windows and only one gas-tight door. Third, even if Mr. Irving were right that it was used for gassing objects and corpses, the concentration of hydrogen cyanide required for this would have been comparatively high, with the consequence that the need for tight fitting apertures which could be opened and closed quickly and easily, would, for the protection of those throwing in the pellets, have been all the greater."

But there is also something perfunctory about the whole speech, as if Rampton were still reluctant to go beyond his written submission. Perhaps he feels restrained by his subject matter. Or perhaps he's just tired. Deliberate or not, there is a lack of drama in his presentation that is striking coming from a man with such rich resources of voice and expression.

Rampton's breakneck speed doesn't allow for much in the way of nuance or complexity. And his bluff matter-of-fact manner, though perhaps tactically sound, also mutes any recognition that the circumstances in dispute in this case are often themselves at variance with reason. "The picture of SS personnel running from their barracks, round the perimeter wire, in full gear, one and a half miles to the crematoria, under a hail of bombs, is just plain daft!" he says at one point. True enough, but in dealing with the mechanics of genocide, common sense doesn't take you very far. The image of the SS running to the crematoria is crazy, but not nearly as crazy as what the SS actually did in the camp—not least in connection with those same crematoria.

In his peroration, Rampton says that since the evidence—both eyewitness and documentary—is so overwhelming "some other reason must be sought to explain [Irving's] devotion, over many years, and even in this court . . . to the bizarre idea that no significant numbers of people were murdered in the homicidal gas chambers at Auschwitz–Birkenau." But he doesn't develop the theme beyond a series of truncated syllogisms.

"Mr. Irving is an anti-Semite; Holocaust denial, in the form in which it is purveyed by Mr. Irving, is an obvious expression of anti-Semitism, and is music to the ears of the neo-Nazis and other right-wing extremists to whom he purveys it. Mr. Irving is a Hitler partisan, who has falsified history on a staggering scale in order to 'prove' Hitler's innocence; this, like Holocaust denial, is obviously very appealing to his fellow travellers—after all, if the Holocaust were a 'myth,' then, obviously, Hitler could have no responsibility for it."

Rampton gives one final tug to the knot that ties his arguments together: "How far, if at all, Mr. Irving's anti-Semitism is a cause of his Hitler apology, or vice versa, is quite unimportant. Whether they are taken together, or individually, it is clear that they have led him to prostitute his reputation as a serious historian (spurious though it can now be seen to have been) for the sake of a bogus rehabilitation of Hitler and the dissemination of virulent anti-Semitic propaganda." And then, at 11:25 a.m., Richard Rampton sits down. He has been speaking for less than an hour.

The judge has a few "points I think I need to clarify," and within seconds Rampton is back on his feet. The first relates to van Pelt's document about cremation capacity, which Irving has challenged. The second is about deportation. "Leaving aside the extermination," the judge asks, "which is a separate issue and I understand what Mr. Irving says about that, you do not understand there to be any argument or dispute between the Defendants and Mr. Irving as to the fact that the deportation took place, and indeed also as to the fact that Hitler knew about it, because it is Mr. Irving's case that that was all that was involved?"

Rampton answers both questions easily. And if they seem to indicate that, at the very least, the judge is still taking Irving's arguments seriously, the next question—more of a request, really, for the defense to furnish a chronological summary of the "setting up of the gassing in the Reinhard camps" with supporting documents—points in the other direction.

Gray's last question has a long buildup. "Part of your case against Mr. Irving is that he is a racist, leaving aside anti-Semitism, that he is a racist and you have a number of quotations from his speeches?"

"Yes."

"How does that bear," the judge wonders, "on (a) the words complained of, and (b) the meanings that you seek to justify?"

"If one looks at the general evidence," Rampton explains, "as an objective, open-minded, careful, dispassionate historian, that Hitler was, indeed, responsible, knew all about it, and authorized it, the conclusion is irresistible that he did. Mr. Irving has shut that window, as it were, and has got on with the shut window behind him with the falsification of history so as to exculpate Hitler."

"So this is again another instance of deliberate manipulation which kind of runs through—?"

"It is a kind of deliberate blindness to the evidence. What he does not like, he ignores," says Rampton.

"Deliberate blindness?"

"Yes, it is deliberate blindness."

"So it is telescope to the wrong eye?" asks Gray.

"What I say . . . is that his denials of the Holocaust have been made without any reference whatsoever to any reliable evidence," says Rampton. "This means that his denial must have another agenda."

"This is an area," Gray asks, "where you put it as being deliberately perverse blindness and acting in pursuance of what is, effectively, a neo-Nazi agenda, is that right?"

In itself, the question is not ominous. Indeed, Rampton's answer almost takes the judge's agreement for granted. "Looking at the way in which he expresses Holocaust denial and the audiences to whom he expresses that denial and the things that he says on those occasions, one is driven to the conclusion that the hidden agenda, the reason for the historical incompetence, if I can call it that (though there is a much stronger word that I could think of), is that he is at root deeply anti-Semitic and a neo-Nazi, as your Lordship just said."

But what the judge says next shatters Rampton's complacency. "Well, that raises the last question that I wanted to canvass with you, and it is anti-Semitism and, indeed, the racism and the extremism and all the rest of it. I find it a little—and I find it throughout the case—a bit difficult to see how, if at all, those allegations against Mr. Irving dovetail with the general allegation that he falsifies . . . deliberately the historical record. Because it seems to me—and I just want to know how you put it—that if somebody is anti-Semitic, and leave aside racism, but anti-Semitic and extremist, he is perfectly capable of being, as it were, honestly anti-Semitic and honestly extremist in the sense that he is holding those views and expressing those views because they are, indeed, his views."

Rampton is too stunned by this to do more than utter "Yes."

However Gray's bombshell hasn't quite finished detonating. "Now, it seems to me that probably, if you come down to it, that the anti-Semitism is a completely separate allegation which really has precious little bearing on your broader and perhaps more important case that Mr. Irving has manipulated the data and falsified the record. Or do you say that they are connected in some way and, if so, how?"

Gray's portrayal of an "honest" anti-Semite suggests the possibility of a three-way split, a finding that, though Irving is indeed an extremist—or "honest extremist"—and may have misrepresented the larger historical record, Irving's motives were sincere. Any such split decision would be a disaster for the defense. And if Rampton hasn't even gotten the link between Irving's racism and historical dishonesty across to the judge, there is little reason to be confident about Auschwitz, either.

Barristers are paid to think on their feet, and Rampton does so now. "The bridge between the Holocaust denial and the Hitler apology from anti-Semitism is a very easy one to build," he says, "because what more would a historian who is an anti-Semite want to do in exculpation of Hitler . . . than to deny the Holocaust?"

For Gray, this still seems a bridge too far. "Yes, but he might believe what he is saying," he insists. "That is the point. That is why it is important."

At the end of testimony, Irving had considerable ground to make up. Rampton's withering final cross-examination exposed him as a chancer, a man practically addicted to "trying it on"—telling lies with the intention, but not necessarily the well-founded hope, of being believed. Like the dishonest waiter in his example, Irving had been repeatedly caught giving incorrect change—always in his own favor. Or so it seemed. On the way into court that morning Irving himself, an eternal optimist, rated his chances as "no better than fifty-fifty."

His closing argument is Irving's swan song, his moment in the light—perhaps his last chance to make his case as well as plead his suit before the assembled representatives of the world's press. Irving is determined to make the most of it. "To show who's in command," he writes in his diary, "I propose that the Court adjourn for five minutes." The judge agrees.

Since there is still a crowd waiting to get in, and none of us dare leave our seats, the foreseeable consequence of Irving's request is to heighten the discomfort of what was already a cramped, stifling atmosphere. When Irving begins to speak, his first words, written the night before, are hesitant and full of trepidation: "My Lord, this is rather like going over the top at Gallipoli. My father was in that battle so I know what it is like."

But Irving's voice is clear and strong. Perhaps braced by Gray's comments, by the time he reaches his written text, Irving's cadences are passionate, his words spoken with conviction: "The Defendants in this action, the publisher Penguin Books Limited and the American scholar Deborah Lipstadt, have sought to cast this trial as being about the reputation of the Holocaust.

"It is not.

"The world's press have also reported it in this way. Again, it is not.

"This trial is about my reputation as a human being, as a historian of integrity, and—thanks to the remarks made by Mr. Rampton—as a father."

As Irving continues speaking Mr. Justice Gray's final challenge to Rampton seems to still echo in the courtroom: "Yes, but he might believe what he is saying." Irving knows perfectly well that his father, a career naval officer, never went "over the top" at Gallipoli.* That's just "author's license." But when he tells the court "a judgment in my favor is no more than a judgment that disputed points which I have made about some aspect of the [Holocaust] narrative are not so absurd, given the evidence, as to disqualify me from the ranks of historians," he may actually believe it. At least at the time.

"A judgment in my favor," he continues, "does not mean that the Holocaust never happened; it means only that in England today discussion is still permitted. My opponents would still be able, just as now, to produce other documents if they can; to expound alternative interpretations. They would be as free as ever to declare that they think that I am wrong and all the other things that have been said about me today. They would be impeded in one way only: they would not be able to say in a loud and authoritative voice that I am not a historian, and that my books must be banned."

This, of course, isn't even close to the truth. A judgment in Irving's favor would not only muzzle Lipstadt and destroy her book, it would intimidate anyone else inclined to criticize Irving along similar lines. It would also be a major victory for the self-styled "revisionists." And, at least in court, no one has called for Irving's books to be banned. Yet it is far too simple to say that Irving can't possibly believe he is fighting only to clear his own reputation and to defend his right to express his views. Part of him clearly does believe it. And that part of him speaks with all the eloquence inspired by his grievance.

Nor, it should be said, is Irving's grievance entirely imaginary. Publishers have treated him shabbily. Not just St. Martin's, foolish enough to appraise him at his own measure and then craven when they found that others were less gullible.

* In his diary entry for March 15, 2000, Irving writes that his father was "aboard one of the bombarding British battleships, so he probably had it rather cushier than the grenadiers who were ashore." See Action Report, 17 (July 20, 2000), p. 29.

His British publisher, Macmillan, flattered him to his face even as they circulated a memo authorizing editors to let prospective authors know Irving was on the way out: "If this helps you to reassure any prospective authors we are happy for you to say it (although not too publicly if possible)." Then they pulped his backlist.

As for Irving's charge that his enemies conspired against him, did so across national borders, and were in many cases Jews—this, too, cannot be dismissed as entirely the figment of a paranoid imagination.

"The real defendants in this case," Irving complains, "are not represented in this court but their presence has been with us throughout, like Banquo's ghost." In his written statement, Irving names the Jewish groups he considers his tormentors; in court he merely alludes to "the people who commissioned the work complained of and provided much of the materials used in it."

His tact doesn't obscure his meaning: the Jews have destroyed his livelihood. Several times during the trial Irving tried to cross-examine witnesses about what he called "Bundle E"—his dossier on the "global" conspiracy to ruin his reputation. Rampton repeatedly objected on the grounds of relevance, but in the end the judge said Irving could introduce his evidence "by way of submission." Now is his chance, and though most of the material is indeed extraneous to the issues in dispute, Irving spends about a third of his written statement rehearsing his injuries at the hands of various Jewish groups.

The injuries are real enough. Letters were written, pressure—discreet and less discreet—was brought to bear. Information—not all of it scrupulously attributed or verified—was circulated around the globe. Though the chief aim of the campaign was to change the climate of opinion sufficiently to force publishers tempted to profit from Irving's notoriety to revise their calculations, Irving couldn't be certain his opponents would confine their efforts to verbal protest. "For twelve months after our young child was born," he tells the court, "we lived with a wicker Moses basket in the furthest corner of our apartment, near a window, attached to a length of wire rope in case the building was set on fire and we had to lower her to safety."

Indeed in other circumstances Irving might be entitled to a measure of sympathy. The Anti-Defamation League in the United States maintained dossiers not just on Irving, but on African-American groups like the National Conference of Black Lawyers, on leftist organizations like the National Lawyers Guild and the Committee in Solidarity with the People of El Salvador, and even on the American-Arab Anti-Discrimination Committee; in October 1999 the ADL agreed to pay to settle a class-action lawsuit accusing it of illegally spying on these groups.[1] In the wake of the assassination of Israeli Prime Minister Yitzhak Rabin, it would also be naïve to dismiss the cruder manifestations of the campaign against Irving—such as the placard "Gas Irving," seen in a demonstration outside his Mayfair flat—as mere rhetorical excess.

Where Irving's reasoning goes off the track is not in seeing himself as the object of an organized campaign, but in his apparent surprise that this should be so. Not because he threatens Jews, or their livelihood, but simply because he offends them. One consequence of the unhappy history of Jews in the first half of the twentieth century is that there will always be some Jews who feel the need to make the point that now, in the second half of the century, they no longer have to suffer in silence when someone offends them.

As Irving seeks to rebut the historical part of the defense case, he illuminates the grounds for offense all over again: the Jews who recounted what they saw and heard and lived through at Auschwitz "turned out to be liars." Those who, despite the "uniformly poor evidentiary basis," persist in believing their relatives were murdered at Belzec, Sobibór, or Treblinka have been duped by "deliberately inflated death tolls." Even the Jews sent from Berlin to Kovno are miraculously restored to life when Irving—as if still in ignorance of their fate, as if Longerich had never informed the court that they were shot on arrival—refers yet again to the "curious British decodes which revealed the provisioning of the deportation trains with tons of food for the journey . . . and even the deportees' 'appliances.'"

In the place of all these fraudulent victims, Irving offers the story of his own martyrdom: "I have been outlawed, arrested, harassed, and all but *vernichtet*—destroyed—as a professional historian." This should seem grotesque. Indeed, it is grotesque, as is Irving's accusation that his opponents, whom he has dragged into court, are guilty of McCarthyism: "My general response to this attempt at 'guilt by association' which we have seen a lot over the last few weeks, is to compare it with the worst excesses of the inquisitions conducted by Senator Joseph McCarthy. . . . Hollywood's finest scriptwriters, many of them Jewish, had their careers *vernichtet*, to use that word again, by the reckless allegation that they had associated with known Communists. Now come these Defendants leveling the mirror image of these same charges at me."

Irving has never been more shameless—or more eloquent— than in this, his final gambit. Amid such passion, Irving's slip in addressing the judge as "Mein Führer," which he does at one point, barely registers. Irving revisits all his apparent concessions during the trial—the systematic nature of the genocide, the memorandum to Hitler detailing the number of Jews killed—and, one by one, he qualifies them out of existence. He minimizes, yet again, the death toll at Auschwitz, while piously declaring: "If it is one million or 300,000 or whatever the figure is, each of them means that many multiples of one individual. I never forget in anything I have said or written or done the appalling suffering that has been inflicted on people in camps like Auschwitz."

After all we've seen and heard to claim—and beyond that to believe, as Irving seems to—that "I am on the side of the innocents of this world" is a remarkable achievement. At 4:30 p.m.,

Irving asks the judge for "damages, including aggravated damages for libel and an injunction restraining the Defendants" from publishing similar words about him ever again. Then, some five hours after he started speaking, David Irving sits down.

Now comes the waiting. Rampton asks the judge for a week's notice before the date of judgment to allow interested parties, particularly from overseas, to be present in court. Irving, who plans to spend much of the interval out of the country, agrees.

As anyone who bothers to read the defense's written closing statement soon realizes, the evidence supporting Lipstadt and Penguin's claim to justification is mountainous. Presented in outline form and following the judge's "List of issues in dispute between the parties," the document is divided into five headings: "Meaning," Irving's reputation, his claim for damages, the legal principles behind a plea of justification, and "Justification—facts." The first four take up fewer than 10 pages. But the defense version of the facts fills up a two-inch ring binder.

The historiographical criticisms alone—at 90 pages nearly as long as Irving's entire closing statement—range in chronological order over 19 separate allegations of distortion, from Hitler's trial in 1924 to Irving's charge that the "gas chamber story" was invented by the British Propaganda Warfare Executive. The section on Hitler's role in the Final Solution—and Irving's stratagems for obscuring Hitler's culpability—extends to five additional subheadings. Auschwitz, Holocaust denial, Irving's anti-Semitism and extremism, his misleading depiction of the Dresden firebombing, and his conduct in regard to the Goebbels diaries—each of these topics is dealt with at length and in particular.

In all of this damning detail, however, one item is never addressed: Irving's state of mind. Irving is described as "an anti-Semite and a racist"—two charges which, though never made in Lipstadt's book, form crucial elements of the defense case. But no attempt is made to determine whether Irving's prejudice is a matter of conviction or convenience. Doubtless this is because to Anthony Julius, who drafted that section of the statement, it makes no difference. For Julius what matters is not the anti-Semite's intention, but the injury he causes.

In his query to Richard Rampton, between Rampton's concluding argument and Irving's, Charles Gray appeared to take a different view. After hearing Rampton argue that Irving's anti-Semitism provided the motive for his denigration of the Holocaust, Gray insisted: "Yes, but he might believe what he is saying. That is the point. That is why it is important."

"Believe what he is saying about what?" asked Rampton.

"About the Holocaust."

As much a surprise to Irving as it was to his adversaries, Gray's remark seemed to indicate a feeling that not only had the connection not been made, but that it was irrelevant. This in turn suggested at least the possibility that Gray might rule that Irving was indeed mistaken about many incidents in the history of the Second World War—but that his statements about the Holocaust were misguided rather than knowingly malicious, the expressions of a man "honestly anti-Semitic and honestly extremist." Where that would leave the defense case on other matters, like Auschwitz, it was impossible to predict. Gray's list of issues was non-committal on Auschwitz, inviting the defense to set out the evidence for gas chambers and Irving to give his reasons for rejecting that evidence.

"Never underestimate the ability of a British judge to miss the point," said one veteran reporter during the luncheon recess.

If Charles Gray's remarks caused a certain amount of foreboding, one item on the judge's own résumé provided fuel for anyone prone to wonder whether a courtroom was the proper forum for resolving historical disputes. In the spring of 1987 a pamphlet appeared charging that Lord Aldington, a former deputy chairman of the Conservative Party who held the semi-honorary post of Warden of Winchester College, had "played a decisive and unrepentant role in the massacre of 70,000 men, women and children" during the final days of the Second World War. Entitled *War Crimes and the Wardenship of Winchester College* the pamphlet called Aldington a war criminal who personally arranged for Russian Cossacks and Yugoslav soldiers and their families, who had surrendered to the British, to be handed back to Stalin and Tito. Many of these men had fought on the German side; others were merely on the wrong side in the Yugoslav civil war. Most were killed shortly after repatriation.

Among the pamphlet's 10,000 recipients were the current teaching staff at Winchester, the parents of boys at Winchester, Old Wykehamists, the members of the House of Commons and the House of Lords, the Chief Rabbi, the Prince of Wales, and the Queen. A more public act of defamation could scarcely be imagined, and Aldington duly sued for libel—which was just what the pamphlet's authors had intended. One of them, Nigel Watts, had a long-standing grievance against Aldington as chairman of the Sun Insurance group, which had refused to pay on his brother-in-law's life insurance policy. Watts's co-author—and co-defendant—Nikolai Tolstoy, was author of *Victims of Yalta*, a study of the forced repatriations, and *The Minister and the Massacres*, which blamed the handover on Harold Macmillan, at the time political adviser to Field Marshal Alexander. Though he'd interviewed Aldington for the latter book, Tolstoy hadn't been satisfied by his answers. The self-styled "Count Tolstoy," who likes to stress his kinship with the author of *War and Peace*, could hardly wait to get Aldington under oath.

But when the two sides faced each other, Justice Michael Davies warned: "This is a trial for an action for libel, and not an historical commission or some sort of inquisitorial process. This is not an inquiry into what happened in May 1945 to the

Yugoslavs or the Cossacks."[2] The judge's remarks were aimed at Tolstoy, who was represented in court by his solicitor, Michael Rubinstein, and his barrister, Richard Rampton. Doubtless they also made an impression on opposing counsel, Aldington's fellow Old Wykehamist, Charles Gray QC, who argued that his client was merely following orders.

Gray's advocacy resulted in the largest ever award for libel damages by a British jury: £1.5 million. Yet as Ian Mitchell, author of a recently published book on the trial, writes, "this did not put an end to the controversy." According to Mitchell, "critical evidence for the Defence was kept from the court" by Aldington's fellow Tories in the Ministry of Defence and the Foreign Office. The charge of a cover-up is echoed by author Robert Harris, who contributes a foreword to Mitchell's book citing *Aldington* v. *Tolstoy* as emblematic of "the baroque absurdities and vast costs of British justice."[3]

Despite their history of professional antagonism, during the Irving trial Gray had given no sign of anything except high regard for Rampton, who of course returned the compliment. Nor did anyone suggest either that Gray himself had been aware of any allegedly withheld evidence in the Aldington trial, or that either side in the present dispute had improperly concealed anything from the court. All the same, it is impossible to read Mitchell's book and not come away with a sense that historical truth and British justice are two very different kettles of fish.

As if to underscore this distinction, only a few months before the Irving trial began another former Tory official, novelist and politician, Jeffrey Archer, was forced to resign as the party's candidate for London mayor when he faced charges that his victory in a famous 1987 libel trial was the result of perjured testimony. Not long before that Jonathan Aitken, a former cabinet minister, suddenly dropped his own libel suit against the *Guardian* newspaper and Granada television when they came up with documentary proof that he, had lied under oath—as had his wife and daughter. Until he was caught by a fortu-itously discovered hotel bill Aitken, who ended up going to prison for perjury, had been so confident of victory he rejected numerous settlement overtures—which, presumably, he reviewed with his counsel, Charles Gray.

11

A reasoned judgment

Courtroom 36 is the largest in the Royal Courts of Justice, and it is here, at 10:30 on the morning of April 11, that judgment is handed down in the case of *David Irving* versus *Penguin Books Ltd. and Deborah Lipstadt*. Unlike the trial's previous venues, Courtroom 36 is unmodernized. Its high, coffered ceilings, wood-paneled walls, and tall, gothic, stone windows lend an almost ecclesiastical tone to the trial's last scene—an effect enhanced by the choir loft at the rear, its three rows of seats now filled with reporters and a very few members of the general public. Outside the rain is pelting down, and the court benches are once again piled high with sodden coats.

On one side of the room Deborah Lipstadt, wearing a somber black suit and white blouse, sits chatting with Anthony Forbes-Watson. Heather Rogers, Richard Rampton, and Anthony Julius are behind them. On the other side the more favored members of the press crowd into the jury box, with the considerable overflow filling most of the scarred wooden benches below the choir loft. At precisely 10:29 David Irving pushes through the double doors and makes his way to his seat near the jury box. Irving is jacketless, his blue-and-white striped shirt and blue-and-yellow striped tie partially covered by a grey, chalk-striped waistcoat with a red silk back. This departure from his usual costume is not, it turns out, an attempt to emphasize his status as a "shirtsleeves historian" but the result of an encounter with egg-throwing hecklers outside the building.

The phalanx of law books and loose-leaf binders that lined Irving's desk during the trial are gone, and after exchanging a few words with Rae West, the portly, chronically unshaven man who runs his website, Irving sits with his elbows on the empty table, his hands folded, his chin resting on his hands. It is not the posture of a man who expects good news.

The judge's clerk passes out extracts of his judgment, and like impatient schoolboys we turn to the last page: "In the result therefore, the defense of justification succeeds." But under the heading "VERDICT" the space is left blank.

Once Charles Gray begins to speak, however, any lingering suspense is soon dispelled. He begins with one more half-hearted effort to keep history in its place: "I do not regard it as being any part of my function as the trial judge to make findings of fact as to what did and what did not occur during the Nazi regime in Germany." This is followed by an immediate concession: "It will be necessary for me to rehearse, at some length, certain historical data. The need for this arises because I must evaluate the criticisms of or (as Irving would put it) the attack upon his conduct as a historian in the light of the available historical evidence." Yet Gray insists, "It is not for me to form, still less to express, a judgment about what happened. That is a task for historians."

Those are the last confusing words Gray utters. For the next two hours, as he continues to read out portions of his 333-page decision, Gray's low, lugubrious voice delivers a judgment that is broad in scope, closely reasoned, clearly argued—and absolutely devastating to David Irving.

At times, the judge's language is surprisingly blunt: Irving's claim, he says, "is that he is the victim of an international Jewish conspiracy determined to silence him." Though this is exactly what Irving claimed, his own tact—and Rampton's objections—meant that the question was seldom posed so openly at the trial.

Acknowledging these objections, Gray explains "the latitude which I allowed Irving in developing this theme. They [the defense] contend, correctly, that in the ordinary run of litigation, the rules of evidence would have prevented him advancing any such case. However, for a number of reasons, I thought it right not to take too strict a line. Irving has represented himself throughout (demonstrating, if I may say so, very considerable ability and showing commendable restraint). This has not been a trial where it has been possible or appropriate to observe strict rules of evidence. Furthermore Irving has been greatly hampered in presenting this aspect of his case by the unexpected decision of the Defendants, in full knowledge of the allegations which Irving was making about the conduct of Lipstadt, not to call her to give evidence and to be cross-examined by Irving. It goes without saying that the Defendants were perfectly entitled to adopt this tactic but it did place Irving, acting in person, at a disadvantage."

Gray says that in order to prove a conspiracy, Irving had to show that both Defendants were implicated. He finds that "on the evidence of the contents of the book itself, I accept that it does indeed represent a deliberate attack on Irving, mounted in order to discredit him as a historian and so to undermine any credence which might otherwise be given to his denials of the Holocaust." But Irving failed to show that Penguin bore him particular hostility. Besides, says Gray, Lipstadt's intentions only become a factor in assessing damages.

Irving has argued that owing to the seriousness of the allegations against him, "a higher standard of proof should be applied" than a simple balance of probabilities. Gray agrees. As the judge reads on, however, even this small victory soon turns hollow.

In 245 paragraphs Gray lays out the evidence concerning

Irving's treatment of historical evidence. Scrupulously even-handed, he takes each disputed topic—from Hitler's 1924 trial, *Kristallnacht*, and the shooting of the Jews in Riga to the Schlegelberger note, Hitler's meeting with Horthy and the confessions of Hans* Aumeier—in turn, first summarizing the defense case and then giving Irving's response. This is followed by another 133 paragraphs doing the same for Hitler's attitude toward the Jews and his involvement in the Final Solution. Here again, Gray is heroically faithful to both the evidence heard in court and to the historical record: "The Defendants recognize," he writes, "that the documentary evidence for implicating Hitler in any policy for the systematic shooting of Jews is sparse. There is no 'smoking gun.' A large number of documents were destroyed, many of them on the orders of Heydrich, so the documentary picture is a partial one. However, the Defendants do highlight a number of documents which, they contend, point, albeit not unambiguously, to Hitler's complicity."

He turns next to Auschwitz, in doing so abandoning the charade of keeping history outside the courtroom: "The overall question which I have to decide is whether the available evidence, considered in its totality, would convince any objective and reasonable historian that Auschwitz was not merely one of the many concentration or labor camps established by the Nazi regime but that it also served as a death or extermination camp, where hundreds of thousands of Jews were systematically put to death in gas chambers over the period from late 1941 until 1944."

Holocaust denial, Irving's racism and anti-Semitism, the charge that he associates with right-wing extremists, his description of the bombing of Dresden and his conduct in obtaining the Goebbels diaries—each area of contention comes in for the same painstaking dissection, with each assertion and

* For some reason identified as Kurt Aumeier in the judge's text.

its contrary neatly separated into discrete paragraphs and laid out for consideration. When definitions are called for, Gray supplies them, although in the case of Holocaust denial, he quotes Evans on the deniers' credo:

(i) that Jews were not killed in gas chambers or at least not on any significant scale;

(ii) that the Nazis had no policy and made no systematic attempt to exterminate European Jewry and that such deaths as did occur were the consequence of individual excesses unauthorised at senior level;

(iii) that the number of Jews murdered did not run into millions and that the true death toll was far lower;

(iv) that the Holocaust is largely or entirely a myth invented during the war by Allied propagandists and sustained after the war by Jews in order to obtain financial support for the newly-created state of Israel.

Here again, the pretense that Gray's dilemma is anything but historical is quietly laid aside: "It is necessary also to consider whether and, if so, to what extent, what Irving has said and written is consistent with or borne out by the available historical evidence. For, as the Defendants accept, there can be no valid criticism of Irving for denying that a particular event occurred unless it is shown that a competent and conscientious historian would appreciate that such a denial is to a greater or lesser extent contrary to the available historical evidence."

More than three-quarters of the way through his judgment Gray still hasn't said a word about how he sees the evidence. But as he arrives at section 13, "Findings on Justification," Irving, who got the decision last night and knows what's coming, sits up in his chair as if to brace himself.

His ordeal begins with an encomium: "As a *military* historian, Irving has much to commend him. For his works of military history Irving has undertaken thorough and painstaking research into the archives. He has discovered and disclosed to historians and others many documents which, but for his efforts, might have remained unnoticed for years. It was plain from the way in which he conducted his case and dealt with a sustained and penetrating cross-examination that his knowledge of World War Two is unparalleled. His mastery of the detail of the historical documents is remarkable. He is beyond question able and intelligent. He was invariably quick to spot the significance of documents which he had not previously seen. Moreover he writes his military history in a clear and vivid style. I accept the favorable assessment by Professor Watt and Sir John Keegan of the caliber of Irving's military history . . . and reject as too sweeping the negative assessment of Evans."

At this Irving squeezes out a brief smile, but his triumph over Evans is extremely short-lived. "The questions to which this action has given rise do not relate to the quality of Irving's military history," says Gray. What matters instead is Irving's integrity as a writer and presenter of historical evidence, and here the judge finds Evans's devastating appraisal completely persuasive: "In the course of his prolonged cross-examination, Evans justified each and every one of the criticisms on which the Defendants have chosen to rely."

Irving's attempt to divert the blame for *Kristallnacht* from Hitler to Goebbels "is at odds with the documentary evidence." His account of Himmler's November telephone call regarding the train load of Berlin Jews is "in error" and there is "no evidence" for his attribution of the call to Hitler's intervention. "Whilst I accept that a historian is entitled to speculate," says Gray, "he must spell out clearly to the reader when he is speculating rather than reciting established facts."

The judge finds that Irving's treatment of Hitler's responsibility for the destruction of the Jews has "a distinct air of unreality." On the Schlegelberger Memorandum, though

Irving's arguments "are worthy of consideration," the judge finds his eagerness to present the document as incontrovertible evidence both unseemly and unwarranted.

As for his account of Hitler's meetings with the Hungarian Regent, "In my judgment," says Gray, "Irving materially perverts the evidence of what passed between the Nazis and Horthy." Item by item Gray weighs Irving's historical judgment in the balance and finds it wanting. But he hasn't yet said whether these distortions were conscious and deliberate.

Instead, the judge again turns to Auschwitz: "I have to confess that, in common I suspect with most other people, I had supposed that the evidence of mass extermination of Jews in the gas chambers at Auschwitz was compelling. I have, however, set aside this preconception when assessing the evidence adduced by the parties in these proceedings."

Gray says he recognizes "the force of many of Irving's comments" about the evidence for the gas chambers, such as thinness of the documentary record and the paucity of references to the use of gas, many of which might well be explained by the incidence of typhus. He also accepts that the aerial photographs which the defense claimed showed the holes in the roof of Crematorium 3 are "hard to interpret." He even grants that Irving "had some valid comments to make" about the eyewitness testimony, pointing out instances where the evidence was either obviously mistaken or exaggerated. Irving "suggested various motives why witnesses might have given false accounts, such as greed and resentment (in the case of survivors) and fear and the wish to ingratiate themselves with their captors (in the case of camp officials). Van Pelt accepted that these possibilities exist. I agree."

Without sweeping these inconsistencies aside, Gray remarks that "what is to me striking about that category of evidence is the similarity of the accounts and the extent to which they are consistent with the documentary evidence. The account of, for example, [*Sonderkommando* Henryk] Tauber, is so clear and detailed that, in my judgment, no objective historian would dismiss it as invention unless there were powerful reasons for doing so. Tauber's account is corroborated by and corroborative of the accounts given by others such as Jankowski and Dragon. Their descriptions marry up with Olère's drawings. The evidence of other eye-witnesses, such as Höss and Broad, would in my view appear credible to a dispassionate student of Auschwitz.

"My conclusion," said the judge, "is that the various categories of evidence do 'converge' in the manner suggested by the Defendants. . . . Having considered the various arguments advanced by Irving* to assail the effect of the convergent evidence relied on by the Defendants, it is my conclusion that no objective, fair-minded historian would have serious cause to doubt that there were gas chambers at Auschwitz and that they were operated on a substantial scale to kill hundreds of thousands of Jews."

Though Irving has already lost on historiography and Auschwitz, the worst is yet to come. So far the judge has referred only to Irving's claims, not his motivation. He follows a similar line in finding, in the fastidious language of the judgment, "that the statements made by Irving which are apostrophized by the Defendants as Holocaust denials are false" and that "Irving's denials of these propositions were contrary to the evidence."

Not until he gets to Irving's anti-Semitism does the judge allow a note of anything stronger than regret into his voice. Referring to the anthology of offensive quotations prepared by the defense, Gray says "It appears to me to be undeniable that . . . in the absence of any excuse or suitable explanation for what he said or wrote, Irving is anti-Semitic. His words are

---

* As for the argument stressed most by Irving at the trial: "The apparent absence of evidence of holes in the roof of Morgue 1 at Crematorium 2 falls far short of being a good reason for rejecting the cumulative effect of the evidence."

directed against Jews, either individually or collectively, in the sense that they are by turns hostile, critical, offensive and derisory in their references to Semitic people, their characteristics and appearances." In one case Irving claimed his remarks were intended as a joke; if so, says Gray, "it was an anti-Semitic joke.

"I have more sympathy," he continues, "for Irving's argument that Jews are not immune from his criticism. . . . Irving gave as an example what he claimed was his justified criticism of the Jews for suppressing his freedom of expression. Another legitimate ground of criticism might be the manner in which Jews in certain parts of the world appear to exploit the Holocaust. I agree that Jews are as open to criticism as anyone else. But it appears to me that Irving has repeatedly crossed the divide between legitimate criticism and prejudiced vilification of the Jewish race and people. The inference which in my judgment is clearly to be drawn from what Irving has said and written is that he is anti-Semitic."

By now Irving has slumped down into his chair, and glares at Gray under half-closed eyelids. "I have concluded," the judge goes on, "that the allegation that Irving is a racist is also established for broadly analogous reasons."

Gray expresses some reservations about Hajo Funke, whose report, he says, "made reference to a bewildering array of organizations and individuals. . . . But Irving's association with many of those organizations is tenuous to say the least. I am satisfied that Irving has had no significant association with a great many of them. The same applies to the individuals named by Funke." Nevertheless the judge, citing the disputed Halle video as evidence of "Irving's willingness to participate in a meeting at which a motley collection of militant neo-Nazis were also present" and his regular contacts with Zündel, Faurisson, the National Alliance and a handful of German extremists, finds "in my judgment that Irving shares many of their political beliefs."

There is one ray of consolation for Irving when the judge finds the Defendants have failed to prove he broke an agreement with the Moscow archives. He also rules they haven't proved Irving's handling of the glass plates containing the Goebbels diary exposed them to any undue risk.

But there is nothing at all comforting to Irving when the judge returns to what he calls "the central issue of Irving's historiography," namely whether "he has *deliberately* falsified and distorted the historical evidence." This is not a question of Irving's competence, but his integrity. And here again the judge leaves no room for doubt:

"Certain of Irving's misrepresentations of the historical evidence might appear to be simple mistakes on his part. . . . But there are other occasions where Irving's treatment of the historical evidence is so perverse and egregious that it is difficult to accept that it is inadvertence on his part."

After giving a series of examples, Gray takes up the various concessions Irving made—and then retracted—during the trial. "What is the significance of these alterations . . . in relation to . . . Irving's motivation?" The judge concludes that Irving's apparent willingness to concede when confronted with the evidence suggests he knew the falsity of his position all along, while his subsequent retractions "manifest . . . a determination to adhere to his preferred version of history, even if the evidence does not support it.

"It is not difficult to discern a pattern," says Gray summing up his findings: "Over the past fifteen years or so, Irving appears to have become more active politically than was previously the case. He speaks regularly at political or quasi-political meetings in Germany, the United States, Canada and the New World. The content of his speeches and interviews often displays a distinctly pro-Nazi and anti-Jewish bias. He makes surprising and often unfounded assertions about the Nazi regime which tend to exonerate the Nazis for the appalling atrocities which they inflicted on the Jews. He is content to mix with neo-Fascists and appears to share many of their racist and anti-Semitic prejudices. The picture of Irving which emerges from the evidence of his extra-curricular activities reveals him to be a right-wing pro-Nazi polemicist."

He concludes: "It appears to me that the correct and inevitable inference must be that for the most part the falsification of the historical record was deliberate and that Irving was motivated by a desire to present events in a manner consistent with his own ideological beliefs even if that involved distortion and manipulation of historical evidence."

Though the defense haven't proved every part of their case, the judge rules that what they haven't proved—Irving's conduct in the Moscow archives, the portrait of Hitler alleged to hang over his desk—is covered by section 5 of the 1952 Defamation Act, which provides "in respect of words containing two or more distinct charges against the [claimant], a defence of justification shall not fail by reason only that the truth of every charge is not proved if the words not proved to be true do not materially injure the [claimant's] reputation having regard to the truth of the remaining charges."

"In my judgment," says Gray, "the charges against Irving which have been proved to be true are of sufficient gravity [that the remaining charges would] . . . not have any material effect on Irving's reputation. In the result therefore, the defense of justification succeeds."

Gray fills in the final blank: "It follows that there must be judgment for the Defendants."

At this Irving rises: "My Lord, on the issue of costs. I think there should be a hearing on the issue of costs."

Having won on every significant issue—and in the clearest and most convincing terms imaginable—no one on the defense side rises to object. But as he grants the motion, Gray warns Irving: "The defense are going to have the bulk of their costs." And when Irving also asks Gray's permission to appeal his verdict (which would virtually guarantee review by a higher court), the judge refuses.

Still digesting the magnitude of his defeat, Irving gathers up his soiled jacket and leaves the court through a back entrance. Responding to a reporter's shouted question he describes the judgment as "perverse" but otherwise offers no immediate comment.

The Defendants have hired a room at a nearby hotel for a press conference that quickly becomes a victory celebration. Now free to speak to the press, Lipstadt reads from a brief statement: "I am very pleased that what I wrote has been vindicated." As she continues, thanking "Penguin and Pearson for standing with me shoulder to shoulder through this process," Penguin publicity representatives fan out through the room passing out copies of a press pack containing profiles of Lipstadt, her lawyers, Penguin executives, Penguin's lawyers, and a seven-page "Essence of the Judgment." There is also a glossy photo of Lipstadt, a copy of Rampton's opening statement, and a statement by Penguin, which Anthony Forbes-Watson now reads.

"This has been a hugely expensive case and whilst we will take active steps to recover our costs, we will certainly be left significantly out of pocket."

Pressed for a figure, Forbes-Watson estimates the trial has cost Penguin about £2 million. When a Canadian reporter asks if the certainty that Penguin won't ever recover the bulk of its costs doesn't represent a victory of sorts for Irving—on the supposition that the next publisher, faced with a winnable but ultimately costly case will decide not to go ahead—Forbes-Watson disagrees. "Sometimes principles override financial considerations," he says, and though the reporter is tactless enough to wonder whether Pearson's shareholders will agree, the questions quickly shift back to Lipstadt.

Like Irving, the defense lawyers had been given a text of the judge's decision the night before. But Lipstadt herself only learned of her triumph a half-hour before the judge began speaking. "What went through my mind was a moment of intense joy, gratitude," she said.

As for her opponent, "I'm not sure whether he shouldn't be allowed [in the United States]," she says confusingly. But when the next questioner solicits Lipstadt's support for the campaign to make Holocaust denial illegal in Britain, she declines: "I don't think those laws really work. I think sometimes they tend to make martyrs of deniers."

Nor does she think the judge's decision is likely to be the last word. "There is no end," she says, "to the fight against racism, anti-Semitism, and hatred." And if the judge, though completely vindicating her characterization of Irving, seemed nonetheless reluctant to adopt Lipstadt's terminology, using the phrase "Holocaust denial" only either in quotes or when attributed to Lipstadt or her lawyers, she has no intention of complaining. Besides, she says, "I'm writing a book on this trial; this is not the only time I'm going to have my say."

David Irving's silence doesn't last very long. On the way into court that morning Irving, who already knew he'd lost, told a correspondent for the *Washington Post* that in the long run he thought his reputation would be enhanced by the trial. He'd said much the same thing to me a few weeks earlier. By 10 o'clock on the evening of his defeat Irving has appeared on Australian television, the *Today* program, and *Newsnight*, and in countless radio interviews. On the following day the cycle continues, including a radio debate with Alan Dershowitz in the United States.

Though editorial response in Britain is uniformly hostile to Irving, the *Daily Telegraph* prints an article by John Keegan declaring that Irving's loss "will send a tremor through the community of 20th century historians." Despite their differences over Hitler's involvement in the Holocaust, Keegan says that Irving has "many of the qualities of the most creative historians. He is certainly never dull." Keegan concludes with a sniff at Lipstadt, "dull as only the self-righteously politically correct can be. Few other historians had ever heard of her before this case. Most will not want to hear from her again. Mr. Irving, if he will only learn from this case, still has much that is interesting to tell us."[1]

At the end of closing arguments, the judge asked Irving, who'd been nodding in agreement to Rampton's request for advance notice of his decision, "You are going to forfeit the last word, are you?" That, clearly, was a forlorn hope.

12

Numbers

A sophist, says Aristotle, is "one who makes money from an apparent but unreal wisdom." This description comes from the opening of his treatise *On Sophistical Refutations*, by which the philosopher means those arguments that "appear to be refutations but are really fallacies instead."[1]

This is a very old game, and though most of the essential moves were analyzed by Aristotle both here and in his *Rhetoric*, new variations are always possible—and often profitable. History does not tell us whether Dio Chrysostom, who lived and wrote some four hundred years after Aristotle, composed his "Eleventh Discourse" as a work for hire. Nor is it known if the "Trojan Discourse," as it is also called, was intended as a kind of advertisement for his talents as a sophist—considerable enough to earn him the name Chrysostom (Golden-Mouth)— or as a cautionary example of the dangers of sophistry, written after its author's conversion to Stoicism. What can be seen, nearly two millennia later, is the rhetorical brilliance with which Dio, a Greek-speaking native of Asia Minor, sets out to convince his contemporaries in Ilium (Troy) that they have been duped by Homer into believing that their ancestors lost the Trojan War.

According to Dio, the poet's tale of Helen, taken against her will to Troy, and her subsequent rescue after ten years of war, is just so much Greek propaganda. Instead of her abductor, Paris was really Helen's lawful husband. Even Homer couldn't dispute his good looks—and as heir to the throne of Troy, chief city of Asia Minor, he was a great catch. But if Helen and her family were happy, the rest of the Greeks were not, and it was their jealous rage at the famed beauty's choice of a foreign husband that launched the thousand ships—though in Dio's version there were far fewer, owing to the unpopularity of the Greeks' unjust cause.

With "no other means of refuting [Homer] than his own poetry," Dio argues that the *Iliad* is a tissue of lies whose falsehood should be evident from the way Homer includes details no mortal could have known, such as the domestic disputes between Zeus and Hera. He points to the improbability of the poem's hero Achilles refusing to rescue his fellow Greeks, and to the suspicious fact that the death of Achilles isn't even mentioned. Nor for that matter is the supposed capture of the city which gives the epic its name. Instead Homer ends with the burial of Hector—a bald stratagem to cover up what actually happened, as recounted to Dio by "a certain very aged priest in Onuphis," which the editor identifies as a "city in Egypt whose location is uncertain."[2]

In this "revisionist" *Iliad*, the dead body inside Achilles' armor belongs to Achilles—not, as in Homer, his friend Patroclus. Their greatest warrior slain, the Greeks sue for peace. But Hector is reluctant to let them get away, and it is only when Odysseus, a member of the Greek peace mission, proposes leaving behind "a very large and beautiful offering" in the form of a statue of a horse, that the Trojans agree. It was this peace offering, so massive that a portion of the city wall had to be removed to allow it to pass inside the gates of Troy, that, says Dio, accounts for "the ridiculous story of the capture of the city by the horse."[3]

Dio never uses the phrase "blood libel on the Trojan

people." Nor does he accuse the Greeks of conspiracy. He merely purports to show how a legend, arising out of the vicissitudes of war, gained a life of its own. But he does suggest to his putative audience in Ilium that "you . . . should be grateful and hear me gladly, for I have been zealous in defense of your ancestors."

No record survives to tell us how the discourse was received. We do know that Dio visited Rome during the reign of Vespasian (when he became a Stoic), fell afoul of Domitian (who banned him from Rome), and became friendly with Trajan. We even know (or so scholars believe) that Dio was involved in a lawsuit in his birthplace of Prusa (now known as Brusa, in Turkey), over some improvements he hoped to make in the town. But it is probably safe to assume the ups and downs of Dio's career were unconnected with what might be called his *Iliad* denial.

On one view, David Irving is simply Dio Chrysostom in a three-piece suit, offering an outwardly plausible, internally consistent fiction that plays on the prejudices of his audience. At times I have heard similar arguments from Irving's critics—and from his defenders. In my own view, these dismissals underestimate both Irving and what he represents.

If Irving were simply a "clown"—as one academic I know argued, complaining about the media's fascination with the trial—it would hardly have been necessary to commission a team of scholars to oppose him. Indeed, such a contest would have been grotesque. It would arguably have been similarly excessive if he were merely the harmless Führer-fancier depicted in *Selling Hitler*, Robert Harris's amusing account of the "Hitler diaries" fiasco. Though Richard Evans prevailed in the end, the 28 hours he spent demolishing Irving's scholarship in the witness box was not just an academic exercise.

But for all his command of historical detail, at times Evans seemed to show little understanding of why the details matter.

In his book *In Defence of History* Evans draws an uncharacteristically crude connection between "the increase in scope and intensity of the Holocaust deniers' activities since the mid-1970s" and "the postmodernist intellectual climate, above all in the USA, in which scholars have increasingly denied that texts had any fixed meaning . . . and in which attacks on the Western rationalist tradition have become fashionable."[4] As his quotation from *Denying the Holocaust* on the same page makes clear, Evans was here following Lipstadt, who laments that "an atmosphere of permissiveness toward questioning the meaning of historical events . . . fosters deconstructionist history at its worst. . . . Holocaust denial is part of this phenomenon." Surely even a curmudgeon like Evans, sworn foe of "fashionable" cant, ought to balk at the notion that Holocaust denial is merely an epiphenomenon of postmodernism?

David Irving is no postmodern prince of our disorder. His distaste for theory of any kind is far too strong for that. If Irving has any critical beliefs, they are far more likely to be in line with his comrade Faurisson's insistence that "every text has only one meaning or it has no meaning at all."[5] That false choice, restricted in the present instance to the Holocaust as either evidence of the Jews' malignity, or a collection of meaningless numbers, comes much closer to what was really at stake in this trial. "You may disagree with me," Irving told the judge, remarking on the disparate numbers he has given for the dead at Auschwitz, "but I see no difference between these figures."

And if Evans's apparent confusion can be explained by his reliance on Lipstadt, her own invocation of "deconstructionist history," though it glances at the discredited figure of Paul DeMan,* is really there just to spice up her argument that

---

* A leader of the "Yale School" of deconstructionist criticism, DeMan died in 1983. Four years later it was revealed that as a journalist in occupied Belgium during the 1940s DeMan had written 180 articles for a collaborationist newspaper, several of them on anti-Semitic themes.

Holocaust denial "is not an assault on the history of one particular group. Though denial of the Holocaust may be an attack on the history of the annihilation of the Jews, at its core it poses a threat to all who believe that knowledge and memory are among the keystones of our civilization . . . [and] to all who believe in the ultimate power of reason."[6] In other words, it's not just a problem for Jews.

Like a lot of the arguments in Lipstadt's book, her conclusion is correct, but her premises are deeply flawed. "At its core," that is when considered as a set of propositions about how it really was during the Second World War, Holocaust denial is, as van Pelt observes in his report, a series of wild surmises that never add up to a coherent narrative. Exposing them all may be tedious—and, when done before a judge in a court of law, incredibly costly—but the idea that Irving and his band of "cracked anti-Semites" at the Institute for Historical Review pose some kind of threat to "our civilization" or the "Western rationalist tradition" is simply absurd.

They do, however, pose a threat to Jews. This is a claim that, perhaps paradoxically, Lipstadt and the defense seemed reluctant to make. Indeed, the desire to avoid making this claim is what appears to be behind Lipstadt's bizarre assertion that those who describe the Holocaust as a hoax are not committing "an assault on the history of one particular group." In that sense, at least, Irving was right to speak of the "real defendants." His quarrel really is with Jews. Of course it is not only with Jews.

Yet this is an argument that the defense has almost seemed afraid to make: that you can't isolate Irving's anti-Semitism from his writing without isolating Jews from the rest of humanity. It might even be said that effecting this isolation is precisely the anti-Semite's aim. That was why the judge's question about whether Irving was an "honest" anti-Semite was so troubling— and so irrelevant. Whatever its rationale, to deny the reality of the Holocaust is *prima facie* an attack on Jews, and should be treated with just as much seriousness as any other racist attack. Or as little.

Which may be the rub. There are two possible grounds for appealing to the world when Jews are attacked. One is guilt. Addressing non-Jews, guilt says: "You abandoned us to Hitler, and now you owe us." Or, when speaking to fellow Jews: "You didn't do enough to save your brethren from the Nazis. Now you must be blindly loyal (for example) to the current government of Israel, whether or not you believe in the wisdom or justice of its policies."

The link between guilt over the Holocaust and support for Israel is so obvious as to hardly bear repeating. As everyone knows, Israel itself was born out of the world's guilt toward Jews. So it comes as something of a shock to read Peter Novick's patient dismantling of these myths in *The Holocaust in American Life*.

It is true that after the war, when the dimensions of the Jewish catastrophe became clear, Zionists moved quickly to turn guilt into political capital. What is notable about this effort, says Novick, is that it failed. With the possible exception of Britain, where fear of being compared to the Nazis may have prevented a more forceful response to the Zionists' unilateral declaration of independence, countries responded to the birth of Israel on the basis of their own national interests. The Soviet Union, eager to undercut British influence in the Middle East, supported it. Countries with ties to the Arab states—like Britain—did not. President Harry Truman, who recognized Israel over State Department opposition, may have been motivated by domestic political considerations—or by a sincere concern for Jewish refugees. But there is no evidence that guilt played any part in his decision.[7]

Indeed, the initial responses to the Eichmann trial revealed a mistrust of Israel's motives which, coming little over a year after President Dwight Eisenhower had condemned Israel's actions in the Suez Crisis, was perhaps understandable. Novick barely mentions Suez, which is a shame since the whole episode provides strong support for his view that, at least in the 1950s, the Holocaust provided Israel with no useful "moral capital."[8]

Novick also appears not to notice that just as the Cold War shaped American responses to the Holocaust it also shaped responses to Israel. Because until June 1967 it was far from clear that Israel was on "our" side. Israel's founders were socialists. In their war for independence the Israelis were armed with Czech machine guns; from 1956 to 1967 Israel bought the bulk of its weaponry from France, a country whose discontent with American power (and British servility) actually led it to withdraw from NATO's military command.[9] Only after the Six Day War did Norman Podhoretz argue that Israel was the religion of American Jews. Until that point, support tended to come from the left, from places like *The Nation* and the newspaper *PM*, whose columnist I.F. Stone was an early and vocal advocate for the new state.[10]

After 1967 everything changed. Novick doesn't draw an explicit connection between Israel's debut as America's strategic asset in the Middle East and the explosion of Holocaust discourse in the United States, but what he does say is suggestive. The image of Jews as military heroes effaced "the stereotype of weak and passive victims which . . . had previously inhibited Jewish discussion of the Holocaust."[11] More importantly, in Cold War terms Israel was now unambiguously on America's team. And if circumstances made it easier for American Jews to talk about the Holocaust—to draw on the "moral capital" which Israel had miraculously accumulated— that was just as well.[12] For in its determination to hold on to the territories gained in battle, Israel began to forfeit whatever sympathy it had attracted as an underdog.

The view from London has always been slightly different. For one thing, British Jews never had the political influence of their American counterparts. And the combination of oil and empire meant that Arab voices were always heard more sympathetically in Britain—at least when their grievances were directed at the Jews. But in both countries by the late 1970s the organized Jewish community devoted a large portion of its efforts to defending the "moral capital" supposedly represented by the Holocaust.*

One way of doing this was by fetishizing the "uniqueness" of the disaster. To Israel Gutman, co-director of Yad Vashem and author of the article on "Holocaust Denial" in the *Encyclopedia of the Holocaust*, "tendentious and trivializing claims that the Holocaust was not unique and that there had been precedents" are tantamount to denial. Comparisons with the Cambodian genocide and the slaughter of Native Americans have both drawn fire from Jewish groups; the government of Israel, in response to pressure from its military ally Turkey, has even attempted to quash efforts to recognize the Armenian genocide. Lipstadt herself seems of two minds, writing that to question the uniqueness of the Holocaust "is far more insidious than outright denial," while assuring me, "You have to make comparisons. We only learn by comparisons."[13]

Another is by stifling debate. When Norman Finkelstein and Ruth Birn published a book pointing out the many scholarly defects of Daniel Goldhagen's *Hitler's Willing Executioners*, they were subjected to a sustained campaign of personal abuse. Their book, *A Nation on Trial*, was no more extreme in its condemnation than Raul Hilberg, whose essay deploring "The Goldhagen Phenomenon" in *Les Temps Modernes* described the Harvard professor's work as "lacking in factual content and logical rigor" and casting a "cloud . . . over the academic landscape."[14] That didn't keep Abraham Foxman, head of the

---

* As Anne Karpf points out in her fascinating and brutally frank memoir, *The War After*, such efforts did not extend to much in the way of help for actual Holocaust survivors, who were "left largely to their own devices."

Anti-Defamation League, from trying to discourage the publication of *A Nation on Trial*.*

Journalists who exposed "Binjamin Wilkomirski's" bogus memoir of his childhood in Auschwitz and Majdanek found their motives impugned. Hadn't Goldhagen himself certified *Fragments* a "small masterpiece"? Israel Gutman still defends the imposture: "Wilkomirski has written a story which he has experienced deeply, that's for sure. So that, even if he is not Jewish, the fact that he was so deeply affected by the Holocaust is of huge importance. . . . The pain is authentic."[15] It isn't only anti-Semites who, in T.S. Eliot's infamous phrase, find a "large number of free-thinking Jews undesirable."[16]

The lever of guilt doesn't work. More importantly, to continually insist that Jewish suffering is a special case is to collaborate in the very isolation that anti-Semites like Irving seek to accomplish. And when frustration turns that lever into a club, whether

---

* In his letter to the book's editor, Foxman argued that Finkelstein's views on the Holocaust are "tainted by his anti-Zionist stance." Though Finkelstein is indeed a fervent anti-Zionist, there are several ironies in this line of argument. The gas chambers, after all, did not distinguish between Zionist and anti-Zionist Jews. And as the son of Holocaust survivors, Finkelstein was certainly entitled to his views—which were, in any case, far more representative of the scholarly consensus on the Holocaust than Goldhagen's. But the final irony is that much of the animus toward Finkelstein stems from an essay he published in 1984, while still a graduate student at Princeton. The subject was Joan Peters's *From Time Immemorial*, a book purporting to show that the Palestinians never existed as a people and that consequently their claims on Israel were essentially baseless. Using a technique similar to Richard Evans's examination of David Irving, Finkelstein demonstrated that the book, which had been hailed as definitive by the *New Republic*, "the historical truth" by Lucy Dawidowicz, and a "historical event in itself" by Barbara Tuchman, was little more than a farrago of fraud, distortion, and plagiarism. Finkelstein's refutation of the book's "Palestine denial" still rankles, and is I believe at least as relevant to the controversy over his recent attack on *The Holocaust Industry* as the author's deliberately provocative tone and occasional exaggerations.

directed at Jews or Gentiles, whether wielded by Jews who feel the Holocaust belongs to them alone or by Zionists seeking to preserve Israel's "moral capital," the result is a blurring of distinctions between memory and propaganda that serves only the interests of the Nazi perpetrators and their political legatees.

So why not give it up? Perhaps because there is no guarantee an appeal not grounded in guilt will be heard either. And while guilt assumes that Jews owe the rest of humanity nothing— Novick quotes an Anti-Defamation League memorandum advocating increased emphasis on the Holocaust as a "bill 'for Sufferings Rendered'" —the alternative, an approach based on what might be called "solidarity," imposes obligations that may not be so congenial.

In *Facing the Extreme*, his finely drawn study of moral life in the camps, Tzvetan Todorov distinguishes between "caring" and "the solidarity felt by members of a group among themselves." He prefers caring, since "solidarity with our own implies the exclusion of all others." I disagree. It may be that as a refugee from Bulgarian Communism Todorov hears the word differently than do I, the grandson of a garment worker, brought up in a household where "we don't cross picket lines" was as much an article of faith as the Exodus from Egypt or the story of Esther and Haman. But I accept Todorov's observation that "solidarity is a political, not a moral, act."[17]

Indeed it is precisely as a political act that I wish to commend solidarity as a response to attacks on the reality of the Holocaust and as a replacement for appeals based on guilt, which are also political acts. Solidarity says: "We are in this together." As Todorov notes, solidarity is based on the anarchist principle of mutual aid, and though this may be inadequate to the Hobbesian nightmare of the camps, in the world outside it seems less demeaning to begin by treating others as equals than as either instruments of our deliverance or objects of charity.

In concrete terms an ethic of solidarity says that when Jews are offended as Jews, they should stand up and say so. They would then have a right to expect from the rest of the community exactly that degree of outrage and sympathy which they have afforded others. In America, this might mean talking less about the Holocaust and listening more to those for whom the artifacts of racism and oppression are not yet shut away in a museum. In Britain, it might mean a greater willingness to speak out on issues like police brutality or justice for asylum seekers. What does it say when the two recent Home Secretaries—one Conservative, one Labour—who have done most to restrict the rights of refugees are themselves respectively the son and grandson of Jewish refugees?

Jews would face a choice. They could own up to—even enjoy—the prosperity and access to power that have come to large numbers of Jews since the end of the Second World War. Or they could—as a political act, an existential gesture, a religious observance, even a moral choice—throw in their lot with the excluded. But they couldn't have it both ways—wearing the Holocaust as a badge of martyrdom on the robes of power, a kind of amulet to ward off criticism and secure a share in whatever consolations society affords its disadvantaged members.

The basic idea is, whenever possible, to substitute the complex web of mutual obligation and association that constitutes civil society for the coercive powers of the state. In the United States, with its free-speech tradition and plethora of Jewish organizations, state action would be needed rarely if at all. In countries where anti-Semitism was still a real danger—or where the general problem of incitement to racial hatred was still considered a serious threat to public safety—the state's role might be greater. Even there, though, it would be far better to give people the chance to respond themselves rather than assuming the government will step in to enforce the limits of permissible expression.

One of the strengths of solidarity as a political principle is that it must always begin locally—in a neighborhood, an ethnic group, a religious community—and can only spread outward through mutual consent. This is a long way from the perpetual defensiveness entailed by, in Hannah Arendt's phrase, the "doctrine of eternal anti-Semitism" which was also such an article of faith for my parents' generation.[18] But the alternative—to call for yet more coercion on the part of the state, not only to outlaw Holocaust denial, and hate speech generally, but to use such laws as tools for breaking down the protections erected around speech and writing over hundreds of years—seems far more risky. And more naïve. In a forum held after the judgment, David Cesarani, director of the Wiener Library, suggested the media response to Irving's defeat showed that such laws were indeed necessary. Freedom of speech, he argued, was a relic of eighteenth-century liberalism—a luxury we could no longer afford. His remarks struck me as more dangerous than anything David Irving has ever said or written.*

Yet Irving does represent a real danger. Partly this is political. The laundry list of names Hajo Funke read out in court aren't primarily concerned with Jews. Chances are, most of the skinheads we saw marching and chanting in the Halle video have never even met a Jew. For them, Holocaust denial is just a means to an end, a verbal sign of recognition that sorts out the hard cases from the fellow travelers. Their end—Irving's project—is the rehabilitation of Fascism. And given Jörg Haider's success in facing down his critics in the European Union, and Jean-Marie Le Pen's durability on the French political scene, and the rising fortunes of neo-Fascists in Italy, an American must at least hesitate before assuming that fears of a far-right resurgence in Europe are purely delusional.

* Cesarani's comments seemed so off the wall I sent him a note asking if he meant them in earnest, and if I might have a text in order to quote him precisely. Cesarani responded that he did not want to be quoted.

But not all of Irving's defenders are Fascists, or anti-Semites—or even right-wingers. For every cretin who laughs at Irving's jokes about the one-man gas chamber there are probably thousands, like John Keegan, who assume Irving is wrong about the Holocaust but wonder why they should be expected to mind. For every goose-stepping neo-Nazi in thrall to Irving's rhetoric there are hundreds of readers drawn in by his narratives. And for every Michele Renouf (the mysterious blonde at Irving's table throughout the trial, an Australian taxi-driver's daughter who, thanks to a six-week marriage to the late Sir Francis "Frank the Bank" Renouf, a New Zealand financier, now styles herself "Lady Renouf") affecting interest in "open debate" but suspiciously alert to Jewish peculiarities, there is a Christopher Hitchens, whose genuine commitment to freedom of speech (and a fondness for seeing "egg on faces" even greater than Irving's) led him to forget the sound advice he'd once offered Noam Chomsky.

There is, Hitchens once wrote regarding Chomsky's role in *l'affaire* Faurisson, "no obligation, in defending or asserting the right to speak, to pass any comment on the truth or merit" of what the speaker says. Indeed, as Hitchens gently reminded Chomsky, the suggestion of something rank about a person's views is "all the more reason not to speculate" about those views. True enough. So why call Irving "a great historian of Fascism"? Perhaps because the urge to speculate is too strong to resist. As is the urge to doubt. Despite the trial, despite the facts, despite the verdict, doubt persists. To pretend otherwise is to deceive ourselves.

It is after all one thing to say, as Charles Gray did in his judgment, "no objective, fair-minded historian would have serious cause to doubt that there were gas chambers at Auschwitz." It is another thing to *know* that in a given building hundreds of thousands of people were murdered. How do we know anything beyond what we ourselves have experienced? How do we put our doubts to rest?

Several months before the trial opened, the *London Review of Books* ran a newspaper reporter's account of her attempts to corroborate accounts of atrocities in Kosovo. Her tale was inconclusive, honorably so. But her final words made me deeply angry: *Maybe the truth here is not one thing: but I don't want to be an accomplice to a lie. . . . Nobody much wants to return to Jean Cocteau, but there was something soothing in the words my friend quoted. "History is a combination of reality and lies," he said. "The reality of history becomes a lie. The reality of the fable becomes the truth."*[19]

That seemed to me a fancy argument for letting herself off the hook. Maybe she couldn't find out what happened. Maybe she should have tried harder. And if she believes that reporting the facts makes no difference to whether the fable becomes the truth, and even finds the prospect "soothing," then maybe she should find another line of work. Still, I understood the temptation.

I had nothing but sympathy for the reporter who sat through Irving's "no holes, no Holocaust" argument feeling "like a man in some kind of Kafkaesque dream." After reporting Irving's insistence that the elevator to the ovens simply couldn't have carried as many bodies as van Pelt had claimed, he confessed:

> on the way home in the train that night, to my shame, I took out a pocket calculator and began to do some sums. Ten minutes for each batch of 25. I tapped in. That makes 150 an hour. Which gives 3,600 for each 24-hour period. Which gives 1,314,000 in a year. So that's fine. It could be done. Thank God, the numbers add up. When I realised what I was doing, I almost threw the little machine across the compartment in rage.[20]

Even for those of us who never thought Irving might be right, there was still doubt. Not about the facts, but about what would happen if the facts somehow made no difference.

What pulled me back was a memory: I am six years old and

my father has brought his best friend home for dinner. After we eat, the friend takes the back off our television set and shows me the tubes lighting up inside. One is burned out, and as he replaces it I notice a line of numbers on his arm, just below the wrist. "What are those, Uncle Mike?" He tells me that the Germans put them there when he was a little boy "so I wouldn't get lost."

My Uncle Mike was never a little boy. When he was 12 or 13, the Germans occupied Hungary, and his entire family was put on a train to Auschwitz. Big for his age, and claiming to be older, he was sent to work in the mines. This was 1944, and Auschwitz was liberated by the Red Army in January 1945. By then the rest of his family had been gassed.

The truth is, I can't be certain of all these details, and my Uncle Mike has been dead for some time. I was reminded of him while listening to Irving's response to the obvious questions: What happened to the missing Jews? If they didn't die in the camps, where were they? Irving talks about "the large number that turned up in the state of Palestine, what's now the state of Israel," and sometimes, as if acknowledging that this number isn't nearly large enough, claims that others might have been killed in Dresden. The rest, he suggests, fled to the Soviet Union or the United States. As a simple matter of accounting, this is preposterous. As an explanation it is also monstrous. Because the assumption behind it is that, lured by the good life to the United States, or chasing the workers' paradise in Russia, or seeking the Zionist dream in Israel, people like my Uncle Mike would simply forget that they had once had mothers, fathers, sisters, brothers, grandparents, children, and wouldn't bother to look for them, which is why so many Jews are still unaccounted for. In other words, it presumes that Jews are not human beings.

No one knows this better than Raul Hilberg. *The Politics of Memory* tells the story of Hilberg's Uncle Josef, interned by the Vichy French in 1940:

My father, by then in New York, received Josef's frantic
appeals for help, but there was no money for tickets which
might have enabled Josef to escape to America. When the
deportations from the Vichy-French zone began in 1942,
Josef disappeared. "The blood of my brother is upon me,"
my father would say.

Hilberg, who spent years of his life in archives, never forgot
his Uncle Josef. In 1978 he found him, on list of deportees
from France: Joseph Gaber. "He was deported on August 19,
1942 and arrived in Auschwitz two days later. Since he was
already forty-eight years old, he must have been gassed immediately."[21]
    Yet when St. Martin's canceled Irving's contract, Raul
Hilberg stood up for David Irving. "If these people want to
speak," he told Hitchens, "let them. . . . I am not for taboos and
I am not for repression."[22] Hilberg reaffirmed these views to
me over the telephone in the summer before the trial, with
two minor modifications: "Denial hurts people. There are survivors. That should not be forgotten." Speaking personally, "I
believe in the freedom not to be responsible. But that doesn't
mean I endorse it."

The Holocaust happened in history. The rape of Helen, as the
classicist M.I. Finley reminds us, did not. Archeology may
furnish evidence about a city in a place we can identify with
Troy, but the stories in the *Iliad* happened "once upon a time."
There are lots of numbers in Homer—ships, warriors, even
dates—but none of them, says Finley, allows us to attach the
story to any larger chronology. [23]
    When I arrived at Raul Hilberg's house in Vermont a few
months before the trial, we began by talking about numbers. In
The Destruction of the European Jews, Hilberg lists one million
Jews killed at Auschwitz. His total number for the Holocaust,
however, is 5.1 million, not 6 million, a conclusion that led

David Irving to cite his work at the trial, and which has caused Hilberg no end of trouble. Does it really matter? I asked.

"Yes it matters," Hilberg said. "It matters on a variety of counts. When you segment these losses by country, you find that the major difference between my count and those who say six million . . . is the Soviet Union. Which means, if they didn't die they're there. . . . That matters—because you are talking about a substantial part of Jewish history. And you're talking about current Jewish history!"

Hilberg launched into a learned and fascinating lecture on the vagaries of the Soviet census, the politics of census data, and the dangers of accepting unsourced estimates. "The German statisticians called it a house number, whenever a number like that appears [that] you can't prove."

I asked about gas chambers. Irving devotes so much energy to creating doubt about gas chambers. Why? "People are shot or hacked to death in other countries, even after World War Two—Rwanda, for example. You built the gas chamber with a view to killing a mass of people. Once you have a gas chamber, you have a vision, and the vision is total annihilation. In a gas chamber, you don't see the victim. So the gas chamber in that sense is more dangerous, the gas chamber is more criminal. The gas chamber has wider implications. So when you deny the gas chamber, you deny not just a part of the event, you deny one of the defining concepts. Auschwitz has become the synonym for the Holocaust. And of course you deny, apart from anything else, the death of several million people."

At the trial, Irving also cited Hilberg in support of his claim that Hitler never ordered the Jews killed. It's true that while earlier editions of *The Destruction of the European Jews* refer to an "order," more recent editions do not. But as Hilberg explains, he made this change in the interest of precision about the evidence, not because he agrees with Irving: "The prevailing notion in Germany is that Hitler did it. As it happens, this is also my notion, but I'm not wedded to it."

Hilberg does have strong views. "The way in which the Holocaust is now spread in the high schools and so on makes me gag. To teach the Holocaust to people who don't know where Hungary is!" He is disturbed by "people who misrepresent history, who talk about resistance as though there was a massive attempt. . . . The resistors were, first and foremost, confronted by Jewish opposition. That was their first obstacle." The rhetorical posturing and pressure tactics employed by some of the lawyers and politicians who campaigned to force Swiss banks to pay reparations offended him deeply. And he is still scathing about Goldhagen's "turgid book, with its endless repetitions, lack of substantiation."

Whatever we talked about, though, we seemed always to come back to numbers. "These numbers do matter," Hilberg said. "They also matter for the very simple reason—call it religious if you like." At this point he saw my gaze shift from the Teletubbies magnets on his refrigerator to the menorah balanced on top of his television set.

"I'm an atheist," he said. "All these things belong to my wife, not me. I am an atheist. But there is ultimately, if you don't want to surrender to nihilism entirely, the matter of a record. Does the record matter? In my judgment it is not discussable, it is not arguable. It matters because it matters to me—it's my life."

The sanctity of facts. As the trial wore on, I often found my mind returning to the afternoon I'd spent with Hilberg gazing out over his weathered deck to the trees in his garden, just beginning to take on their fall foliage. After a lifetime of studying brutality, inhumanity, murder on an industrial scale, after personal tragedy and professional conflict, this is what he has to hold on to: the sanctity of facts. Was that enough?

Charles Gray's reasoned judgment ratified every major proposition the defense sought to establish. David Irving had indeed been shown to be a liar, a bigot, and a distorter of historical evidence—a man whose word could no longer be relied upon for the smallest detail, let alone a reliable interpreter of major historical events. It had also established, if only by implication, the right of Jews and other maligned ethnic groups to respond robustly, and in an organized manner, when they are attacked. Indeed it affirmed their right to do so even when the attacks are "merely" verbal—so long as the response is also limited to speech. And, despite considerable reluctance, the judge also issued a number of findings on the destruction of the European Jews, holding that, solely on the basis of the evidence available to David Irving—not the totality of the evidence, or even all the evidence presented in the trial—the "historical data" were clear enough to compel the conclusion that the Holocaust had indeed happened, that Hitler had at the very least been aware of what happened, and that only a prejudicial cast of mind could account for the refusal to acknowledge the reality of the gas chambers at Auschwitz.

Insofar as it was attainable under the laws of libel, justice had been done. Was that enough?

Irving's ability to disturb Jews has been diminished, and will probably be curtailed further as he is forced to either pay his opponents' costs or submit his finances to the bankruptcy court—a far harsher regime in Britain than America, which would likely result in the loss of his home. His fellow "revisionists," too, will now have to do without Irving as their respectable frontman. But it is doubtful the judge's arguments will themselves make any impact on the paranoid adherents of Holocaust denial or other believers in Jewish conspiracy. Their views are, by their very nature, impervious to reasoned judgment. Within months of his loss, Irving was already being received in the United States as a martyr to their cause. To the deniers, the magnitude of Irving's defeat merely demonstrates the power of the forces arrayed against them.

Nor does it seem likely that even this triumph will encourage Irving's opponents to relax their eternal vigilance.

Lipstadt's backers among Jewish organizations have their own reasons for making sure the struggle continues. And though she and her publishers deserved to win, the encouragement their victory will give to groups like the Anti-Defamation League or the Board of Deputies in their efforts to police public discussion, not just of the Holocaust but of American and Israeli policies, is no cause for celebration.

But there was something else that troubled me, something beyond my own political unease and my inability to fully embrace Raul Hilberg's heroic pessimism. There was something, I realized, that struck me as missing all along: witnesses. I understood perfectly why Lipstadt's lawyers had decided that calling witnesses would be a distraction. They had a case to win. Besides, they quite rightly sought to avoid giving Irving a chance to vent his hostility on people who, by definition, had already suffered more than enough.

But Irving's whole approach to history was based on the premise that witness testimony is essentially worthless. Sure, he used it when it suited him—and, as the defense proved, ignored it when it didn't. But on the larger question of whether we can really understand the Holocaust—or any historical catastrophe—without witnesses, the lawyers, and the judge, mostly went along with Irving's premise. The only challenge to this consensus came from Robert Jan van Pelt, whose report quoted extensively from witness testimony, but even he, under cross-examination, seemed embarrassed about the need to rely on that kind of evidence.

In his essay on "Archaeology and History" M.I. Finley argues that "unless one is prepared, in the study of the past, to abandon all interest in change, growth . . . or the interrelationships among different aspects of human society, I see no virtue in the insistence that any one type of evidence" be elevated above the rest.[24] Arnoldo Momigliano, urging a history based on original authorities, explains: "By original authorities we mean eyewitnesses, or documents and other material remains that are contemporary with the event they attest."[25] As classicists, Finley and Momigliano presumably found witnesses harder to come by than historians of the Holocaust, yet they saw no grounds for minimizing their importance—Momigliano placed them first on his list.

This must be right. As a reporter, I know perfectly well that witnesses can mislead—not always innocently. But without them—or our own eyewitness testimony—there would be nothing to report. Even if there were sound reasons for not calling living witnesses, there might have been a place found in court for the voice of Salmen Gradowski, a member of the *Sonderkommando* at Auschwitz who was killed in the fall of 1944. Knowing that his own death was imminent, Gradowski took the notes he'd managed to make during the previous nineteen months and put them inside a metal canister, which he buried in a pit of human ash. Found after the war, Gradowski's journal asks: "Dear discoverer of these writings! I have a request of you: this is the real reason I write, that my doomed life may attain some meaning, that my hellish days and hopeless tomorrows may find a purpose in the future."[26]

Facts are crucial. Facts are sacred. Facts are indeed what give history its dignity. But they are not the whole story. The struggle to find the right way to describe the destruction of European Jewry is sometimes depicted as a contest between history and memory.[27] And as we have now all been taught, memory is a terribly unreliable guide to *wie es eigentlich gewesen ist*, "how it really was."

And so we take refuge in history, in documents, in facts—cool, detached, silent, precise.

Thanks to Deborah Lipstadt and her lawyers the facts about the Holocaust are indeed safer—and for that perhaps we should be grateful.

But witnesses, memories, *testimony*—all that was left outside the courtroom. And that seems to me cause for regret.

Witnesses are always partial. Memory is by definition

selective. And testimony—not the sworn responses of expert witnesses, but the still-vivid responses of people whose history is lived, not studied—can be treacherous.

Yet without witnesses, without human voices to put flesh on the facts, we have something that, while it may pass muster as history, can never tell the truth.

Afterword

On June 20, 2001 the dramatis personae of *David Irving* versus *Deborah Lipstadt and Penguin Books* convened once again at the Royal Courts of Justice. The occasion was Irving's final attempt to gain leave to appeal against Mr. Justice Charles Gray's devastating judgment. For nearly four days a panel of three high court judges heard Irving claim, yet again, that his views on the destruction of European Jewry were eminently reasonable, or, if not, were the result of "poor judgment" rather than a wilful and malicious distortion of the evidence.

Deborah Lipstadt returned from Atlanta with many of the friends and supporters who accompanied her at the original trial. Joining them, on the left hand side of Court 73—the same court where most of the trial took place—were Richard Rampton, Heather Rogers, Anthony Julius and James Libson as well as Helena Peacock from Penguin Books with Kevin Bays and Mark Bateman. Richard Evans, Robert Jan van Pelt and Hajo Funke were in the row behind. Irving himself sat just across the aisle, with the ever-loyal Michele Renouf seated nearby. This time, however, Irving prudently retained a barrister, Adrian Davies, a minor figure on the right of the British political scene and an able and convincing advocate for Irving's views.

A portly, balding man with an unctuous manner, Davies made his first appearance on Irving's behalf at the costs hearing the previous summer, when he persuaded Charles Gray to reduce Irving's "payment on account" (the amount he was required to pay pending a final assessment of his opponents' costs) from £500,000 to £150,000. He also managed to defer enforcement of that order while Irving's application to appeal was still pending.

Though the stakes were as high as ever—if Irving won the right to appeal the defense would have to revisit and possibly re-fight every point gained during the trial—the atmosphere in the appeal hearing was distinctly anti-climactic. Gray's judgment left little room for arguments on points of law. And the questions of fact had been so thoroughly aired during the trial it was difficult to imagine any new evidence, even if it had been available, making much difference. Irving did submit a 384 page affidavit by Germar Scheerer—one of the many pseudonyms used by Germar Rudolf—the German chemist who claimed to have duplicated Leuchter's results. The defense duly commissioned a further 202 pages from Robert Jan van Pelt, but in the end neither document was formally introduced in evidence.*

Instead, Irving's appeal focused on those aspects of the case which were of most importance to him: a defense of his treatment of historical evidence, an attack on the expertise of Robert Jan van Pelt and on the integrity and expertise of Richard Evans, and a last, desperate attack on the evidence for mass gassings at Auschwitz. Indeed, in a challenge that stands as a stinging rebuke to those (including Irving) who claimed that this trial was never really about the Holocaust at all, Davies told Justices Mantell, Pill and Buxton: "If at any point my

---

* Only evidence not available at the time of the trial can be introduced on appeal, and Irving told me he realised that the "Scheerer" affidavit would be inadmissable on those grounds.

opponents can show that David Irving was not just negligent but perverse and wilfully blind [to the evidence on Auschwitz], not just in 1988 or in 2000 but at any point in between, then I must lose." Effectively Irving was willing to stake his entire case on Auschwitz.

The appeal also revealed those aspects of the case of least concern to Irving. At the trial, the defense contended that Irving was a racist and an anti-Semite, as well as a right-wing extremist. Charles Gray found each of those characterizations to be fully justified, furnishing part of the motive for Irving's distortions. As the appeals judges noted, Irving did "not seek to challenge those findings which go to motive only." Nor did he challenge Gray's finding that Irving's record of contacts with the far right "indicates that he shares their political beliefs."

Instead, Davies offered the concessions that, in some cases, had been wrung out of Irving during the trial as evidence of his client's integrity and regard for evidence. "David Irving," Davies told the court, "has never denied that the Nazis murdered millions of Jews. Not hundreds of thousands, but millions of Jews." But of course Irving, on numerous occasions rehearsed during the trial, had denied exactly that. Davies also described the view that Jews were murdered in gas chambers by the Nazis as "common ground".

Rampton was having none of this, but perhaps out of deference to Davies's professionalism seemed willing to let pass the sorts of claims that, when advanced by Irving during the trial, would instantly have brought him to his feet. Besides, it soon became clear the three judges' skepticism needed no prompting. That Irving's arguments on Auschwitz were doomed was obvious from the moment one of the appeals judges interrupted Davies to describe Charles Gray's approach to the famous "holes in the roof" of Crematorium 2, which Davies had been attacking as, "crushingly obvious common sense." As for Irving's treatment of historical evidence, Mr. Justice Mantell, who as trial judge in the Rosemary West serial murder case took a mere forty words to sentence Mrs. West to life in prison, was equally succinct, calling the current dispute "a simple question of reportage. If a man says 'I stopped beating my wife in public with a cane,' it is perverse to report him as saying 'I stopped beating my wife.'"

When the appeal court's decision was finally handed down, on July 20, 2001, Irving didn't even bother to attend. It was left to Adrian Davies, and a pair of rather embarrassed looking solicitors from Amhurst Brown, to hear the terms of Irving's latest comprehensive defeat. The judges appeared to have some difficulty with the concept of Holocaust denial. "We are not persuaded", they wrote, "that the expression [Holocaust denial] can be given any precise technical meaning or that 'Holocaust denier' defines a class of persons precisely." Even so, "we agree with the judge that the applicant may be described as a Holocaust denier."

They also agreed with Charles Gray on Auschwitz, holding that he "was fully entitled to reach" his conclusions on "the factual issue" concerning Auschwitz, which Gray had described as "the central question". In each of the further ten instances where Irving had challenged Gray's criticism of his approach to historical evidence, the appeals judges found Gray's criticisms fully warranted. Irving's application for permission to appeal was refused.

In the normal course of events, David Irving's defeat in the appeal court would be the end of the story. Indeed the stay on Irving's cost order was immediately lifted, forcing him to make a payment of £150,000 towards his opponents' legal costs within six weeks or face bankruptcy proceedings. Those six weeks have now come and gone, and Irving has yet to pay a penny. Nor has he been made bankrupt, though Penguin say they will move against Irving as soon as he returns to Britain. Mishcon de Reya have said they plan to apply for Deborah Lipstadt's costs as well.

But the truth is that beyond the huge self-inflicted wound of the trial itself, making Irving "pay" is not a simple task. The process for assessing costs in Britain—done by a special judge known as a "taxing master" who scrutinizes attorneys' bills, expert fees and expenses—is itself both time-consuming and expensive. And given the long list of mortgages and charges already registered against Irving's principal asset—his London apartment—there is little likelihood of ever recovering the trial costs, let alone any further expenses.

Irving may have assets beyond the reach of British courts—in the United States, for example—where he has spent most of his time since the appeal. Indeed, if Irving is made bankrupt in Britain, where the law can force him to forfeit his home and all personal property except "the tools of his trade", it is entirely possible that he will simply move to the United States, where he continues to appear as a fixture on the right-wing lecture circuit.

Ironically, one factor keeping Irving from abandoning Britain is his professed desire to aggressively pursue his case against Gitta Sereny and the *Observer* newspaper. Given his defeat in the Lipstadt suit the odds, even under British libel law, would now appear to be against him. Yet Irving vows to press on, his pursuit of Sereny hampered only by his newly-announced intention to embark on litigation aimed at Richard Evans and his book *Lying About Hitler*, which Irving claims is libellous.

The spectacle of this disgraced figure still harrying his enemies through the courts would be ludicrous were the consequences not so serious. Readers of this book will know that I have my disagreements with Evans, though those tend to be more about questions of theory than matters of fact. Nor have I been uniformly admiring of his conduct as a witness, though again, readers of this book should be in no doubt about the devastating effectiveness of Evans's attack on Irving's methodology and integrity as a historian. Speaking personally, I have also felt that in his public responses to this book Evans has not always been either completely candid or as scrupulously fair as he might have been. Nonetheless, when I first heard that, faced with the threat of a libel action by David Irving, the British publisher of *Lying About Hitler* had cancelled the contract, my initial disbelief quickly gave way to outrage. That Irving should be allowed to censor public debate in this way is intolerable; that he should be able to do so with such effectiveness, despite the judgment against him, is the strongest possible rebuttal to those who would see in the Irving judgment a vindication of British libel laws.

One more thing needs to be said, and that concerns the brave and principled stand taken by Penguin Books and its parent company, Pearson, in defending Deborah Lipstadt. If during my narrative of the trial I have seemed excessively skeptical of the publishing company's motives, I can only say that excessive skepticism is a reporter's *deformation professionel*. But if readers have mistaken that skepticism for dismissal, or if in consequence I have apparently understated Penguin's courage—or the hard work and commitment of its attorneys— let me make amends for that now.

Our knowledge of the Holocaust remains incomplete— necessarily so. Because the gaps in our knowledge are not incidental, to be filled in later like the sequences of the human genome project. They are not even, though we sometimes pretend otherwise, like the missing clues which will condemn the guilty and exonerate the innocent. These gaps are essential to the event itself, and though some of them may indeed be closed by the efforts of historians and archivists, others are only now becoming apparent. Others have yet even to suggest themselves.

This is frustrating, but this is also history. Those who, like David Irving, seek to diminish or deny the reality of the destruction of European Jewry on the basis of this gap in the record or that apparent contradiction in the evidence are guilty of many things, not least a moral callousness that lets them treat such great suffering as a mere instrument, either of state policy in the past or of ideological combat during the present. But they, and Irving's shrinking-yet-persistent band of defenders in the academy, are also subject to a misunderstanding about the nature of the past.

Talking with Anthony Julius after the trial, I asked whether he wasn't troubled by the Judge's references to an "objective historian". Julius replied that, personally, he didn't find the implied distinction terribly helpful. "My sense is that if you want to write about something, you have to do that thing justice. You have to embrace it in all its elements . . . It's not a question of being subjective or objective. It's a question of not doing justice to his subject, by focusing on one tiny aspect," he said.

This struck me as very much a lawyer's view: true as far as it went, yet still short of the truth. Surely a narrow focus could sometimes be useful. Wasn't the problem really, I asked, that Irving treats the tiny aspects—the contradictions in witness accounts, for example—as if they were the whole story.

"Which," returned Julius, "is the problem of fetishism. A fetishist is a person who does not understand metonymy. Irving is a fetishist. We are metonymists."

Another way of putting it is in terms of the Heideggerian concept of a *Zeugganzes*—a complex of elements forming a system that functions as a totality, so that a change at any one point entails a change at every point. The philosopher Arthur Danto cites the impact of the rifled gun barrel, the conical bullet and the percussion cap on modern warfare as an example.* But the Holocaust, like the American Civil War or indeed any complex historical event, is not a *Zeugganzes*. If Mussolini had never attempted to invade Greece, or if he had succeeded, or even if Hitler had simply declined to send in the *Wehrmacht*, it is likely that most of the 60,000 Greek Jews who perished in

* Arthur C. Danto, "Gettysburg", *Grand Street* VI:3, Spring 1987, pp. 98–116.

the Holocaust would have survived the war. Conversely, if the Bulgarians had been less resourceful in deflecting German pressure to deport that country's 50,000 Jews, or if it hadn't been clear by the end of 1943 that the Germans were not going to win the war (thus encouraging the Bulgarians to continue to hold out) Bulgaria's Jews might well have ended up at Auschwitz alongside their Greek neighbors. But none of these rather large contingencies would have changed anything essential about the Holocaust. Nor would the addition or subtraction of fifty or 60,000 dead make Auschwitz any less, or more, of a terrible place.

Except, of course, for the Greek Jews, or the Bulgarians. From their point of view the catastrophe would have been completely different: it would have happened *to someone else* (or, in the Bulgarian case, *to them*). To say it would merely have seemed so strikes me as perverse. Some critics of this book's first edition have accused me of being sophomoric or simpleminded in pointing out the obstacles to an "objective" understanding of the past. So at the risk of further obloquy let me simply say that perspective matters, and that the ways in which where we stand shapes what we see—and even what we can see—are not always apparent at the time.

September 25, 2001
London

Notes

Introduction

1 Leon Uris, *Exodus*, London: William Kimber & Co. 1959, p. 146.
2 Leon Uris, *Exodus*, p. 155.
3 Mavis M. Hill and L. Norman Williams, *Auschwitz in England*, London: Macgibbon and Kee, 1965, pp. 15–25.
4 Raul Hilberg, *The Destruction of the European Jews*, (Student Edition), London: Holmes and Meier, 1985, pp. 314–315.
5 Martin Gilbert, *Holocaust Journey: Travelling in Search of the Past*, London: Phoenix, 1998, p. 78.
6 Deborah Lipstadt, *Denying the Holocaust*, London: Penguin, 1994, p. 188.
7 Gilbert, pp. 77–78.
8 Peter Novick, *The Holocaust in American Life*, Boston: Houghton Mifflin, 1999, p. 221.
9 Primo Levi, *The Drowned and the Saved*, translated by Raymond Rosenthal, New York: Summit Books, 1998, p. 11ff.
10 Richard Breitman, *Official Secrets: What the Nazis Planned. What the British and Americans Knew*, London: Penguin, 1998, is judicious, even generous, yet ultimately damning on this question.
1 Louise London, *Whitehall and the Jews*, 1993–1948, Cambridge: Cambridge University Press, 2000, p. 242.

Chapter 1

1 Trial transcripts supplied courtesy of Harry Counsell & Company, Clifford's Inn, London. Gray's remarks occur on the transcript for January 11, 2000 (Day 1), page 2, lines 15–16; *Irving v. Lipstadt*, **1:2:15–16**.

Chapter 2

1 Irving's account can be found on his website at: http://www.fpp.co.uk/Online/98/10/RadDi141194.html

2 My notes of a telephone conversation with David Irving, June 1999.
3 Richard Evans, Expert Report, Part II, p. 157. (All pagination from expert reports refers not to internal page numbers, but to the page numbers given for the documents in MS Word, US letter-size pages, as read on-screen.)
4 Lance Morrow, "Just an Ordinary Man" (review of *Hitler's War*), *Time*, May 2, 1977.
5 Back-cover blurb for *Hitler's War*.
6 David Irving, *Goebbels: Mastermind of the Third Reich*, reviewed by John Keegan in the *Daily Telegraph* (London), April 20, 1996.
7 Martin Broszat, "Hitler und die Genesis der Endlösung. Aus Anlass der Thesen von David Irving," *Vierteljahreshefte fuur Zeitgeschichte*, 25 (1977), pp. 739–75, reprinted in Hermann Graml and Klaus-Dietmar Henke (eds.), *Nach Hitler. Der schwierige Umgang mit unserer Geschichte. Beiträge von Martin Broszat* (Munich, 1986), pp. 187–229.
8 Charles Sydnor, Jr., "The Selling of Adolf Hitler: David Irving's *Hitler's War*," *Central European History* (June 1979).
9 Gitta Sereny and Lewis Chester, "The $1,000 Question," *Sunday Times* (London), July 10, 1977.
10 David Irving, *Hitler's War*, London: Papermac, 1977, p. xiii.
11 Norman Finkelstein and Ruth Birn, *A Nation on Trial*, New York: Owl Books, 1998, *passim*.
12 Neal Ascherson, "A Bucketful of Slime," *Observer*, March 29, 1981.
13 Kai Bird, "The Secret Policemen's Historian," *New Statesman*, April 3, 1981, pp. 16–18.
14 David Irving, *Torpedo Running*, London: Focal Point, 1990; Christopher Hitchens, "Hitler's Ghost," *Vanity Fair*, June 1996, pp. 72–4.
15 Henry Porter, *Lies, Damned Lies*, London: Coronet, 1985, pp. 141–53. Porter's account of Irving's role and Dacre's reservations is confirmed by "Irving's Backing for Diaries Welcomed," *Times* (London), May 3, 1983, and "New Slant on Hitler's Diaries," *Daily Mail* (London), May 3, 1983.
16 Hitchens, "Hitler's Ghost."
17 "David Irving's Daughter is Killed in Fall," *Evening Standard* (London), September 16, 1999; see also David Irving's diary for September 14, 1999 on his website.
18 Raul Hilberg, *The Destruction of the European Jews*, New York: Holmes and Meier, 1985 (student edition—abridged), p. 157.
19 "The Truth Shall Set You Free," *Dispatches*, broadcast on Channel 4 (UK) on November 27, 1991. A slightly different translation (the speech was given in German) occurs in the transcript at **28: 190: 4–14.**
20 *Irving* v. *Lipstadt*, **14: 97: 17–26.**
21 Marianne MacDonald, "The Nature of the Beast," *Independent on Sunday Magazine*, April 6, 1997, pp. 4–7.
22 See Irving's website, which offers a list.
23 Roger Eatwell, Expert Report, "David Irving and Right-Wing Extremism," p. 30. Though Eatwell never testified at the trial, his report was submitted to the court. It was also posted on Irving's website.
24 Lord Weidenfeld to David Irving, June 16, 1977.

25 Ernst Zündel to David Irving, May 21, 1986; Irving's Further Discovery, quoted in Robert Jan van Pelt, Expert Report, Chapter 9, p. 11.

26 Ernst Zündel to David Irving, November 9, 1987; Irving's Further Discovery, cited in van Pelt, Expert Report, Chapter 9, p. 13.

27 Deborah Lipstadt, *Denying the Holocaust*, London: Penguin, 1994, p. 162.

28 *Ibid.*, pp. 164–5.

29 Richard Evans, Expert Report, Part I, p. 76.

30 David Irving, speech at Chelsea Town Hall, November 1991.

31 Robert Harris, *Selling Hitler*, London: Arrow Books, 1996, p. 189.

32 Gordon Craig, "The Devil in the Details," *New York Review of Books*, September 19, 1996, pp. 8-14.

Chapter 3

1 Art Spiegelman, *Maus: A Survivor's Tale*, New York: Pantheon Books, 1986, p. 12.

2 Deborah Lipstadt, *Beyond Belief: The American Press and the Coming of the Holocaust 1933–1945*, New York: The Free Press, 1986, pp. 254, 256.

3 Peter Novick, *The Holocaust in American Life*, Boston: Houghton Mifflin, 1999, pp. 64–5.

4 *Ibid.*, pp. 38, 41.

5 Tony Kushner, *The Holocaust and the Liberal Imagination*, Oxford: Blackwell, 1994, p. 125.

6 Novick, *The Holocaust in American Life*, pp. 86–7, 94.

7 Kushner, *The Holocaust and the Liberal Imagination*, p. 138.

8 Elena Lappin, "The Man With Two Heads," *Granta*, 66 (1999), pp. 11–13. See also Martin Arnold, "In Fact, It's Fiction," *New York Times*, November 12, 1998.

9 Novick, *The Holocaust in American Life*, pp. 128–36.

10 Raul Hilberg, *The Politics of Memory*, Chicago: Ivan Dee, 1996, pp. 107–8, 117, 124.

11 *Ibid.*, pp. 125–7.

12 Novick, *The Holocaust in American Life*, pp. 135–6.

13 Hannah Arendt, *Eichmann in Jerusalem: A Report on the Banality of Evil*, New York: 1963, p. 125.

14 Novick, *The Holocaust in American Life*, p. 136.

15 Arno Mayer, *Why Did the Heavens Not Darken?*, London: Verso, 1988, pp. 16–18.

16 *Ibid.*, p. 113.

17 *Ibid.*, pp. 234–75.

18 Daniel Goldhagen, "False Witness," *New Republic*, April 17, 1989, pp. 39–44.

19 Novick, *The Holocaust in American Life*, p. 92.

20 Daniel Goldhagen, *Hitler's Willing Executioners: Ordinary Germans and the Holocaust*, London: Little, Brown, 1996, pp. 200, 290.

21 Hilberg, *The Politics of Memory*, p. 25.

22 Novick, *The Holocaust in American Life*, p. 314, n. 36.

23 Mayer, *Why Did the Heavens Not Darken?*, pp. viii–x.

24 Roland Barthes, *Mythologies*, Paris: Éditions du Seuil, 1957, pp. 229, 239.

25 Deborah Lipstadt to Yehuda Bauer, August 15, 1984.

26　Deborah Lipstadt to Adam Bellow, September 3, 1991.

Chapter 4

1　Michael Rubinstein, *Wicked, Wicked Libels*, London: Routledge and Kegan Paul, 1972, p. 124.
2　Anthony Julius, *T.S. Eliot, Anti-Semitism, and Literary Form*, Cambridge: Cambridge University Press, 1995, p. 1.
3　Gabriel Josipovici, "Sheeny Among Nightingales?," *Jewish Chronicle*, October 6, 1995, p. 28, argued in precisely those terms, presumably by way of showing himself to be a Jew impervious to such petty slights.
4　Gitta Sereny, "Spin Time for Hitler," *Observer Review*, April 21, 1996, p. 1.
5　Robert Harris, *Selling Hitler*, London: Arrow Books, 1996, pp. 118–36.
6　Eberhard Jaeckel, "*Noch einmal: Irving, Hitler und der Judenmord*," in Peter Marthesheimer and Ivo Frenze (eds.), *Im Kreuzfeuer: Der Fernsehfilm Holocaust. Eine Nation is betroffen*, Frankfurt: 1979, pp. 163–6.
7　Michael Zander, *Cases and Materials on the English Legal System*, London: Butterworth, 1999, p. 64.
8　Peter Novick, *The Holocaust in American Life*, Boston: Houghton Mifflin, 1999, p. 201.
9　Irving, "Reply to Second Defendant," n.d. [from Irving's website].

Chapter 5

1　John Munkman, *The Technique of Advocacy*, London: Butterworth, 1991, pp. 50, 60.
2　Christopher Browning, *Nazi Policy, Jewish Workers, German Killers*, Cambridge: Cambridge University Press, 2000, pp. 26–32. Browning cites Götz Aly as attributing a "relatively diminished role . . . to Hitler in the decision-making process." This of course is not the same as arguing that Hitler knew nothing about the Final Solution.
3　Pierre Vidal-Naquet, *Assassins of Memory*, New York: Columbia University Press, 1992, pp. xi–xii, 31–9, 50–1, 91.
4　Richard J. Golsan, "Introduction" to Alain Finkielkraut, *The Future of a Negation: Reflections on the Question of Genocide*, Lincoln: University of Nebraska Press, 1998, pp. xxii–xxiii.
5　Gitta Sereny, "Let History Judge," *New Statesman*, September 11, 1981, p. 12.
6　Christopher Hitchens, "The Chorus and Cassandra," *Grand Street*, Autumn 1985, reprinted in *Prepared for the Worst*, New York: Hill and Wang, 1988, pp. 59–77.
7　Vidal-Naquet, *Assassins of Memory*, pp. vi, ix–x.
8　*Ibid.*, pp. 58–9.
9　Deborah Lipstadt, *Denying the Holocaust*, London: Penguin, 1994, pp. 220–1.
10　Vidal-Naquet, *Assassins of Memory*, p. 122.
11　Gitta Sereny, "Spin Time for Hitler," *Observer Review*, April 21, 1996, p. 1.
12　Lipstadt, *Denying the Holocaust*, p. 180n.

13 John Keegan, *The Second World War*, London: Pimlico, 1989, pp. 238–9.

14 Browning, *Nazi Policy*, pp. 118–20, for example, details the role of General Max von Schenckendorff, commander of the rear Army Area Center, in ordering the slaughter of the Jewish population of Brest-Litovsk, which was carried out in part by the men of Infantry Division 162.

15 Keegan, *The Second World War*, p. 502.

16 Tony Kushner, *The Holocaust and the Liberal Imagination*, Oxford: Blackwell, 1994, p. 12; see also Raul Hilberg, *The Politics of Memory*, Chicago: Ivan Dee, 1996, pp. 70–1.

17 Gerald Reitlinger, *The Final Solution: The Attempt to Exterminate the Jews of Europe, 1939–45*, London: Valentine, Mitchell and Co., 1953, pp. 406–7 and 531, cited in Kushner, *The Holocaust and the Liberal Imagination*, pp. 3, 12.

Chapter 6

1 Robert Jan van Pelt and Debórah Dwork, *Auschwitz: 1270 to the Present*, New Haven and London: Yale University Press, 1996, *passim*.

2 Daniel Goldhagen, *Hitler's Willing Executioners: Ordinary Germans and the Holocaust*, London: Little, Brown, 1996, p. 425.

3 Jean-Claude Pressac, *Auschwitz: Technique and Operation of the Gaschambers*, New York: The Beate Klarsfeld Foundation, 1989.

Chapter 7

1 Arno Mayer, *Why Did the Heavens Not Darken?*, London: Verso, 1988, pp. 363, 365. In another passage ignored by his critics—and by Irving—Mayer said "It must be emphasized strongly that such defects are altogether insufficient to put in question the use of gas chambers in the mass murder of Jews at Auschwitz" (p. 363).

2 Pierre Vidal-Naquet and Limor Yigal, *Holocaust Denial in France*, Tel Aviv: The Center for the Study of Anti-Semitism, n.d., pp. 3–4.

3 Arthur A. Cohen, *The Tremendum: A Theological Interpretation of the Holocaust*, New York: Crossroads, 1981, pp. 1 ff.

4 W.H. Lawrence, "50,000 Kiev Jews Reported Killed," *New York Times*, November 29, 1943, p. 3. Cited in Robert Jan van Pelt, Expert Report.

5 Bernard Wasserstein, *Britain and the Jews of Europe, 1939–1945*, Oxford: Clarendon Press, 1979, pp. 166 ff.

6 Richard Breitman, *Official Secrets: What the Nazis Planned. What the British and Americans Knew*, London: Penguin, 1998, pp. 145–50, 180.

7 Tony Kushner, *The Holocaust and the Liberal Imagination*, Oxford: Blackwell, 1994, pp. 139–41.

8 Breitman, *Official Secrets*, p. 10.

9 *Ibid.*, pp. 113–21.

10 Thies Christophersen, *Auschwitz: A Personal Account*, Introduction by Manfred Roeder, revised edition, Reedy: Liberty Bell Publications, 1979, pp. 15 ff.

11 Wilhelm Stäglich, *The Auschwitz Myth: A Judge Looks at the Evidence*, Torrance, CA: Institute for Historical Review, 1986, p. 47.

12 William C. Lindsey, "Zyklon B, Auschwitz, and the Trial of Dr. Bruno Tesch, *Journal of Historical Review*, 4 (1984), pp. 287 ff.

Chapter 8

1 Bryan Cheyette, *Constructions of "the Jew" in English Literature and Society*, Cambridge: Cambridge University Press, 1993, p. 16.
2 Anthony Julius, *T.S. Eliot, Anti-Semitism, and Literary Form*, Cambridge: Cambridge University Press, 1995, p. 12.
3 Deborah Lipstadt, "Benefits of Belonging," *Hadassah Magazine*, June/July 1993, pp. 14–17.
4 Christopher Browning, *Ordinary Men: Reserve Police Battalion 101 and the Final Solution in Poland*, New York: HarperCollins, 1992.
5 Daniel Goldhagen, *Hitler's Willing Executioners: Ordinary Germans and the Holocaust*, London: Little, Brown, 1996, p. 416.
6 *Ibid.*, p. 48.
7 *Ibid.*, p. 521, n. 81.
8 Raul Hilberg, "Le Phénomène Goldhagen," *Les Temps Modernes*, 592 (February–March 1997), pp. 1–10; Hilberg's English text was reprinted in "The Goldhagen Phenomenon," *Critical Inquiry*, 23 (Spring–Summer 1997), pp. 721–7.
9 David Irving, Action Report, 17 (July 20, 2000), p. 16.
10 Richard Evans, *In Defence of History*, London: Granta, 1997, pp. 76, 101.
11 *Ibid.*, pp. 223, 249.
12 *Ibid.*, p. 125

Chapter 9

1 Martin Gilbert, *Holocaust Journey: Travelling in Search of the Past*, London: Phoenix, 1998, pp. 391–2. At the trial Longerich quoted the first and third paragraphs which I have given in his translation, but only portions of the second, which I have therefore quoted in full from Gilbert's translation. The speech itself goes on for another paragraph and a half.

Chapter 10

1 "ADL Settles a Class-Action Suit," *Forward*, October 1, 1999.
2 David Hooper, *Reputations Under Fire: Winners and Losers in the Libel Business*, London: Little, Brown, 2000, p. 350.
3 Robert Harris, "Foreword," to Ian Mitchell, *The Cost of a Reputation*, Edinburgh: Canongate, 1998, p. ii.

Chapter 11

1 John Keegan, "The Trial of David Irving—and My Part in His Downfall," *Daily Telegraph*, April 12, 2000.

Chapter 12

1 "De Sophisticis Elenchis," transl. W.A. Pickard-Cambridge, in Richard McKeon, *The Basic Works of Aristotle*, New York: Random House, 1941, pp. 208–12.
2 J.W. Cohoon, ed. and transl., *Dio Chrysostom: Discourses I*, London: William Heinemann, 1932, p. 475.
3 *Ibid.*, p. 541.
4 Richard Evans, *In Defence of History*, London: Granta, 1997, p. 241.

5   Alain Finkielkraut, *The Future of a Negation: Reflections on the Question of Genocide*, Lincoln: University of Nebraska Press, 1998, p. xxii.

6   Deborah Lipstadt, *Denying the Holocaust*, London: Penguin, 1994, pp. 19–20.

7   Peter Novick, *The Holocaust in American Life*, Boston: Houghton Mifflin, 1999, pp. 71–2.

8   *Ibid.*, p. 154; see also Peter Grose, *Israel in the Mind of America*, New York: Knopf, 1983, p. 304.

9   Uri Bialer, *Between East and West*, Cambridge: Cambridge University Press, 1990, pp. 180–1.

10 I.F. Stone, *Underground to Palestine*, New York: Pantheon, 1978, and *This is Israel*, New York: Boni and Gaer, 1948, *passim*. See also Paul Milkman, *PM: A New Deal in Journalism*, New Brunswick: Rutgers, 1997.

11 Novick, *The Holocaust in American Life*, p. 149.

12 *Ibid.*, pp. 156, 168–9.

13 *Ibid.*, pp. 330–1, n. 107, citing Lipstadt, "Holocaust-Denial and the Compelling Force of Reason," *Patterns of Prejudice*, 26: 1/2 (1992), pp. 72–3.

14 Hilberg, "Le Phénomène Goldhagen," *Les Temps Modernes*, 592 (February–March 1997), pp. 1–10.

15 Elena Lappin, "The Man With Two Heads," *Granta*, 66 (1999), pp. 11–13.

16 T.S. Eliot, *After Strange Gods*, London: Faber and Faber, 1934.

17 Tzvetan Todorov, *Facing the Extreme: Moral Life in the Concentration Camps*, London: Phoenix, 2000, pp. 82–4.

18 Hannah Arendt, in Ron H. Feldman (ed.), *The Jew as Pariah*, New York, 1978, p. 141, cited in Norman Finkelstein and Ruth Birn, *A Nation on Trial*, New York: Owl Books, 1998, p. 93, n. 87.

19 Audrey Gillan, "What's the Story?," *London Review of Books*, 21: 11 (May 27, 1999).

20 James Dalrymple, "The Curse of Revisionism," *Independent*, January 29, 2000.

21 Raul Hilberg, *The Politics of Memory*, Chicago: Ivan Dee, 1996, pp. 23–4.

22 Christopher Hitchens, "Hitler's Ghost," *Vanity Fair*, June 1996.

23 "Myth, Memory and History," in M.I. Finley, *The Use and Abuse of History*, London: Pimlico, 2000, pp. 14–15.

24 "Archaeology and History," in M.I. Finley, *The Use and Abuse of History*, London: Pimlico, 2000, p. 92.

25 Richard Evans, *In Defence of History*, London: Granta, 1997, p. 93.

26 Todorov, *Facing the Extreme*, pp. 62, 96–7.

27 Leon Weiseltier, "After Memory," *New Republic*, May 3, 1993, pp. 16–26.

Index